costume society of america series

A SEPARATE SPHERE

A Separate Sphere

DRESSMAKERS IN CINCINNATI'S
GOLDEN AGE, 1877–1922

Cynthia Amnéus

With essays by Marla R. Miller, Anne Bissonnette, and Shirley Teresa Wajda

Cincinnati Art Museum

Texas Tech University Press

This book is typeset in Bembo. The paper used in
this book meets the minimum requirements of
ANSI/NISO Z39.48-1992 (R1997). ∞

Designed by Barbara Werden
Principal photography by Tony Walsh

Library of Congress Cataloging-in-Publication Data
Amnéus, Cynthia.
    A separate sphere : dressmakers in Cincinnati's golden
age, 1877-1922 / Cynthia Amnéus ; with essays by Anne
Bissonnette, Marla R. Miller, and Shirley Teresa Wajda.
        p.   cm.
"Published in conjunction with the exhibition 'A sepa-
rate sphere: dressmakers in Cincinnati's golden age,
1877-1922,' organized by the Cincinnati Art Museum,
October 12, 2003-January 4, 2004." Includes biblio-
graphical references and index.
    ISBN 0-89672-507-3 (cloth : alk. paper)
    ISBN 0-89672-515-4 (paper : alk. paper)
    1. Dressmaking—Ohio—Cincinnati—History—19th
century—Exhibitions. 2. Dressmaking—Ohio—
Cincinnati—History—20th century—Exhibitions.
I. Cincinnati Art Museum. II. Texas Tech University.
III. Title.
    TT504.4 .A48 2003
    746.9'2'097717809034—dc21
                                                2003004015

Texas Tech University Press
Box 41037
Lubbock, Texas 79409-1037 USA
800.832.4042
ttup@ttu.edu
www.ttup.ttu.edu

03   04   05   06   07   08   09   10   11 /
9   8   7   6   5   4   3   2   1

Manufactured in China at Everbest Printing Company.

Frontispiece: Kate R. Cregmile (active 1891–1923)
Reception Dress, 1891–1892; silk; Gift of Mrs. Robert
S. Alter, 1963.542a,b.

The Cincinnati Art Museum gratefully acknowledges
Lazarus, the presenting sponsor of the exhibition "A
Separate Sphere: Dressmakers in Cincinnati's Golden
Age, 1877–1922," the Cincinnati Art Museum, October
12, 2003 through January 4, 2004.

    The Cincinnati Art Museum would like to thank
the Friends of Fashion, particularly their charter
members: Mrs. J. Gordon Dixon, Mrs. Graham E. Marx,
Mary Light Meyer, and Mrs. Richard Thayer.

    The Cincinnati Art Museum gratefully acknowl-
edges the generous operating support provided by the
Fine Arts Fund, the Ohio Arts Council, the Institute of
Museum and Library Services, and the City of
Cincinnati.

    Conservation of works in the exhibition was
supported by the generosity of the Taste of Duveneck
2002.

    The Cincinnati Art Museum would like to thank
the following organizations for their generous
sponsorship of the *Year of Cincinnati:* Ashland Inc.,
Bartlett & Co., Frost Brown Todd LLC, and Vorys,
Sater, Seymour and Pease LLP.

Contents

Foreword

OVER THE PAST several decades, we have increasingly come to view the world through a gendered lens. This shift in perspective—motivated in large measure by changing demographics and the emergence of women as a dominant force in the workplace—has been a welcome one, for it has greatly enriched our understanding of contemporary culture and the forces shaping it.

If our view of the present has changed in this regard, it should come as no surprise that so, too, has our view of the past. The research undertaken by a new generation of scholars has been encouraging; it has not only offered fresh and productive ways of looking at familiar subjects but also has prompted a renewed interest in and, more importantly, a reassessment of the significant contributions that women have made in many different disciplines. Understandably, a great deal of attention in the emerging field of women's studies has been focused on the arts, an area in which women have long played a prominent role both as practitioners and as arbiters of taste. Nowhere can this phenomenon be seen more clearly than in

fashion design, because costume is perhaps the most sensitive register of the expression of personal identity and, more broadly, of cultural values.

This work represents a welcome addition to scholarship in this field for two reasons: First, it serves as a groundbreaking study of the organization and economy of fashion design in a prosperous midwestern city in the late nineteenth and early twentieth centuries; second, it examines the demand for, and the production of, fashionable women's clothing during a vibrant and culturally expansive period in the history of Cincinnati from the interrelated perspectives of the many talented dressmakers who prospered here and the affluent patrons who were their principal clients. Set in a larger context, this examination of Cincinnati serves as a microcosm of a national phenomenon.

The fact that *A Separate Sphere* focuses exclusively on Cincinnati is notable and deserves special mention, because this city holds a very important place in the history of American art, and the works of art produced here during this period represent one of the greatest strengths of the Museum's

x

collection. The exhibition that this publication accompanies is the last in a series of exhibitions presented during 2003—Ohio's bicentennial—that celebrate the rich artistic heritage of this city. It is fitting that we end the year with a tribute to this important chapter in the history of the arts in Cincinnati and to one aspect of the pivotal role played by women in their development.

Projects of this scope are made possible only by the generous support of both corporate and individual donors. We are deeply grateful to Lazarus for its presenting sponsorship support. I must also acknowledge with gratitude the Friends of Fashion, particularly their charter members: Mrs. J. Gordon Dixon, Mrs. Graham E. Marx, Mary Light Meyer, and Mrs. Richard Thayer. Special mention should be made of the exemplary efforts of the many individuals who

participated in the preparation of this work: to Judith Keeling, editor-in-chief, and her colleagues at Texas Tech University Press; to Anne Bissonnette, Marla Miller, and Shirley Teresa Wajda, who graciously agreed to contribute essays; to photographer Tony Walsh for the skillful manner in which he captured the essential character of the costumes presented in the exhibition; to Karen Feinberg, who served as copy editor; and to our skillful publications coordinator, Sarah Sedlacek. Our greatest thanks, however, are due to Cynthia Amnéus, the Museum's associate curator of costume and textiles, who conceived of the exhibition and publication, and oversaw the development of both with great intelligence and care.

TIMOTHY RUB
Director
Cincinnati Art Museum

Acknowledgments

LIKE ANY PROJECT of this scope, this publication and the exhibition it accompanies are the result of many individuals' contributions. I cannot claim that it is the product of my work alone. First and foremost, I would like to thank the director of the Cincinnati Art Museum, Timothy Rub, for his faith in my ability to complete this project in time to coincide with Ohio's bicentennial celebration and the opening of the Cincinnati Wing at the Museum. I have appreciated his trust and encouragement every step of the way. Deputy director, Stephen Bonadies, served as counsel and white knight whenever problems arose. His excitement about the project refueled me when I was overwhelmed. Heartfelt thanks go to Anita Ellis, director of curatorial affairs, whose patient mentoring, frank opinions, supportive words, and gentle directorial hand led me through uncharted territories. Her guidance was invaluable.

I am indebted to Wendy Gamber, whose book, *The Female Economy: The Millinery and Dressmaking Trades, 1860–1930,* offers an impressive, in-depth look at the economic role of milliners and dressmakers in the nineteenth and early twentieth centuries. Her scholarly work allowed me to place Cincinnati's dressmakers in context in a way that would not have been possible without her research. The examination of the Tirocchi sisters' lives and work in *From Paris to Providence: Fashion, Art, and the Tirocchi Dressmakers' Shop, 1915–1947,* edited by Susan Hay, provided invaluable information about the workings of a dressmaker's salon, relationships with clients, and the transition to ready-made clothing. In addition, the many scholars who have examined nineteenth-century women's lives and the ideology of the separate sphere opened my eyes to the vital strength of these female entrepreneurs as they sought to forge a place for themselves and their families, while choosing not to yield to societal norms.

More than documentation of an exhibition, this work is the first publication to explore the lives of dressmakers who worked in Cincinnati in the late nineteenth and early twentieth centuries. I am pleased that Marla Miller agreed to lend her expertise as a historian to discuss the challenges facing scholars who research women.

xii

Shirley Wajda has offered her insights into the lives of the patrons who wore the creations of Cincinnati's dressmakers, many of whom were members of Cincinnati's wealthiest families. It is only through these donors' generosity in giving their garments to the Museum that the work of the city's dressmakers has survived. I am grateful, too, that Anne Bissonnette agreed to contribute her original research on the formation and evolution of the tea gown, a highly specialized and most intriguing garment, as part of this work.

I owe a great debt and sincere thanks to Nancy Rexford, whom I am honored to call my friend and colleague. Nancy, along with Otto Charles Thieme, first mentored me and encouraged me to continue along my path as a costume historian. Nancy's expertise in dating the garments illustrated in this publication is incomparable and was indispensable to me. I also thank the previous curators of the collection, Mary Light Meyer, Carolyn Shine, and Otto Charles Thieme, for their foresight in accepting into the collection many of the garments featured here, as well as making a start on the research into Cincinnati's dressmakers. I am honored to be able to bring this long-imagined project to fruition, so that we may all honor these forgotten artists.

In regard to the production of this publication, I gratefully acknowledge the work of Tony Walsh, photographer, who expertly captured the beauty of each garment; Scott Hisey, photo services coordinator, who scheduled and oversaw all of the photography; and Sarah Sedlacek, publications coordinator, who saw me through the publication process despite an inordinately busy schedule and other pressing projects. Karen

Feinberg performed an important task in copy editing the text. I appreciate her thorough and thoughtful considerations. Linda Pieper and Lori Wight, curatorial secretaries, deserve my thanks for solving all my computer problems with ease and wading patiently through the many drafts of the manuscript.

The presentation of the garments would not have been complete without the expertise of Harold Mailand of Textile Conservation Services, who was able to make our most fragile garments beautiful again, and Christopher Daniels, whose sculptural skills customized mannequins to fit our most petite garments. This project would never have been completed on time without the help of my assistant, Lynelle Barrett, whose excellent organizational and technical skills were put to the test with challenging restoration projects, mannequin preparation, hair making, and last-minute changes that I orchestrated.

My research would never have been so complete without the dedication and cheerful assistance of many librarians. I am indebted to Môna Chapin, head librarian at the Mary R. Schiff Library of the Cincinnati Art Museum, and Peggy Runge, cataloger, who patiently sought out and processed the numerous interlibrary loans for the various obscure publications I requested on an almost daily basis. The staff of the Public Library of Cincinnati and Hamilton County in the Departments of History and Genealogy, Magazines and Periodicals, Government and Public Documents, Rare Books, and Art and Music were expert in finding volumes of material whose existence I never would have imagined. In addition, the staff of the Baker Library at

Harvard Business School kindly allowed me to examine the credit ledgers of R. G. Dun and Company, where I found invaluable information. Furthermore, the staff of the Cincinnati Historical Society Library were indispensable in finding the many bits of information that helped illuminate the lives of both the dressmakers and the donors. Reference librarian, Anne Shepherd, deserves special acknowledgment for her dedicated interest in the project and her commitment to going above and beyond the call of duty.

Along with the aforementioned staff members, consultants, librarians, and essayists, a large number of volunteers contributed many hours of specialized work in the form of fine handwork and research skills to make this project possible. Special thanks go to my dear friends Carolyn Juett and Gretchen Vaughn, who always rose to the occasion when I was most desperate. Their support was heartfelt and is very much appreciated. I owe them both a great debt of thanks. Deanna Thompson also dedicated many hours to the project; she searched for the "mother lode" of personal accounts and diaries. This never materialized, but she stuck with me tenaciously to the end. Katherine Yarges also deserves special thanks. Her research skills are without equal. Her intense interest in the project and her unfailing thoroughness illuminated many facts and concepts that never would have been uncovered without her diligence. These four women, along with Connie Barcelona, Shelia Barker, Lisa Bruemmer, Mary Alice Burke, Jean Clendenning, Sally Crane, Janet Haartz, Evelyn Horowitz, Adrienne Juett, Angelyn Krauss, Mary Magner, Janice Morrill, Ellie Nelson, Becky Robinson, and Sandy Williams, are owed great thanks for their dedication and the many different roles they played in keeping this project moving forward.

Last, but certainly not least, I would like to thank my husband, John, and my son, Max, for supporting and encouraging me, even when I was at the library yet again.

CYNTHIA AMNÉUS

A SEPARATE SPHERE

Marla R. Miller

Dressmaking as a Trade for Women

RECOVERING A LOST ART(ISANRY)

The business of a mantua-maker, which now includes almost every article of dress made use of by ladies, except, perhaps, those which belong to the head and the feet, is too well known to stand in need of description.

Book of Trades, 1807

Although the "sewing trades" are too important numerically from the point of view of the employment of women to be entirely neglected . . . the employment of women in the making of clothing is less interesting than in the other industries [since] needlework of any kind except, perhaps, the making of men's garments, has always been regarded as within women's "peculiar sphere."

EDITH ABBOT, *Women in Industry*, 1915

THE BEAUTIFUL, often spectacular garments gathered together in this publication are works of art—objects that display talent and taste, ability and imagination in the pursuit of beauty. But these objects are equally the evidence of artisanship, the work of laborers whose income depended on their skill. Since the American Revolution, the word *artisanry* has come to be associated with work traditionally performed by men, such as silver-smithing, blacksmithing, or woodworking. Women with craft skill traditionally have been viewed as part of the domestic sphere: their work in the clothing trades has been regarded not as skilled craft labor but as an extension of their traditional domestic duties, whereas men with such skill have been placed more easily in the worlds of trade and commerce. But artisans were all of those people in any community, women and men, who knew how to make things that were "aesthetically, functionally, and economically acceptable,"[1] objects as practical as they were beautiful.

Not quite two centuries have passed since the *Book of Trades* found mantua- or

dressmaking almost unworthy of comment;[2] nearly nine decades have passed since early twentieth-century economist Edith Abbot, too, was inclined to skip over any formal study of women's work in the sewing trades.[3] Yet dressmaking has always been among the most important occupations available to American women. Perhaps the longest surviving form of artisanry in the United States, it tells an important story about larger changes in American life from the colonial period to the present. To be sure, the historical study of American dressmakers has advanced greatly since the 1910s, thanks largely to the success of the modern women's movement and the advent of women's history as a thriving field of study, but dressmaking has not yet gained critical purchase in the scholarship of American artisanry.[4]

Part of the reason for this gap lies in present-day definitions attached to artisanal work, which shape the narratives that historians can see in their sources. Also important, however, are the kinds of materials available (and unavailable) for the study of women and work, the limits they impose, and the opportunities they suggest. Because comparatively few documents were generated by early American working women, who typically have lacked literacy and numeracy skills, the historical study of artisanal women is simply more difficult than the historical study of artisanal men. A review of the obstacles facing the student of women's work suggests how one might study dressmaking women over a range of times and places in ways that bring their artisanal work to light. I focus here on the available sources concerning New England in the preindustrial era, because that is what I know best, but such a discussion necessarily touches on the full trajectory of the trade and suggests opportunities for new work in this important area of women's history.[5]

An initial hurdle in studying the dressmaking trade is the exceptionally poor survival rate of the products and tools of women's labor. Generally more perishable and less valuable than those of male craftworkers, the objects produced and the implements used by most needlewomen (with the exception of highly ornamental tools and embroideries) have not traditionally been the stuff of museum collections. Straight pins, needles, shears, scissors, irons, and thimbles have attracted little curatorial interest.[6] As archaeologist Mary Beaudry observed, excavated artifacts related to sewing "more often than not, get relegated to the oblivion of the 'small finds' in archaeological reports. . . . [I]t seems items of needlework are commonly excavated but seldom published and almost never analyzed and interpreted."[7] Nor are the products of this labor themselves available as sources of insight into individual makers; even the best garments bear no maker's mark, because

dressmakers did not "sign" their work with labels before the 1850s. Even in the next half-century, not everyone adopted the practice. Although many dressmakers remain anonymous, the gowns they made survive to document their extraordinary abilities and provide eloquent evidence of early American women's artisanal skill.

Although little can be done to correct for the survival rates of these objects, other forms of evidence—buildings and landscapes—can illuminate early American women's working lives. In her 1992 survey of landmarks of women's labor history, Lynn Weiner observed that although women engaged in an array of commercial activities in early America, "few structures remain standing" that shed light on their work environments.[8] What is more, historians have long considered the presence of a shop a key element of artisanal identity. For many women, however, the work environments were the houses of the local gentry, many of which survive. For example, the Hadley, Massachusetts, farm of Elizabeth and Charles Phelps was home to four Hadley women, from 1770 to the 1820s, but for another sixty domestic servants and needleworkers, including a handful of dressmakers and more than a dozen tailoresses, it was a workplace.[9] Dressmakers' own homes, too, served as work spaces: eight of the twenty-one women whose careers are examined in this publication worked out of their homes. What spaces did they use for their work? What furnishings and tools were deemed essential? The built environment and the material culture of home-based dressmakers can be sources of new insight.

Although many dressmaking women operated from their homes, others, including six of the dressmakers profiled here, estab-lished themselves in shops. Many commer-cial rooms once occupied by the town's dressmaker still remain on main streets across America; these spaces, with careful investigation, may increase our under-standing of dressmakers as local business-women. Cultural resource surveys under-taken by state historic preservation offices routinely identify buildings that once housed dressmakers' shops, and historical societies possess photographs of the propri-etress and her employees gathered in front of the shop's display window. More rarely, records pertaining to these businesses sur-vive, but these sources together remind us that dressmaking was a trade that moved easily from private to public settings. Dress-makers sometimes may appear to be hidden from view because of biases in the docu-mentary record, but, in fact, these women were highly visible members of community life in small towns across nineteenth- and early twentieth-century America.

Evidence from the material world can be extremely useful in gaining insight into past lives, though historians tend to be more comfortable with documentary materials. Yet many of the published and unpublished sources consulted most easily and most often by historians with an interest in labor prac-tices can conceal the true numbers of women working at a trade. City business directories, for example, appear to be records of the men and women active in a given place and time, but these sources are far more commonly available for urban than for rural communities. More important, they appear to be comprehensive records, although they are in truth selective. News-paper advertisements, too, are highly impor-

tant sources in attempts to document the work and sometimes the work sites of mantua-makers and dressmakers, but these appear largely in cities and mask the pres-ence of needlewomen less well attuned or less knowledgeable in the sophisticated world of advertising. For instance, historian Thomas Dublin compared women listed as dressmakers in Boston directories with fig-ures in the census and found that only about one-tenth of them appeared in the pages of the *Boston Business Directory*.[10]

The U.S. Census itself, one of the richest sources of information on both individual craftswomen and the extent of a craft in a given community, did not record American women's (or men's) work before 1850, the first year that information on occupations was gathered by census takers. After that year, however, both federal and state census takers collected information on occupations, which has served as the backbone of much historical work. The appearance of census data on occupations is a tremendous boon, because, for the first time, researchers have access to the ways that women and men identified their own occupational status. Yet, like city directories, even seemingly straight-forward sources such as the census can also conceal as much as they reveal. Middle-class white women, acutely aware of cultural expectations that they not seek paid work, were often reluctant to admit that they were engaged in anything other than respectable housewifery. They regularly reported that they were merely "keeping house," whether or not they were also working for income. Prospective historians must approach docu-ments, such as city directories and newspa-pers, with care, remembering that they reflect the census taker's view, as well as the respondents' self-reportage, because the latter had a stake in influencing how they were perceived by both the stranger standing before them and the federal government itself.

Finally, financial and other business records have long been among the most important sources for historians of work. Account books and daybooks are perhaps the most important sources to consider here, both because they have been misunderstood most often and they hold the most promise for new insights. These documents are excellent sources to examine the daily, seasonal, or yearly rhythms of a man's craftwork, but such records, at least in this form, were rarely kept by women. Historian Gloria Main notes the dearth of account books kept by women and adds that "most rural women born before 1730 could not write, read others' writing, or do arithmetic above the simplest level." Thus, they were unlikely to produce this type of ledger.[11] Indeed, even through the nineteenth century, women in the clothing trades did not necessarily master the pen as well as the needle: Anna Dunlevy, according to federal census records, did not learn to read or write until she was in her fifties, long after she had immigrated to the United States and was well into her career as one of Cincinnati's most renowned dressmakers.[12]

Yet it seems equally plausible that women's lack of access to literacy and numeracy skills caused them to develop other strategies for tracking their debts and indebtedness; such strategies, unfortunately, have rarely found their way into any archive. Some women chose to keep records in forms that we associate today with journals rather than accounts, a practice that has

helped obscure their original purpose: in the 1830s and 1840s, Castleton, Vermont, dressmaker L. H. Guernsey recorded her work cutting and altering clothing for kin and neighbors in the form of a daily diary, with no notations concerning her compensation until the end of the year. At that time, she paused to tally up her annual earnings, which apparently had been tracked elsewhere.[13]

Moreover, many account books kept by men *were* the account books of women. Catherine King Phelps, for instance, was an active Northampton, Massachusetts, gownmaker in the 1740s and 1750s. Her husband, mason Nathaniel Phelps, recorded in the pages of his own accounts that Catherine made riding hoods, made and altered gowns, and made frock bodies, stays, a "manty" (i.e., mantua), and other garments for her family and neighbors.[14] Roughly one in ten of Phelps's 100-plus accounts contains charges for Catherine's work in clothing production. His account book was also hers in part; the value of her time and skill was assessed and charged in precisely the same way.

A generation later, Esther Wright cut, basted, made, and altered more than 180 gowns, frocks, cloaks, stays, and other garments for Northampton residents.[15] She, like Catherine Phelps before her, kept her accounts in a ledger also devoted to the work of a male relative—in this case, Solomon Wright, whose relationship to Catherine is unclear. Certainly, the people of Northampton valued Esther's artisanal skill. If historians have overlooked her presence in the volume, however, it is not because Esther stayed in the shadows; Solomon may have inscribed his name in bold script in the middle of the book's cover, but Esther wrote her name just as boldly beneath his. That the book is cataloged as Solomon's is an artifact of twentieth-century, not eighteenth-century, biases.

Missing from this list are letters and diaries from the dressmakers' own hands. Sources such as these are hardest to find, because, especially early on, working women did not learn to write. Letters also indicate that someone is traveling, another luxury unknown to many early American needle-women. More often, the narrative sources describing dressmakers' work are those of clients, usually women of comparative privilege, who described their experiences with dressmakers in letters to friends or in their own journals. These sources can be most enlightening but must be used circumspectly, because artisans may or may not have shared their customers' views. Teasing out working women's concerns from their employers' words requires careful scholarship and cautious imagination: one must look past what the writer says, and try to puzzle out how the artisan herself may have perceived the same events.

What is added to our historical vision when we explore the artisanal world of American dressmakers? Most important, a close investigation of the dressmaking trades challenges traditional depictions of artisanry as a male preserve, because these women recognized the same range of tasks, skills, and practitioners, from the unskilled to the specialists, found in the more commonly studied early American crafts.[16] Moreover, by including women in the study of artisanry in this way, our understanding of artisanry itself necessarily changes: it expands definitions to accommodate the ways in

which women have long managed to practice their crafts despite legal and cultural barriers to female enterprise.

Thinking about the broader place of these skilled tradeswomen in the sweep of U.S. history opens other doors as well. We see women in the history of technology, finance, social economies, publishing, and design. We see women as employers and employees, clients and craftswomen. The artisanal tradition flourished from at least the eighteenth to the early twentieth century, and it persists today in the work of dressmaking women who still apply craft skill and training to the production of women's apparel.

Yet in tracing the story of American dressmaking, historians must be as enterprising as their subjects. The historian's craft, after all, is not so different from the dressmaker's. Like the dressmaker, the historian must learn and practice technical skills, while remaining watchful for promising opportunities and for new fashions, styles, and ideas made popular by fellow practitioners. Historians, like dressmakers, also must think creatively about the materials before them, observing their properties and determining how to use them to best advantage. And in the end, the products created by both dressmakers and historians reflect discipline, ingenuity, and imagination in equal parts. Long-standing biases and outmoded notions have placed dressmaking women outside artisanal circles for too long; innovative methods and new uses for old materials can help to restore them to their rightful position in the histories of American labor, enterprise, and craft.

6

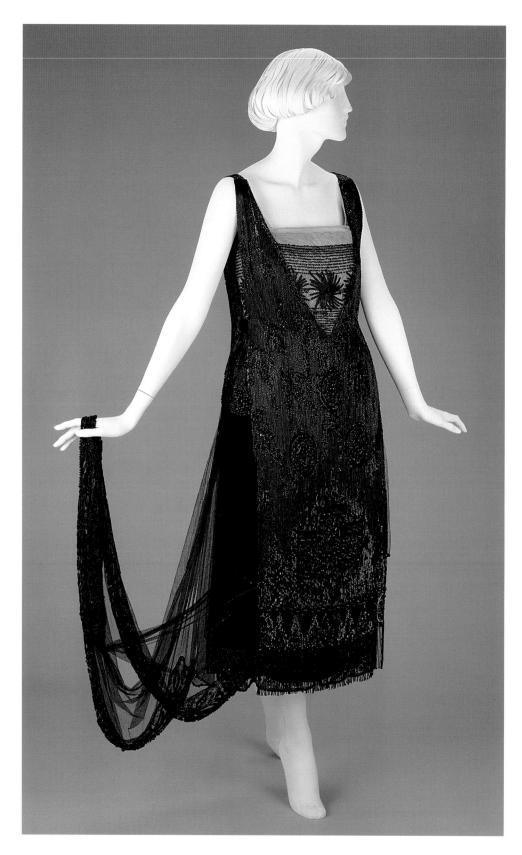

Josephine M. Kasselman (active 1913–1933); *Evening Dress,* 1918–1920; silk, beads, sequins, metallic thread; Label: Josephine 411 RACE ST. CINCINNATI; Gift of William Mack, 1943.23.

The elegant evening dress is covered with thousands of black sequins, faceted beads, and bugle beads. The train can be held in the hand or conveniently snapped to the dress at the waist.

Dressmakers in Cincinnati's Golden Age

AN INTRODUCTION

IN 1854, the editors of *Godey's Lady's Book* quoted a sermon by Gardiner Spring, noted Presbyterian cleric and author, on the topic of "feminology." Spring stated, "[T]he obvious designation of woman to a different sphere of action and influence, from that which is occupied by the stronger sex, suggests the contemplation of excellencies which . . . are delightfully appropriate to her character and condition. There is a feeling of heart, a consciousness of dependence, a natural and amiable timidity, a tenderness and kindness, which unfit a woman for the rude and tumultuous occupations, and which, while they assign to her a more retired sphere . . . constitute her true dignity and glory."[1]

Spring and the editors of *Godey's Lady's Book* were expressing their acquiescence to the prevailing ideology that men and women belonged "naturally" in "separate spheres." Women, considered tender, frail, and inferior to men both physically and intellectually, were intrinsically suited to a different or separate "occupation" in life. The ideology of the separate sphere became a pervasive concept that shaped the destiny

of women in the Victorian era and continues to do so today.

As a result of the immense cultural transformations that accompanied the Industrial Revolution and the shift to an urban society in America in the late eighteenth century, relationships between men and women changed profoundly. These changes were expressed in the separation of occupations or spheres of influence: those viewed as appropriate for men and those suited to women. In the new world of urban living, men were designated the breadwinners. During the working day, they braved a rat race of financial struggles in what was considered a ruthless and evil world. When the day was over, however, a man could find solace in the restorative powers of home, the woman's designated sphere. There, woman provided heightened morality and beauty to the lives of those around her. This "occupation" retired her to the home, free from contagion in the "rude and tumultuous" world, where she cared for her children and her husband, and set an example for her community. Women became, in the words of Barbara J. Berg, "butterflies in amber."[2] They were expected to elevate the community as a whole, through their actions and, in fact, their dress, to a higher level of goodness.

This idyllic arrangement, however, was neither acceptable nor even possible for many women. In 1848, as the rhetoric of the separate sphere ideology flooded women's periodicals, popular fiction, and the pulpit, supporters of the women's rights movement held their first convention. Women desired equal rights, education, and employment opportunities. They did not want to be merely decorative objects whose right to learn the alphabet was debated by male scholars and clerics.[3] They did not believe that "natural" physical limitations barred them from higher learning or from a profession. In 1920, after a struggle lasting seventy-two years, women finally won the right to vote; four more decades passed before the Women's Liberation Movement of the 1960s provided a semblance of equality with the "stronger sex."

The women's rights movement of the nineteenth century was fueled largely by middle-class women who had the education and the leisure time to travel, speak, and write. The many poor women of the working class found other avenues, generally out of dire necessity, to throw off the yoke of the separate sphere. Women went to work in the textile mills of the northeast, they taught school (at less than half the wages of their male counterparts), and they became entrepreneurs. Dressmakers belonged to this latter category. The majority were single, native-born Caucasian women of working-class status. In a social milieu that disdained working women as improper, they chose an occupation that afforded them independence, status, and the opportunity to step out

of their sphere into the world of polite society, intercontinental travel, and high fashion. Dressmakers of the nineteenth century represent the indomitable spirit of women who knew they could fare better than the life society prescribed.

The women who worked as dressmakers in Cincinnati in the late nineteenth and early twentieth centuries are representative of this national phenomenon. By the middle of the nineteenth century, Cincinnati was rich in both industrial and cultural resources. Growing from a frontier town at its founding in 1788 to a thriving metropolis with a population of over 160,000 by mid-century, it was heralded as the nation's fastest growing city. Cincinnati's founding families prospered as meat packers, attorneys, iron-masters, steamboat builders, and bankers; their wealth provided the city with cultural advantages—the art museum, the symphony, the opera, the theater—that rivaled those of the cities on the eastern seaboard. Their daily life of opulence required that the female members of these families be fashionably attired. Although Cincinnati women patronized the most revered Parisian couturiers as early as the 1860s, they also regularly employed the skills of local dressmakers. In a period when custom construction was the only choice for the complex fit of fashionable clothing, the dressmaker was an important figure in the life of the woman of style.

Dressmakers were highly skilled artisans; each gown they created was unique. Called a "noble art"[4] equal to that of the painter or sculptor, custom dressmaking required technical expertise, as well as a highly developed artistic sense that provided clients with stylish gowns.

Fashionable dress played a significant role in the lives of nineteenth-century women; it wielded far more influence than we can imagine today. Sarah Josepha Hale, editor of *Godey's Lady's Book* from 1837 to 1877, described dress as indicating "moral taste and goodness, or their perversion."[5] Correct and fashionable dress indicated a woman's moral excellence and her ability to affect positively those around her.

Every woman, whether in an urban or rural setting, wished to dress fashionably. Mill girls, who earned only a pittance, subscribed to fashion magazines and scrimped to dress in the latest styles. In church, which perhaps was a more appropriate venue for displaying one's spiritual prowess (an important aspect of a woman's prescribed sphere), women wore their Sunday best; everyone was sure to see it there. Although piety decreed that attention should not be given to dress, Lois Banner records the report of one young woman: "We could sing out of hymnbooks looking right at the notes and tell whose ruffle was cut in the new way and how Abby Norton's sleeve was set."[6] In short, dress was a defining element in every woman's life.

Like their counterparts across the country, Cincinnati dressmakers such as Selina Cadwallader, Adelaide Martien, and Anna Dunlevy turned their skills to profits. Research in census records, county vital statistics, credit ledgers, and city directories has rescued these women from anonymity and has yielded a limited amount of information about the artisans whose work is represented in this volume. Their struggles and their successes are documented in these bits of information that provide us with only a glimpse into their lives. Some banded together in family groups, with mothers, sisters, and daughters as their coworkers. Others were solitary: they were widowed or chose not to marry. Some worked for a short time until their businesses failed, always under threat of fierce competition, or until they married. Still others weathered the transition to women's ready-made clothing in the early twentieth century.

Whatever their circumstances, these women chose a life of independence that allowed them to step out of their separate sphere with a determination that we can admire even today.

The Ideology of the Separate Sphere

DURING THE CLOSING decades of the eighteenth century, the idea that men and women operated within separate spheres as a result of inherent physical and mental differences became increasingly central in American thought. According to this ideology, man's sphere of influence was the public realm, "dedicated to production, competition and material gain."[1] Woman, the weaker sex, was relegated to the private sphere of the home. Her role was domestic: caring for the home and the children, and embodying for her family—and for society at large—the moral ideals of virtue and beauty. The contemporary generalization that Victorian women were decorative objects who spent their days sipping tea and attending soirées is a direct result of the ideology of the separate sphere.

Notions of women's general inferiority did not originate in the Victorian era. These ideas were based on the fusion of classical, Christian, and Germanic traditions of the early Middle Ages, which spawned western European culture.[2] In the Victorian era, however, we first encounter the idea that men's and women's work occupied different spheres. This new ideology supported and maintained a rigid separation between work done in the home and that performed outside the home.

Settlers who crossed the Atlantic to the New World brought with them their cultural conviction that women were inherently inferior and therefore subservient to men. The law upheld this conviction. Under common law, married women suffered civil death. Once married, they held no legal rights to property and had no legal standing or existence apart from their husbands. Yet even while women were both ideologically and economically dependent, they figured substantially in the success of men's ventures. In fact, the puritanical colonists encouraged and even expected unmarried women to work. Believing industry to be a virtue and idleness a sin, authorities punished those who did not work. Working women were expected to help defray community expenses by paying a poll tax, but women contributed far more than taxes to colonial society.

Colonial America was an agrarian economy characterized by the small-scale

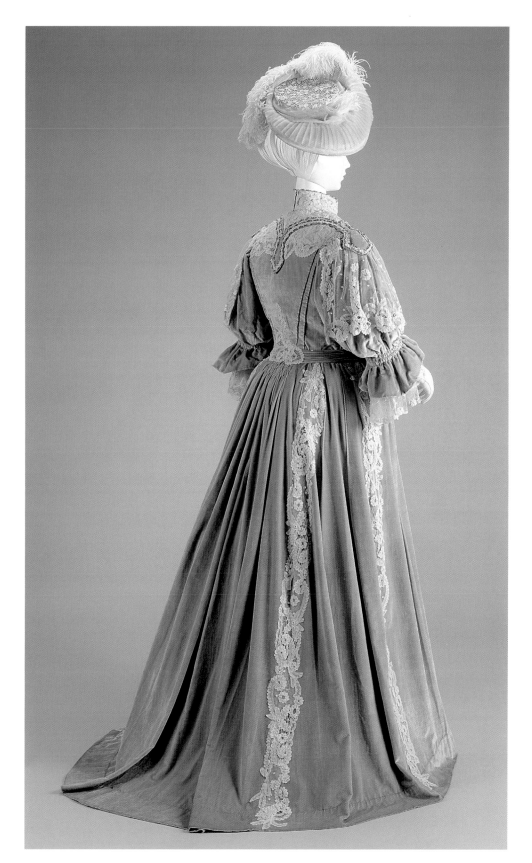

BACK VIEW: Alma
Heimbach; *Afternoon
Dress,* 1902; 1975.52a,b
(see page 119).

---

agriculture and business ventures typical of a preindustrial society. Individuals lived on a subsistence level. In the eighteenth century, farm households were self-contained: each household produced for its needs alone, with the help of itinerant and independent craftsmen such as the tailor, the weaver, and the blacksmith. One's home and place of work were one and the same, and this situation encouraged economic cooperation between husband and wife. In fact, the labor of each individual in the household, male or female, was important and valued as a contribution toward the physical and financial survival of the whole family or household. Men, in their superior position as head of the household, bore the responsibility of providing for their families, but women's labor was crucial to a settlement's prosperity. Women worked side by side with their husbands to "carve homes out of the wilderness." They farmed the fields, built log cabins, and took responsibility for household chores and child care.[3] Women were forced to depend on men to acquire land, but "men had no bread without women baking it."[4] In colonial America, men's economic independence was interwoven with women's essential contribution.

Although tasks almost always were divided along gender lines, a woman was an integral part of her husband's business. Women learned crafts from their fathers and husbands, and more often than not were quite capable of carrying on alone if they were widowed. Social mores permitted women to supplement their husbands' income: "The woman merchant, innkeeper, teacher or printer did her work without apology or sense of restriction, knowing she would be judged on her achievements."[5]

Yet even those women who merely performed "women's work" in the privacy of their home provided essential services for their families and contributed significantly to the household's economic wealth. From 1790 to 1810, Sarah Snell Bryant, an educated farm wife in western Massachusetts, described her daily occupations in her diary. Her tasks included "the sewing of shirts, gowns, and coats—knitting gloves and stockings, baking, brewing, preserving food, churning butter, gardening, nursing the sick, making candles or soap, washing, ironing, scouring, quilting with neighbors, and even entertaining visitors."[6]

Contemporaries of Sarah Snell Bryant who lived in more densely populated areas might have reduced their workload by purchasing goods and services, if they were wealthy enough to do so. Martha Church Challoner, for example, who lived in Newport, Rhode Island, in the 1760s, was well-off enough to buy various articles of clothing and some foodstuffs. She had two servants in her household and hired others to do the washing, mending, spinning, carding, and sewing. She continued, however, to make candles, knit stockings, sell butter and eggs, and sew the linens herself, while supervising the household.[7]

Women's labor, both inside and outside the home, was a highly valued source of goods for family use, as well as for barter or sale. The status of all women was enhanced by society's respect for the varied work they performed. As models of feminine capability, these industrious females enabled women to feel proud of their sex. Despite legal, economic, and personal restrictions, women had the ability to determine their own course in many ways; they exercised a measure of control over their own lives. These opportunities diminished markedly, however, in the last decades of the eighteenth century, when an outpouring of antifeminist writings and thinking began to pervade American society.[8]

At the end of the eighteenth century, the economy of the fledgling republic began to move away from agricultural and household production toward a flourishing commercial and industrial base. The Industrial Revolution, which began around 1760 and continued well into the nineteenth century, transformed the tradition of finely crafted objects made for specific individuals into the practice of multiple production for many in distant markets. Production was transferred from the home to the factory. This shift toward market-oriented production paved the way for the development of the manufacturing and factory system. Previously, a craftsman had been both owner and sole worker in a shop that provided high-quality custom goods for neighbors and relatives; now, the craftsman was boss of many apprentices and journeymen, who produced for retail sale to strangers. The system of piecework or "putting-out" developed similarly. Traditionally, a woman had produced the clothing for her family from start to finish: she carded, spun, and wove the fiber, cut the cloth, and sewed the garment to fit each individual. Under the new system, manufacturers distributed materials to individuals to work on in their homes. The finished pieces were collected, the workers were paid by the piece, and the finished articles were shipped to market to be sold. Large-scale manufacturing produced functional specialization, and division of labor became the norm. In the past, every man

and woman had been a jack of all trades, but, now, labor and laborers became specialized. This new system changed the nature of both men's and women's work.

Women's work had always been centered in the home, in a system in which the family's workplace and its home were one and the same. With the rise of merchant capitalism, however, women's traditional work in household manufacture became less important and less necessary.[9] One of the first areas to be industrialized was textile manufacturing, a primary responsibility for women in subsistence production. In 1760, spinning and weaving tasks began to be contracted out by large-scale manufacturers to women in their homes. The finished yarn and cloth were sent to the factories, which produced the final product. Soon, manufacturers placed the spinning wheels and looms in their factories. In 1789, Samuel Slater introduced industrial spinning machinery, and power looms followed in 1814. By 1830, the industrial manufacturing of cloth had largely superseded home production.

Household manufacture was fast becoming a thing of the past, and money was relied upon increasingly to purchase basic commodities. "Greater population density, commercial expansion, technological advances in transportation and communication, specialization in agriculture, and involvement of rural residents in given-out industry all contributed to the demise of the self-contained household economy." In 1797, Abigail Lyman of Boston complained, "There is no way of living in this town without cash."[10] Residents of smaller towns echoed this sentiment.

As women's traditional tasks were co-opted by the marketplace, their work became centered increasingly on household management and child care. Meanwhile, husbands and sons were drawn away from the home, in an effort to replace their productive labor with work that would produce cash. The cultural transformation that occurred between 1760 and 1835 created a society centered on modern industrial work patterns—patterns that no longer followed the natural rhythms of the day or the seasons. "The replacement of family production for direct use with wage earning, the institution of time-discipline and machine regularity in place of natural rhythms, the separation of work places from the home and the division of 'work' from 'life' were overlapping layers of the same phenomenon."[11]

As a result of this change, the ideology of the separate spheres was designated along traditional lines of work outside the home as man's sphere, and work inside the home as woman's. Perhaps as men were required to adapt to time discipline and specialized occupations, they began to observe fundamental differences between their own work and that of their wives. Perhaps they began to recognize that the work performed by women was premodern and not ruled by the time clock. Women's work in response to immediate and natural human needs, such as the preparation of meals, caring for the sick or child care, seemed nonsystemized and inefficient.

Whereas men's lives had changed enormously, women's lives had remained constant in a sense. Even the piecework that women accepted in the home as productive income-earning work was subject to the momentary and ever-changing needs of the household. Unlike men's work, it could be picked up and put down at a moment's

notice. Increasingly, men began to distinguish women's work from their own by labeling it as the women's sphere. This sphere was separate not only because it was defined within the home but also because it did not contribute to the rational acquisition of the new currency—cash. In that sense, it was worth less than men's work. Women's work integrated labor with life in a traditional manner; it was a remnant of the preindustrial, premodern life in which men no longer participated. It was truly in a separate sphere.[12]

At the heart of the separate sphere ideology was a compound of four ideas: "a sharp dichotomy between the home and the economic world outside that paralleled a sharp contrast between female and male natures, the designation of the home as the female's only proper sphere, the moral superiority of women, and the idealization of her function as mother." These concepts, joined with earlier traditions of female subordination and natural inferiority, shaped new attitudes toward women in the nineteenth century.[13] A flood of writings, both fictional and nonfictional, appeared in nineteenth-century periodicals, novels, and sermons, defining woman's role and telling women how to behave. "Whole books [were] printed to tell them how to set down their feet and how to lift them up again . . . ; how to fix their hands, and which way to hold their heads, when they ride or walk, sit or stand, or lie; and . . . about where to put their stockings when they take them off at night to go to bed."[14]

The definition of women as purely domestic was justified mainly by the contrast between the home and the outside world. Men's sphere, outside the home, was

"The Sphere of Woman," *Godey's Lady's Book* (March 1850).

Sarah Josepha Hale, editor of *Godey's Lady's Book* from 1837 to 1877, ardently endorsed women's appropriate role as confined to the home, even though she herself was employed in the public sphere. *Public Library of Cincinnati and Hamilton County.*

viewed as an arena of fierce competition and economic struggles that drove them to perform less than Christian actions in an attempt to remain financially solvent; it was an exploitive, selfish, degrading place. From this world, man retreated to the solace of home, where he found shelter from the day's cares and anxieties. Home was not only a retreat but also a moral and spiritual haven presided over by women.[15] Women's sustaining morality at home allowed men to negotiate safely the ruthless, debasing world of the marketplace.

No woman more clearly and emphatically put forth the tenets of the separate sphere than Sarah Josepha Hale, editor of the *Boston Ladies' Magazine* from 1828 to 1836, and subsequently of *Godey's Lady's*

Book; the latter periodical was read by women across the country throughout the nineteenth century. "Our men are sufficiently money-making," Hale said. "Let us keep our women and children from the contagion as long as possible."[16]

A paragon of harmony and tranquility, home eased the country's psychological transition from an agrarian society to a nation of industrial and urban growth. Woman became the ballast on the unsteady journey into urbanization, providing a model of stability and comfort in the home.[17] The separate sphere ideology provided early industrial America with a system for ordering, understanding, and adapting to a new way of life. It grew stronger and gained widespread acceptance with the convergence of various concepts that came to the forefront in the eighteenth and nineteenth centuries.

Writings of the early nineteenth century were filled with assertions that woman was the center of the domestic circle. Whereas "men were the movers, the doers, the actors,"[18] women were defined as passive, altruistic, soft, and submissive. As the guardians of both individual and social virtue, their natural purity had to be protected carefully within the home, away from the ruthless world of business and politics.[19] Mrs. A. J. Graves asserted emphatically that women's sphere was the home, and the home alone, in her book *Woman in America,* published in 1855. She wrote, "[H]er domestic duties have a paramount claim over everything else upon her attention— that *home* is her appropriate sphere of action; and that whenever she neglects these duties, or goes out of this sphere of action to mingle in any of the great public movements of the day, she is deserting the station which God and nature have assigned to her. She can operate far more efficiently in promoting the great interests of humanity by supervising her own household than in any other way."[20]

Women's role by no means was viewed as lacking power or influence. In fact, their vocation as the moral standard was exalted, and women rhetorically were accorded immense impact. Woman's role as mother was perceived as the primary force by which she could change the world. In the new social order, children were left at home primarily with their mothers, and a father's influence over his offspring was greatly diminished. Women were entrusted with their sons' and daughters' moral development at a time when the parent–child relationship was becoming much more important.

In previous centuries, childhood had been viewed as a separate stage of life in which children were to be segregated from adults. In the seventeenth and eighteenth centuries, however, attitudes began to change: the parent–child relationship assumed a new importance with regard to moral training. Coinciding neatly with the rise of domesticity and the emphasis on woman's role in the home, a "fearful charge" was placed on mothers. Within the safe haven of her home, woman's most important responsibility was bearing and rearing children. Motherhood took on almost a sacred connotation: "The mother's task was to see to the physical well-being of her offspring, to preserve their moral innocence, to protect them from evil influences, and to inspire them to pursue the highest spiritual values."[21]

A woman's failure to perform these tasks threatened not only her children's destiny but also that of the nation and civilization. The Reverend Winslow asserted that "upon woman depends the destiny of the nations! For she is rearing up senators and statesmen!"[22] Mrs. A. J. Graves, writing in 1841, described home as "the cradle of the human race; and it is here the human character is fashioned either for good or for evil. It is the 'nursery of the future of man and of the undying spirit'; and woman is the nurse and the educator. . . . [S]he may powerfully counteract the evil influences of the world by the talisman of her strong, enduring love."[23] Mothers were called upon to "destroy male sinfulness" by indoctrinating their offspring into a higher, female morality.[24]

Charged with this immense responsibility, women were imbued with moral superiority, even as they remained subordinate and inferior to men in all other matters. Somehow Eve, the cause of man's downfall, was transformed into the Virgin Mary, the vessel of salvation. Woman's great task was to remand her family to God. Women's journals overflowed with essays bearing titles such as "Woman, Man's Best Friend," "Woman, the Greatest Social Benefit," "Woman, a Being to Come Home To," and "The Wife: Source of Comfort and the Spring of Joy."[25] "Wom[a]n replaced nature as the sole repository of goodness and ethicality. . . . Untainted by the corrupt world, she soothed, purified, and nurtured."[26] Nineteenth-century authors, physicians, and clerics agreed that nothing adorned the female character more than "unaffected and deep-toned piety," and asserted that women were naturally prone to be religious.

Lily Martin Spencer
(1822–1902), United
States; *Patty-cake,
1855–1858*; oil on
canvas, 24 × 20 in.
(61 × 50.8 cm);
Museum Purchase:
Bequest of Mr. and
Mrs. Walter J. Wichgar,
1999.214.

"Religiosity, like delicacy, submission, and intellectual inferiority, came to be associated with female nature"; yet another clear delineation was established between men's and women's natural states or spheres.[27]

Woman's ability to inculcate her family with pure morality and virtue was a product of self-abnegation. Women were able to attain such purity and piousness only through all lack of self-interest: "Woman's self-renunciation was called upon to remedy man's self-alienation."[28] Her life was structured by the needs of others, and she was fulfilled through acts of service. The ideal woman was expected to set aside all consideration of herself; her joy would be manifested in the gratification of others.[29] Her work was that of pure affection, with no expectation of reward and no ambition.

Women were able to maintain this superior morality only by keeping busy at uplifting tasks. Fortunately, housework was viewed as uplifting in that it provided opportunities to exercise one's judgment and patient self-possession. Nursing the sick, a duty women commonly were called upon to perform, was considered a particularly gratifying and appropriate occupation: serving as a nurse called upon a woman's higher qualities of patience, mercy, and gentleness.[30] Ernst, a young gentleman in an article in *Godey's Lady's Book* titled "Intellect vs. Affection in Women," recounted the superior nursing care provided by his Aunt Barbara. He reported that she not only made him a bottle of cough syrup, but also that "when I complained of nothing new to read, [she] set to work and wrote some twenty stanzas on consumption."[31]

In addition to raising the children and instilling them with correct religious values,

woman cared for her husband. Battered by daily struggles with the evils of the world, the husband needed his wife's solace and undying devotion; this, too, was a product of self-denial. In T. S. Arthur's fictional story "Bear and Forbear," young Margaret, who was about to be married, conversed with her Aunt Hannah about the requirements of marriage. Aunt Hannah cautioned the bride-to-be to make "Bear and forbear" her motto. Margaret, astonished by her aunt's serious tone, inquired, "Would you have a wife never think of herself?" To which Aunt Hannah replied, "The less she thinks of herself . . . the better. . . . [T]he more she thinks of her husband, the more she will love him and seek to make him happy."[32] Hoping to instill correct values at a much earlier age, a schoolbook titled *The American Instructor* informed young girls that their sole aim should be "to recompense [man's] care with soft endearments."[33] Women could not escape the inexorable message that woman's sole importance consisted of caring for men as mother, daughter, sister, or wife. The Philadelphia *Public Ledger and Daily Transcript* stated this clearly in an article: "A woman is nobody. A wife is everything."[34]

In contrast to European women, Americans were viewed as losing all independence once they entered matrimony. Alexis de Tocqueville, a young French nobleman who visited America in 1830-1831, observed Americans' general character and later recorded his observations. He described American women entering marriage as follows: "Upon her entrance into the world a young American woman finds these notions (of domestic primacy) firmly established; she sees the rules which are derived from them; she is not slow to perceive that she cannot

DETAIL: H. & S. Pogue; *Afternoon Dress*, 1896–1897; 1971.151a,b (see page 159).

depart for an instant from the established usages of her contemporaries, without put–ting in jeopardy her peace of mind, her honor, nay, even her social existence; . . . she has learned, by the use of her independence, to surrender it without a struggle and without a murmur when the time comes for making the sacrifice."[35]

Tocqueville's observations are echoed by those of American writer Samuel Jennings, who outlined the proper behavior of a wife toward her husband in ten points. He sug-gested, first, that she acquaint herself inti-mately with her husband's temper, inclina-tions, and manner, so that she could make herself and their home agreeable to *him*. Jennings made it clear that the wife should adapt to the husband, because "nature has made man the stronger, the consent of mankind has given him superiority over his wife, his inclination is, to claim his natural and acquired rights." Jennings added force to

this statement by quoting St. Paul's dictum: "Wives submit yourselves unto your own husbands, as unto the Lord, for the husband is the head of his wife."[36]

Although both Tocqueville and Jennings described the ideal subjugation of wife to husband, they also "seized upon a central paradox of domesticity, that women were expected to make a voluntary choice amounting to self-abnegation."[37] Marriage was glorified socially as the only avenue to woman's personal self-fulfillment, but a woman's decision to marry was a momen-tous one. Marriage brought society's appro-bation, but it also entailed the willing acceptance of a heavy responsibility that resulted both theoretically and lawfully in the loss of self. Married women could not sign contracts; they had no right to their earnings nor to property, even when it was received as an inheritance or a dowry, and they had no claim to their children in the event of a legal separation from their husband. Indeed, the choice to marry was the most important decision a woman would make and involved the most important consequences for her life.[38] Marriage was described aptly by Lavinia B. Kelly of Northwood, New Hampshire, who called her engagement to J. S. Cilly in 1837 "a serious business."[39]

In the nineteenth century, as in earlier times, marriage was more often than not a union of convenience and financial considerations rather than the result of romantic attraction between the two participants. Certainly, some marriages were based on passionate love. Amanda Wilson of Cincinnati consistently recorded her love for her husband, Obed, in her diary in 1861. Obed Wilson traveled often as a result of his job in publishing; Amanda often stated that she was "Oh so lonely" without him. She wrote that "no one has a better and kinder husband than mine . . . so noble, so good," and she described many happy walks and evenings spent reading to each other.[40]

For every marriage of love, however, there were probably two based solely on convenience, in which the partners either tolerated or learned to love each other. Lavinia Kelly, two months after her marriage to Mr. Cilly, described his absence from home on business by saying, "I miss him a little bit."[41] The bonds of love between husband and wife were expected to grow over time rather than being firmly established when they professed their vows. In most marriages of convenience, the emotional intensity of the marriage probably suffered: passion was not the norm when partners were learning to love each other in a relationship based on inequality.

In addition to the absence of a heartfelt connection between husband and wife, men and women were viewed as basically different, as expressed by the ideology of the separate sphere. Men operated from the intellect; women dealt from the heart. Their approaches to life were believed to be based on completely opposite sets of values, and on biological determinants as well. Women's reproductive organs were believed to determine their physical and emotional well-being. Both biological forces and acutely sensitive nerves purportedly made women affectionate and more emotional than men.[42] Although these inherent differences could be complementary and therefore advantageous in a partnership such as marriage and parenthood, they also implied that women could find satisfyingly reciprocal relationships only with other women: "[J]ust as women were viewed as inferior to men in rationality, men could not be expected to respond in kind to women's feelings."[43]

Through recorded evidence of intense relationships between women, it is clear that this phenomenon did occur. Women were equals to one another, they were inherently alike, and in many ways, they were dependent on each other. "In an era when alimony was rare, women who wished to divorce their husbands leaned on female kin for support. A woman who faced death in childbirth counted on her sisters to protect her children. . . . Young widows turned to their female kin to sustain them and their children; elderly widows counted on their daughters and daughters-in-law to nurse them."[44]

Women were connected intimately by a commonality of social and economic restrictions, a shared domestic vocation and a sexual destiny, experiences that united them both physically and emotionally. Other women were their peers, whereas, in essence, the closest relationship possible between a woman and a man was that of subordinate to superior. Women sought out, and found deeply satisfying, friendships with other women. In their diaries, many women recorded such friendships as their closest relationships and frequently used the word *love* in describing their feelings.[45]

Such relationships afforded women in the nineteenth century a sisterhood that was a result of their social and emotional separation from men. Unable or perhaps unwilling to create such bonds with their husbands, they were sustained by heartfelt friendships with other women. Supported by their churches, clubs, or religious affiliations, women found in their role as moral superiors a commonality that could not be satisfied in their unequal relations with men.

Relations between men and women were reshaped by the ideology of the separate sphere, a response to profound social and economic changes. Although these changes began in the late eighteenth century and were realized in the early decades of the nineteenth century, the ideas that they spawned continued to affect society through the early twentieth century.

The Separate Sphere and the Women's Rights Movement in the Latter Half of the Nineteenth Century

In 1848, the first Women's Rights Convention in America was held at Seneca Falls, New York. Sixty-eight women and thirty-two men signed the Declaration of Sentiments, which stated, in part, "We hold these truths to be self evident; that all men and women are created equal." Twelve resolutions were passed; three of these were particularly relevant to barriers faced by women.

RESOLVED, That woman is man's equal—was intended to be so by the Creator, and the highest good of the race demands that she be recognized as such.

RESOLVED, That woman has too long rested satisfied in the circumscribed limits which corrupt customs and a perverted application of the Scriptures have marked out for her, and that it is time she should move in the enlarged sphere which her great Creator has assigned her.

RESOLVED, That the speedy success of our cause depends upon the zealous and untiring effort of both men and women, for the overthrow of the monopoly of the pulpit, and for the securing to woman an equal participation with men in the various trades, professions, and commerce.[46]

The Seneca Falls Convention initiated the first phase of the women's rights movement in the United States. Meeting almost yearly from 1848 until the outbreak of the Civil War, proponents of women's rights succeeded in bringing the issue before the public and convincing a small number of men and women of the necessity of organizing to promote equality between the sexes. Equality was hard-won, however; the women's rights movement did not focus on a single goal, the right to vote, until the turn of the century, and that goal was not realized until 1920.

The women's rights movement, which developed in the years leading up to the Civil War, emerged from two sources: women's growing dissatisfaction with their

22

DETAIL: H. & S. Pogue; *Wedding Dress,* 1898; 1973.503a,b (see page 57).

assigned place in society, as outlined in the 1848 convention resolutions; and antebellum reform politics, particularly the antislavery movement. This movement offered a moral goal outside the home to those women who were most discontent with their subordinate domestic position. For women, championing this cause was a natural outgrowth of the separate sphere ideology. Charged with the moral responsibility to preserve and heighten social virtue, women found that abolition, much like temperance, was a natural fit with their allegedly superior morality and pious nature that were part of their sphere. Women's involvement in the push for the abolition of slavery enabled them to imagine social change for themselves: if the slaves could be freed, so could they.

Although women's suffrage has come to be synonymous with winning the right to vote, it was hardly an issue in these early years. The Seneca Falls Convention of 1848, organized by Elizabeth Cady Stanton, Lucretia Mott, and several other women, focused on women's legal rights to control their own property and earnings, guardianship of their children, divorce, educational and employment opportunities, and legal status in general. The convention was a mixture of womanly modesty and feminist militancy. Faced with the task of composing a manifesto expressing their demands, the organizers, in Stanton's words, felt "as helpless and hopeless as if they had been suddenly asked to construct a steam engine."[47]

The women who both organized and attended the convention, including Stanton, were not free from their own domestic responsibilities. Like their nonfeminist sisters, they lacked the necessary skills for operating in public; they were often opposed by their fathers, brothers, and husbands; they still bore their domestic and child-rearing responsibilities; and they feared the consequences of their actions. Susan B. Anthony, one of the foremost women's rights activists, was one of the few women who remained single. Even Stanton, who was married and had seven children, questioned her ability to carry on after the birth of her 12½-pound son, Robert. Lucy Stone and Antoinette Brown were both married *after* they had become prominent women's rights advocates. All these women found it difficult to balance their political goals with their domestic responsibilities.

The annual meetings of the women's rights conventions held between 1850 and 1860 provided a forum in which women could state their dissatisfaction and attempt to reach some agreement about what they wanted to achieve. What *was* a woman's proper sphere? How equal *were* men and women, and how could that equality be manifested socially and legally? How and when *should* divorce be permitted? These early reformers showed little interest in gaining the vote; their immediate concerns were legal, educational, and employment rights.

Susan B. Anthony, along with a handful of volunteers, managed to win the first victory for women's legal rights. In her first campaign, Anthony asked the New York legislature for three reforms: women's control of their own earnings; guardianship of their children in case of divorce; and the vote. Her method of collecting signatures on a

petition, though commonplace now, was revolutionary at the time.

The response to Anthony's petition by the New York Legislature's Judiciary Committee was ludicrous. The bachelors on the Committee conceded to the married men's experience in such matters. The Committee stated that women "always have the best place and choicest tidbit at the table. They always have the best seat in the cars, carriage and sleighs; the warmest place in the winter and the coolest place in the summer. They have their choice on which side of the bed they will lie, front or back. A lady's dress costs three times as much as that of a gentleman; and, at the present time, with the prevailing fashion, one lady occupies three times as much space in the world as a gentleman."[48] The Committee's report concluded that the gentlemen, not the women, were the sufferers, and the petition was denied.

Nevertheless, in 1860, four years later, Stanton once again presented a joint session of the two Houses with a bill: the Married Woman's Property Act. This bill became law: it granted women the right to own property, to collect their own wages, to sue in court, and to enjoy property rights, upon widowhood, similar to those of a man when his wife predeceased him. In the same year, fourteen additional states passed some form of women's property rights legislation. In Ohio, the legislation was passed in 1871.

Although these women were advocates of women's rights, they did not fundamentally reject the ideology of the separate spheres. In fact, many women endorsed the belief that women were not inferior to men, but inherently different. The feminist movement contributed to the transformation of

23

women's social roles, but it did not reject the idea of a separate, unique female identity connected to domesticity—an identity that most women were unwilling to relinquish. The ideology of separateness was deeply ingrained, and both men and women feared the demise of the female sphere and the important functions performed in it. Even the most radical feminists, Stanton and Anthony, "recognized the importance of maintaining the virtues of the female world while eliminating discrimination against women in public."[49] The concepts of female moral superiority and sisterhood remained relevant for these women, and they affirmed the separateness of woman's nature.

The concept of man and woman as separate and different was supported in the mid-nineteenth century by two prominent theories. First, Charles Darwin's theory of evolution, set forth in 1859 in *The Origin of Species,* powerfully reinforced the separate sphere ideology by justifying it in biological terms that were accepted as scientific truth. Darwin's theories gained further authority upon publication of his *Descent of Man* in 1871. He asserted that survival of the fittest and the process of natural selection gave certain individuals in a species a competitive advantage over others. Men, whose metabolic rate was higher than women's, generated more variations among their sex and were more aggressive; therefore, men evolved into the stronger and more intelligent members of the species. In contrast, women's reproductive role made them more dependent on men. It was believed that women had smaller and less highly developed brains than men, which performed at the lower level of instinct, whereas men's brains operated in the higher range of

mental function, namely, reason.[50]

Second, in addition to the notion that women were separate and different because of lesser intellectual capability, the age-old idea that a woman's mind was limited by her weaker body gained new strength after the Civil War. Perhaps anxious that the changes beginning to occur in the traditional division of sex roles would further weaken a social fabric already strained by the Civil War, individuals in America championed this idea more fervently than at any other time. Women were plagued by a host of various ailments, probably related more to factors such as lack of exercise, restrictive clothing, and insufficient fresh air and intellectual stimulation. In general, they were viewed as sickly and fragile. Male doctors, however, directed their attention to the uterus and held women's reproductive system responsible for most of their medical problems. According to English philosopher Herbert Spencer, the body was a closed system: if one part of the system suffered undue stress, another part would fail. The uterus was believed to exert paramount power over a woman's physical and moral system, creating "a weak, submissive, uncreative, emotional, intuitive and generally inferior personality."[51] In 1870, one physician stated that it was as though "the Almighty, in creating the female sex, had taken the uterus and built up a woman around it."[52] The uterus usurped much of a woman's energy during menstruation and pregnancy. During these periods, women were relegated to rest and to reduced mental and emotional strain. The female sexual organs bore the onus for many common ailments, including headaches, nervous disorders, indigestion, insomnia, depression, and backaches.[53]

One strong advocate of this position, Dr. Edward Clarke, a member of Harvard's Board of Overseers and a former member of the university's medical school faculty, warned that too much mental stimulation, such as the educational advances that women sought, would destroy a woman's health and reproductive capabilities. He supported this view with scientific evidence, citing the work of Darwin and Spencer, as well as several cases of invalid women who had attempted a college education. In an attempt to pacify feminists, Clarke did not claim that women were inferior, only that they were greatly different from men. He did not question the idea that "whatever a woman can do, she has a right to do."[54] The question was what *could* a woman do? Clarke believed that subjecting women to the intellectual stimulus of a college education, especially at puberty, would result in a feeble body and quite possibly in nervous collapse and sterility. He suggested that women should study one-third less than men, and not at all during menstruation.[55]

Even when they abided by the constrictions of the separate sphere ideology, women in the antebellum period saw a great need for enhanced education. Part of their insistence rested on a growing understanding of the stages of child development and on the belief that sophisticated skills were needed in the important task of child rearing. These beliefs ushered in the concept of "educated motherhood." Within their sphere, women were responsible for the attentive care and rearing of their children. This required knowledge—knowledge that went beyond maternal instincts and required "maternal insights." A mother was responsible not only for meeting her children's physical needs but

also for nurturing their "budding intelligence." To do this, she needed to "read, think, study and apply" what she learned.[56] In order to read, think, study, and apply, however, women needed to be educated. The concept of educated motherhood seemed to make a college education almost indispensable.

Unfortunately, avenues to high-quality education were not open to women. For a young man, a good education was an important, well-established tool for success in a vocation or career. A young woman's education, however, was generally inferior, sporadic, often interrupted when household duties called, and focused on preparing for marriage and child bearing. Feminists fighting for educational opportunities faced a threefold problem: "They had to win the right to learn, the right to teach, and the right to think." In the pre–Civil War era, the arguments and demands for better and higher education for women challenged patriarchal prejudices and institutional restrictions.[57]

At this same time, large numbers of women were entering the workforce as teachers. Teaching school, even in the early years of the republic, was considered respectable work and provided many single women the opportunity to earn wages in a postagrarian society. It was one of the few instances of the expansion of nondomestic occupations for women. The growth of the public school system in the early decades of the nineteenth century provided women with ample opportunities to teach in traditional summer schools, in the growing numbers of academies for girls, and finally, in the 1830s, in traditional winter terms, in which they instructed both boys and girls. Women finally were awarded this last position in part because they accepted a much lower salary than men in the same position, often one-fourth to one-half as much. Women were considered natural teachers; the fact that they accepted wages approximately 60 percent less than those of men was a bonus. One Ohio school superintendent stated, "As the business of teaching is made more respectable, more females engage in it, and the wages are reduced. Females do not . . . expect to accumulate much property by this occupation; . . . I, therefore, most earnestly commend this subject to the attention of those counties which are in the habit of paying men for instructing little children, when females would do it for less than half the sum, and generally much better than men can."[58]

By 1888, 63 percent of all teachers were women. Even so, their own education was minimal. The Midwest seemed to lead the movement to open exclusively male college and university programs to women. Oberlin College, located in Oberlin, Ohio, and established in 1833 as a teachers' college, was the first to grant undergraduate degrees to women. In 1852, Antioch College in Yellow Springs, Ohio, also became coeducational. Until the time of the Civil War, Cincinnati was considered a regional educational center for women with the establishment of Wesleyan Female College and Glendale Female Seminary. Other institutions began slowly to open their doors to women.

Many of the institutions that admitted women in those early years did so as a result of political and financial pressure. They educated women for traditional female occupations and prepared them for marriage. The great majority of their female students were enrolled in education and home economics programs, and received a poorer quality education than their male counterparts.

Despite mandatory exercise regimens and other precautions, higher education for women in the 1860s and 1870s was considered a hazardous proposition. As one alumna of Vassar recalled, "It was impressed upon the whole family that the higher education of women was an experiment, and that the world was looking on, watching its success or defeat."[59]

Women pushing for higher education were energized by their progress but haunted by Dr. Clarke's book *Sex in Education*, published in 1873, in which Clarke described his concerns about the toll of advanced education on women's health. His warnings were heard and heeded by those who feared what might happen to their health if they pursued their education. "At the University of Michigan where women had been studying for only three years, it was reported that everyone was reading Clarke's book and that two hundred copies had been sold in one day."[60] At the University of Wisconsin, where women's presence on campus was not widely accepted, although they had studied there since the Civil War, the regents explained in 1877, "Every physiologist is well aware that at stated times, nature makes a great demand upon the energies of early womanhood. . . . It is better that the future matrons of the state should be without university training than that it should be produced at the fearful expense of ruined health."[61] One can only imagine the fears of young women contemplating a college education while

Anna Dunlevy (active 1889–1913); *Afternoon Dress,* 190–1907; silk, cotton; Gift of Anna E. Winston, 1954.414a,b (see page 103).

28

faced with Clarke's grim predictions of dys-menorrhea, ovaritis, prolapsed uterus, hysteria, and neuralgia.

Feminists fought back against Clarke's claims by disputing his findings as faulty and conducting their own surveys of women who had earned college degrees. Some feminists agreed overall with Clarke and Darwin regarding women's inferior physical and intellectual abilities, yet maintained "that women's special qualities justified their higher education and that their constitutions were sufficiently hardy to withstand the rigors of intellectual exercise."[62] These women also feared the potential harm to "the natural harmony" caused by barring females from higher education. They believed that without the female influence, there was a great risk of social upheaval through the unbridled expression of male aggression, individualism, rationalism, and competition.[63]

By the latter half of the nineteenth century, women had won, to varying degrees, two of their three goals. They had succeeded in gaining legal rights to their property, their money, and their children, and they had made significant progress toward equal education. They continued to fight for the realization of their third goal: freedom in choice of profession. Women who sought an occupation or profession did so for many reasons. College-educated women had experienced the exhilaration of learning and wanted to put their education to use. Middle-class women and unmarried girls often needed to supplement their husband's or father's earnings. Spinsters and widows needed to survive and often had dependents who relied on them for income. For some, it was the need for intellectual stimulation; for

others, it was the need to eat. In any case, women in the antebellum period began to demand the same freedom in choice of occupation as that enjoyed by men.

In 1853, feminist and antislavery advocate Jane Swisshelm ridiculed men who opposed women's entrance into the workforce: "It is well known that thousands, nay, millions of women in this country are condemned to the most menial drudgery, such as men would scorn to engage in, and that for one fourth the wages. . . . But let one presume to use her mental powers—let her aspire to turn editor, public speaker, doctor, lawyer—take up any profession or avocation which is deemed honorable and requires talent, and O! bring cologne, get a cambric kerchief and feather fan, unloose his corsets and take off his cravat! What a fainting fit Mr. Propriety has taken!"[64]

Women who wanted or needed to work faced the barriers of limited opportunity and lack of social acceptance. The definition of an appropriate female occupation was based on the prevailing views of propriety. Feminist Lucy Stone recalled, "When I was a girl I seemed to be shut out of everything I wanted to do. I might teach school. . . . I might go out to dress-making or tailoring, or trim bonnets, or I might work in a factory or go out to domestic service; there the mights ended and the might nots began."[65]

Women as well as men were divided on the subject. Some saw employment for unmarried girls as a deterrent to a hasty and unwise marriage. Others feared corruption and destruction: they described young girls who were lured to the city by employment, who could not possibly make enough money to support themselves, and who fell into prostitution. Although the number of women entering the professions increased between 1860 and 1920, it lagged behind the number of women graduating from college. Professions open to women, such as nursing or teaching, were most often extensions of their "proper" female role; opportunities in medicine, law, the sciences, or the ministry were severely restricted. Between 1890 and 1920, the number of professional degrees awarded to women increased by 226 percent. In 1920, women still were only a tiny proportion of practitioners in the learned professions. Men did not welcome women into careers. Also, although the number of women choosing to remain single increased, as did the divorce rate, the majority of women still chose marriage and motherhood over actually utilizing their education in a professional career.

In most cases, feminists in the second half of the nineteenth century were able to advance women toward greater equality with men, perhaps to a "separate but equal" condition. Nonetheless, neither men nor women were yet willing to relinquish their separate spheres, and both sexes clung to the idea that they were inherently different. The concept of separate spheres deflected conflict and gave women a guise under which to move ahead.

Women's clubs were one way in which women maintained their separate sphere outside the home. Although such clubs had existed previously, those founded after the Civil War were formal in organization and national in scope. They were formed with the intent to "fulfill the principles of virtuous womanhood" and to "elevate the moral character of society,"[66] but they provided women with an organized and united network. The General Federation of

Women's Clubs, organized in 1892, had 495 affiliates and one hundred thousand members.

Such clubs were initially founded to offer a forum for literary discussion. They provided continuing education either for women who had not attended college or for those who had done so and wished to maintain their intellectual life. Clubs were places where women could teach and be taught; they were mutual improvement societies and support groups. If nothing else, they provided a sympathetic forum in which women would be heard and accepted, where they could gain confidence in speaking before an audience and have the opportunity to express their thoughts freely and logically. Here, women could nurture their own culture without the disruptions of male dominance.[67] The meetings offered marvelous opportunities for members to establish and maintain friendships, and the members believed that women could achieve social betterment through intellectual and social activity.

By the turn of the century, nationally based clubs such as Sorosis and the Woman's Christian Temperance Union had launched a multitude of social reform programs. These activities politicized traditional women and forced them to define themselves as citizens, not simply as wives and mothers.[68] In this way, the clubs served as an extension of the feminist movement and opened the door of understanding to scores of women who previously had dismissed the movement as disruptive and destructive.

Summary

The ideology of the separate sphere played a defining role in women's lives throughout the nineteenth and early twentieth centuries. Even when the suffrage movement succeeded in winning women's right to vote in 1920, women were neither truly equal nor free. Many would question whether this is the case even today. Over the course of a century or more, however, women made significant progress in breaking out of a sphere that had been defined for them—perhaps by men, perhaps by social upheaval, perhaps to some extent by themselves, and by a desire to maintain equilibrium in the midst of drastic change. Women were reluctant to relinquish their sphere even when the opportunities presented themselves. A satisfaction with their role as saviors in a world of wickedness, a biological need to be maternal and care for both their children and each other, a fear about how their lives and those of their children would be changed—these and many other possible factors certainly existed, exacting a steady

but slow movement toward a more equal status between men and women.

By the end of the eighteenth century, women had been transformed from subservient but rugged helpmates to fragile, physically weak, and intellectually inferior but morally superior fashion plates. By the early years of the twentieth century, women had become more confident and politically active beings who were beginning to find their voice. Although progress had been made, a great deal of work remained; much of this would not be complete until mid-century. Although women were severely restricted both physically and intellectually by the separate sphere concept, they manipulated it to their own advantage. They managed to use their separateness to bond, to gain strength, to create avenues to social betterment, and to challenge the social mores that bound them.

Women in the Workplace

THE TRANSFORMATION from an agrarian to an industrial and urban society ushered in a new era for women and work. As women's traditional occupations were usurped by mechanical substitutes, women's work adapted and evolved. While married women remained in their prescribed sphere of household management and child care, their single daughters went out to work, providing cash revenue in place of home labor. Their employment was viewed as a fulfillment of family obligations prior to marriage. Single women did not have the responsibilities of managing their own household; their work was socially accepted as a contribution to the family's financial security. Therefore, even while the ideology of the separate sphere dictated that a woman's place was in the home, the early American economy depended on a steady supply of female workers.[1]

The spinning and weaving mills of New England are a prime example of young women's movement into the workplace. In the 1820s and 1830s, mills such as those in Lowell, Massachusetts, were filled with single women. Francis Cabot Lowell and other mill owners devised a respectable route for women entering the working world. They primarily recruited from farm families the daughters between the ages of fifteen and thirty. Working twelve-hour days, six days a week, the mill girls, or operatives, as they were called, tended the machines in cramped rows amid deafening noise and generally unsafe conditions. Until the early 1850s, they were expected to live in supervised boarding houses, observe an evening curfew, and attend church services. This structure provided a "proper" environment in which young women could provide their families with financial support.

Schoolteaching was another early form of employment that was socially acceptable for women. Young women who themselves had only a basic education were qualified to teach young boys and girls the basics of reading, writing, and mathematics. Unfortunately, in the mills, the schools, or any other place where women worked, their wages were abysmally low.

The mid-nineteenth century was not an easy time for workers, male or female.

Hundreds of thousands of working-class Americans lived in overcrowded, polluted slums. "In 1851 Horace Greeley, editor of the *New York Tribune*, estimated that $10.37 was the minimum weekly wage necessary to support a family of five."[2] This amount would pay for rent, food, fuel, and clothing, with nothing left to cover medical bills or other unforeseen expenses. Few, however, made even this paltry wage. Shoemakers and printers averaged $4.00 to $6.00 per week; cabinetmakers made about $5.00; male textile workers averaged $6.50. If a lower-class family was simply to survive, every member was required to work and contribute to the family's resources.[3]

Working women, however, found their wages to be especially meager. In almost every industry, even the most highly skilled women earned 50 to 60 percent less than their male counterparts. "Wage inequities were reflected in an 1833 Philadelphia survey that showed three-quarters of that city's women workers earning less for 78 hours of work a week than journeymen received for one 10-hour day."[4] In 1846, straw hat workers, who were exclusively women and children, averaged only twenty-five cents a day. Artificial flower makers worked eighteen hours a day in their homes and earned $1 to $3 a week.

A flood of women into any trade caused poor wages to fall even lower. Women stitchers who did piecework competed ruthlessly. Those who earned twenty-five cents for handstitching a pair of pants and sixteen cents for stitching a shirt were quickly underbid by others, who agreed to make the same articles for less. In Pittsburgh, women spent an entire day making one shirt and received 12½ cents for their

efforts. In Cincinnati, widows were destitute and could not meet their basic needs because they could not find work; if they did so, they did not receive fair compensation for their labor. "Working as hard as they could, they made nine shirts in a week at 10 cents per shirt."[5]

Working for the same poor wages, and facing the same expenses, but without the support of family members, single women were especially hard-pressed. Rent alone averaged $1.50 to $1.75 per week, leaving only a small sum for food, clothing, medicine, church contributions, leisure activities, and savings. Even a brief period of unemployment due to illness or loss of one's job could be disastrous. In 1869, one experienced seamstress stated, "I have worked from dawn to sundown . . . for twenty-five cents. I have lived on one cracker a day when I could not find work, travelling from place to place in pursuit of it."[6]

When insufficient wages reduced women to starvation levels, many turned to prostitution as their only recourse. In 1859, William Sanger, a social investigator, surveyed two thousand prostitutes serving prison time in New York City. More than half of those he interviewed had earned an average of $5 a month or less before resorting to prostitution. Three-fourths of these women were single or widowed.[7] At least one schoolteacher in Cincinnati quit her poorly paid position at the Second District School for prostitution, a more lucrative profession.[8] The fact that some women became prostitutes only reinforced the beliefs that women should not be working. Women who worked were susceptible to temptation, and were viewed as immoral as a result.

Josephine M. Kas-
selman (active 1913–
1933); *Evening Dress,*
1917–1920; silk, cotton,
metallic cloth; Label:
Josephine 911 NEAVE
BLDG. CINCINNATI;
Gift of Mrs. William
Vollmer, 1985.18 (see
page 126, right).

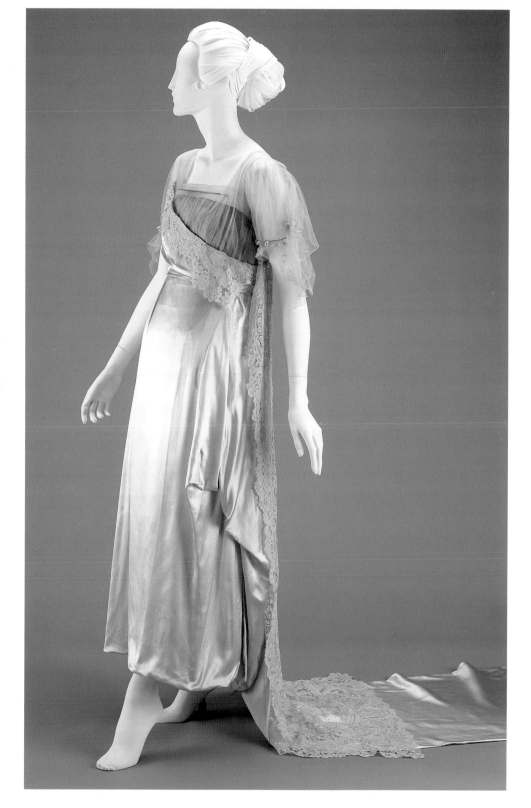

34

Employers justified the inequality between men's and women's wages, because they viewed women as temporary workers: almost certainly, they would leave the workforce as soon as they married. This "fact" was echoed by the 1907 report on working women compiled by the U.S. Census Bureau, which stated that the adoption of an occupation by women was "far from customary," exceptional in the well-to-do classes of society, and "more often temporary than permanent."[9] Indeed, most women, even as late as the turn of the twentieth century, ceased working outside the home when they married. Some were dismissed by their employers, but most gave up their jobs voluntarily before the wedding, as a matter of custom.[10]

According to the Census Bureau, marriage for women was analogous to an occupation for a man, "and it has been said with some truth that marriage is woman's occupation or profession."[11] Generally, only the poorest women continued to work after marriage, and they did so out of pure necessity. Based on the belief that the man should be the primary (if not the only) breadwinner in the home, it was held that a man should be able to make a living wage—enough to support a nonworking wife and their children. When women began working in larger numbers, the question of a living wage for the single woman, whether unmarried or widowed, became an issue. "Budgets included in legislative discussions of a woman's living wage were set at near-starvation level. . . . A woman's wage was enough to keep [her] from starving but not enough to make leaving home attractive."[12]

The Civil War strongly influenced women's progression into the workforce. In the years following the war, thousands of women were driven to work by the absence of working fathers, husbands, and brothers who had either become disabled or died in the war. There had always been an underclass of women in this predicament, but the Civil War exacerbated the problem, drastically reducing the number of potential husbands and transforming otherwise respectable wives into poor widows. In rural areas, women were forced to take responsibility for the family farm and support their families without the help of male relatives. In urban settings, they found jobs in the factories in ever-increasing numbers. The 1850 census recorded 225,922 women at work in factories; by 1870, that number had risen to 323,370. Others glutted the sewing trades. For the first time, females were employed as civil servants, office workers, and retail clerks, and many became teachers. Nursing also became a viable female occupation. During this period and in the late nineteenth century, the sex stereotyping of occupations was established in a pattern that persisted well into the twentieth century. "This was the moment when typists, stenographers, department store clerks, and school teachers all became prototypically female."[13] Nevertheless, opportunities were expanding: in the 1830s, Harriet Martineau observed that only seven occupations were open to women. By 1900, women could be found in 295 of the 303 occupations listed in the U.S. Census.[14]

The surplus population of women who needed work to survive after the Civil War depressed their wages, which already were barely adequate. Using this situation as a lever, women pleaded for help: through no fault of their own, they found themselves outside their socially prescribed bounds and left to fend for themselves. They pushed for higher wages, more diverse employment opportunities, and the protection afforded by unions. "How inhuman," wrote a seamstress to a labor paper, "to refuse employment to women on the pretext that possibly they may marry. Many women now asking for employment gave up their husbands to die for the country."[15]

The expansion of new fields of employment in the postwar years prompted discussion of the types of proper jobs for women. Women's employment needed to be compatible with their physical strength (or weakness); it had to accommodate the needs of the home and enable a woman to remain virtuous. Suitable work for women was "defined in terms of values appropriate to future home life: neatness, morality, cleanliness, sex segregation, and clean language all defined appropriate women's jobs."[16] Naturally, most jobs open to women, even in an expanding market, were those related to women's traditional domestic and caretaking roles, such as teaching, nursing, sewing, operating a boarding house, and domestic service. For women with few skills and little or no education, the choices were even more limited: factory work, waiting on tables, and domestic service were among their few options.

Women chose jobs not only on the basis of the required skills but also according to the "type of girl" the position tended to attract, sometimes despite the poor wage the position would pay. Factory girls, perceived by some as immoral, felt superior to menial domestic workers, but factory work in turn was viewed as inferior to working in a department store. Clerks in dry goods or mercantile houses were considered more genteel, and women often chose retail jobs over others that could pay twice as much.[17] Women, seeking to remain desirable as marriage partners, created their own hierarchy of positions by attaching home-related virtues to particular types of work. For most women, it was important to maintain at least a semblance of loyalty by adhering to the separate sphere ideology.

Other nineteenth-century women, however, even at the risk of being scorned, moved out of their prescribed sphere into occupations that were not considered appropriate. The professions were opened to those with more education—slowly and in the face of great resistance. In 1856, Harriet K. Hunt, one of the first female physicians in the United States, published her autobiography, *Glances and Glimpses or Fifty Years Social Including Twenty Years Professional Life*, in which she chronicled her struggles to enter a male-dominated profession. Irene W. Hartt, in her 1895 book, *How to Make Money Although a Woman*, not only outlined ways of earning pocket money but also discussed the successes of women in professional fields, including artists, architects, designers, writers, and journalists. In chapter 9, titled "Some Untrodden Paths," Hartt encouraged women to be inventive in making their way in the world by "cultivating [their] powers of observation, and being quick to seize upon a new idea."[18] She related the stories of women who earned their living in occupations that were clearly outside socially acceptable roles, such as embalming, woodworking, bill collecting, blacksmithing, and selling real estate. One woman reputedly made a fortune sorting and reselling bottle corks! Hartt, like many

Mary Cassatt (1844–
1926), United States;
Mother and Child (ca.
1889); oil on canvas,
28¹³⁄₁₆ x 23⁹⁄₁₆ in. (73.2
x 59.8 cm); John J.
Emery Fund, 1928.222.

female authors in that period, encouraged every woman to have a profession or occupation with which she could support herself, if necessary. "Every girl should be taught one thing well, no matter what her circumstances are. . . . [I]f poverty should come, they will be prepared to meet and conquer it."[19]

Periodicals and authors offered (on one hand) much helpful advice to women in search of work, and (on the other) much criticism. In the late 1890s, articles in women's magazines, such as "How Some Girls Have Earned Money," "The Social Position of the Girl Who Works," "Hints for Money Making Girls," and "Women's Chances as Bread Winners," provided suggestions of occupations, advice on how to succeed in the working world, and examples of common mistakes to be avoided.[20] In fact, in 1890, the *Ladies' Home Journal* posted an advertisement in a competing women's magazine, *Harper's Bazar* (as it was spelled originally), seeking "Bright Girls and Active Women" who might be interested in "a splendid money-making position" selling subscriptions for the *Journal*.[21]

Most authors on this subject suggested a wide variety of possible genteel, home-based businesses such as caring for pets, mounting fans, teaching voice, ironing, reading to invalids, teaching sewing, designing book covers, and creating dinner table decorations. Indeed, it was proposed that any young girl who had any type of talent could turn it into a profitable business. These articles also offered advice on how to dress properly; specific practical instruction, such as how to apply to a nursing school; and hints on proper manners at work. Ruth Ashmore, a regular contrib-

utor to the *Journal*, assured young women in 1897 that "the civilization of to-day recognizes and respects the working-girl."[22]

Whether or not this was true, most articles were written with the intention of encouraging those who were *compelled* to work outside the home. Although the working woman was considered "vulgar" in all situations, society looked charitably on women who had to work. Those who worked by choice, not out of necessity, encountered much criticism. The woman in business was the subject of the hour; the editors of the *Ladies' Home Journal* counseled "every woman, young or old, to keep miles and miles away from the business world, unless actual necessity drives her to its borders."[23] The editors warned against the drudgery of the business world; in comparison, they described home duties as a "perfect elysium of leisure." They strongly suggested that working does not bring the "life of independence" that young women think it will provide.[24] Indeed, it was believed that those who chose to work out of a desire for independence or for pin money were taking jobs away from those who needed them, condemning themselves to a life of drudgery and, at the same time, emasculating the men who were there to support them.

In 1897, the *Ladies' Home Journal* printed an article titled "On Being 'Old-Fashioned,'" in which the anonymous author praised the woman who continued in her traditional role and ridiculed the "progressive woman." "In domestic life the 'progressive woman' has had a very busy time. She began by upsetting the old sewing-basket. It was narrowing to a woman, she discovered one dark morning.

Likewise were cooking, and the care of children. A woman who stayed at home and looked after the comfort of her husband and children was 'wishy-washy'; she cramped her life, dwarfed her intellect, narrowed her horizon. Clubs by the score, societies by the hundred, schemes and plans by the thousand were started, organized and devised to rid 'poor woman' of her 'thraldom.'"[25] Although the numbers of "progressive women" statistically were on the rise at the turn of the century, this author, like many others, insisted that more and more women were returning to traditional roles in the home—their "proper" place.

Late nineteenth- and even early twentieth-century women's magazines were filled with articles that praised the traditional woman and fiercely challenged the validity of woman's push for equality in all areas. They questioned women who attempted to "improve upon those elements in life which are God-ordained."[26] In 1895, the Reverend Charles H. Pankhurst, in an article titled "Andromaniacs," defined *andromania* as "a passionate aping of everything that is mannish." Referring to progressive women as andromaniacs, Pankhurst echoed the warnings of Dr. Edward Clarke, and contended that woman was "misconstruing her own nature and doing herself an irreparable injury."[27] Pankhurst's series of articles, which continued in the spring and summer months of 1895, dealt with the "true mission" of woman, college training for women, women and the vote, marriage, and the father's "domestic headship," with a consistently critical view of the nontraditional woman.[28] In an article published in 1900, the editorial staff of the *Ladies' Home Journal* argued that women's health indeed

had been damaged by the strain of both education and of working outside the home. The authors concluded by saying that the division of labor was returning full circle to its natural and divine states—that of men in business and women in the home.[29] It is clear that even at the turn of the twentieth century, there was a great social desire, and perhaps a psychological need, for women to return to their traditional roles in the home.

Women who wished or even needed to work faced not only a lack of opportunity and grossly unfair wages but also the pressure of social propriety. The ideology of the separate sphere was deeply ingrained in American society and culture, and it continued to plague women who did not wish their life's work to be defined in terms of marriage and motherhood. It seemed that society simply could not be reconciled psychologically or morally with the idea of women in the workplace.

In reality, the feminists' push for the vote, legal rights, higher education, and equal employment opportunities affected different classes of women in different ways. The small minority of truly upper-class women were wealthy enough to be "above" issues of employment. These women were financially able to maintain the lifestyle that reinforced the concept of woman as frail, idle, submissive, and subservient. Their worth was based on their decorative value alone. The conspicuous leisure of these women provided urban men with an effective means of displaying their financial and social success. Women's fashionable dress precluded the possibility that these women could participate in the "vulgarity" of productive employment.

The upper-class woman's work, beyond

managing her household and maintaining social connections, was often philanthropic. Only she had the leisure time to devote to such noble causes. Even the raising of her children was delegated to governesses and wet-nurses. In her 1846 novel *Two Lives*, Maria McIntosh described the life of a young mother, Grace, who had planned to nurse her new baby. But Grace was "so ridiculed by everyone who heard of it that she soon gave it up. Indeed, it would have been quite impossible as she soon found to fulfill the two characters of a lady of fashion and a nursing mother."[30]

Middle-class women aspired to the position held by the upper class. In fact, the ideology of the separate sphere gave them hope that in being forced out of the labor market and confined to the home, they could attain a similar status—that of decorative object. Unable, in most cases, to afford as much domestic help as her wealthier sisters, the middle-class woman was resigned to caring for and instructing her children herself, while both managing and participating in the daily household regimen.

It was primarily middle-class women who participated in the women's rights movement of the mid-nineteenth century. Confined to their "proper" sphere in the home, they lacked the intellectual stimulation they needed, wished to further themselves, and saw the possibility of advancement through education and employment. Unlike the wealthy few, they had much to gain by enlarging their sphere. Supported materially if not intellectually by their husbands, they had the time and financial independence to pursue such activities. Yet the middle-class woman's feminist activities benefited others as well. Their desire to earn

a college education and their wish for a career were the primary motivators, but they also spoke vividly about the plight of lower-class women, for whom working was not a matter of choice.

In 1893, at the World's Columbian Exposition in Chicago, women's rights advocate Lucy Stone spoke to an assembly in the Woman's Building, heralding a new era for women—women who had broken out of the confines of their sphere. She cited several examples of women who had stepped beyond the prescribed world of domesticity: who had moved successfully into the working world and had broken the stereotype of woman in her singular role as caregiver and nurturer. "When Mrs. Tyndall, of Philadelphia, assumed her husband's business after his death, importing chinaware, . . . the fact was quoted as a wonder. When Mrs. Young, of Lowell, Mass., opened a shoe-store in Lowell, though she sold only shoes for women and children, people peered curiously in to see how she looked. Today the whole field of trade is open to woman."[31] Stone praised the hard work done by many women to bring about these and other advances in legal status and education. She concluded by saying, "These things have not come of themselves. They could not have occurred except as the great movement for women has brought them out and about. They are part of the eternal order, and they have come to stay. Now all we need is to continue to speak the truth fearlessly, and we shall add to our number those who will turn the scale to the side of equal and full justice in all things."[32]

The Columbian Exposition represented a milestone for women. The presentation of their work was organized by the Board of

Lady Managers, the first body of women legally appointed by any government to act in a national capacity. The intent of the exhibitions housed in the Woman's Building was to focus on the progress made by women throughout the past four hundred years, as well as on the recent "increased usefulness that has resulted from the enlargement of their opportunities."[33] By presenting statistics and data pertaining to women's work, the Board aimed to showcase women breadwinners and the new avenues of employment open to women, to demonstrate the social value of such work, and to report which types of work received the best wages and what type of education would be most helpful in obtaining such positions.[34]

Much discussion centered on whether the women's exhibits should be segregated in a separate building; the word *separate* raised many red flags. Some members of the Exposition's Board of Directors viewed a Woman's Building as a waste of money and "utterly without warrant." They believed only one visitor in fifty thousand would enter it. Although there are no statistics regarding attendance in the Woman's Building, popular accounts described it as a highly visited attraction. Kate Field, editor of *Kate Field's Washington*, a national weekly newspaper with a circulation of ten thousand, wrote, "If popularity be a sign of approval, the Woman's Building outranks all others. I never entered its portals without being oppressed by an overflow of humanity. Every woman who visited the Fair made it the center of her orbit. Here was a structure designed by a woman, decorated by women, managed by women, filled with the work of women."[35] Special corre-

spondent Marian Shaw wrote a series of articles on the Exposition for an obscure North Dakota newspaper. On October 27, 1893, she praised the Woman's Building and described its contents: "Woman's achievements in every branch of industry is [*sic*] found within these walls. They form an object lesson in the history of woman's intellectual development, and present an unanswerable argument to those who have been wont to deny her ability to excel in any line of work outside that of light fancy work or household drudgery."[36]

The exhibitions indeed displayed a remarkable collection of products and statistical information designed to herald women's accomplishments in industry, manufacturing, science, art, literature, and the professions. The building itself had been designed by architect Sophia Hayden; the interior decoration was overseen by painter and textile designer Candace Wheeler. The Cincinnati Room included "the best works in the lines of woodcarving, sculpture, painting, [and] pottery."[37] The work of acclaimed woodcarver Agnes Pittman was featured in that room, as were the pottery of Louise McLaughlin and the products of the internationally recognized Rookwood Pottery.

Even while the Woman's Building was showcasing women's progress, the Exposition made a major effort to show the continuing predominance of woman's work in the conventional roles of child rearing, education, the "divine art of healing," and cooking. Exhibits of woman's traditional work included lacemaking, weaving, basketry, embroidery, leathercraft, and all types of fancywork. Overall, the Exposition presented a dual portrait of women at the close of the nineteenth century; although "much was claimed for woman's ability to compete fully and equally with man in the world outside the home, the traditional view of woman . . . was pervasive."[38] The speeches, exhibits, and activities of the Woman's Building reflected quite accurately America's conflicted view of women in 1893.

Nevertheless, throughout the nineteenth century, more and more women had moved into the labor market, both out of need and desire. According to the 1870 U.S. Census, 1,645,188 women ages sixteen and older were engaged in gainful occupations. By 1900, this number had risen to 4,833,630; by 1920, it had almost doubled to 8,202,901—more than 25 percent of all women in the United States.

Cincinnati's female labor force reflected that of the nation overall. In general, the earlier the time period, the lower the proportion of women in the workforce. In the city's first two decades, Cincinnati women were engaged primarily in unpaid household work. Before 1870, women represented less than half the local population. This gender imbalance encouraged women to marry earlier and consequently to engage in housekeeping and child care at a younger age. In addition, shortages of male laborers in new western cities on the frontier, such as Cincinnati, led to relatively high wages for men, and women had no compelling financial incentive to enter the labor market. Thomas Carter, who settled in Cincinnati in 1803, wrote enthusiastically to his family in Reading, Massachusetts, about the opportunities in his new home. In June 1803, he wrote, "A shoemaker may earn more in one day here than in three days there." In January 1806, he again related his easy success

by saying, "I have twenty dollars here where I had one in Reading; I take from five dollars to one hundred and thirty-five dollars a day in general. I am not in want of money; come on, and you may get some too."[39]

As Cincinnati entered its boom period, however, women increasingly entered the labor pool. The tremendous growth of the ready-made men's clothing industry in the 1830s created a great demand for low-wage workers. This type of work was a "natural" fit for women, because it mirrored their traditional household tasks. It also allowed married women with household and child-rearing responsibilities to work at home. Sections of clothing cut in the factory were assembled at home by women as piecework.[40]

The shift of Cincinnati's economy in the second half of the century, from a commercial to an industrial focus, continued to transform the workforce toward increasing reliance on women. From 1860 to 1900, the proportions of women in gainful occupations rose quickly, resulting in a workforce that was increasingly female. This increase may have been related in part to the decline in men's wages at midcentury. As immigrants poured into the city, men's wages decreased, and women felt the need to supplement the family income with revenue-producing work. By 1890, the labor rates for women in Cincinnati were approximately 50 percent higher than those throughout the United States. Of course, at that time, Cincinnati was an urban center with a population of nearly 300,000, whereas almost 80 percent of Americans lived in rural areas or towns with a population of less than 30,000. But Cincinnati also surpassed other cities in the region in this respect, including Cleveland, with a population of 260,000, and Chicago, with 1.1 million inhabitants. Two factors may have contributed to this phenomenon: the continued presence of a major clothing industry in the city and the timing of the increase in immigrant populations. Daughters of immigrants tended to work for pay in higher proportions than first-generation immigrant women, and Cincinnati, by the end of the century, had a higher percentage of second-generation immigrants than did nearby cities.[41]

Women in Cincinnati were employed in a variety of positions, particularly in the manufacturing sector. In the 1840s, 1850s, and 1860s, they found jobs in furniture factories caning chair seats, painting, and varnishing. They were hired in publishing houses to fold and sew book bindings. Boot and shoe manufactories hired women to perform stitching and binding tasks. By 1880, 40 percent of the workers in the highly mechanized carriage factories were women and children; cigar factory employees were 36 percent female. By the end of the century, women had moved increasingly into clerical jobs: in 1900, 10 percent of the total female labor force was employed as clerks, salespeople, and bookkeepers. Office work was feminized by the

mechanization of office procedures and the upward mobility of the men who had formerly performed these tasks.[42] In fact, Cincinnati's successes in manufacturing depended largely on its female workforce.

Cincinnati's women obviously were moving beyond their sanctioned role as homemakers; yet, like all women, they were limited in their choices. Although opportunities for women were diversifying faster than those for men, only a handful of occupations still were open to women, in contrast to the wide variety of options available to men. "In fact, by 1900 the basic occupational profile of today's women was already in evidence. Women who worked for pay, then as now, were highly likely to be employed in one of the following areas: clothing production, personal service, clerical and sales, teaching, nursing, or factory work."[43]

Like others across the country, Cincinnati women were viewed as temporary workers waiting to be married, or were already engaged in household management and child care. They experienced widespread sex discrimination in the form of legal and cultural barriers that virtually prevented them from entering man's sphere.

Dressmaking as a Trade

ALTHOUGH WOMEN's options for employment increased as the century progressed, the occupations that naturally attracted many working-class women were those related to their domestic duties; sewing was one of these. A woman could make a living with her needle in various ways, such as doing piecework in the home or the factory, making straw hats, or mending, but dressmaking was at the top of the needlework hierarchy in both prestige and pay.[1] Dressmakers designed, cut, and fit fashionable gowns, whereas their employees, the seamstresses, "merely" sewed the seams and attached the trimmings according to the designer's instructions.

In an era when fashion required garments for women to be custom-made, the dressmaker who could fit a dress accurately to her client's body was esteemed. Having a gown that fit so well that it distinguished one from the "puckered, gaping, baggy masses"[2] was often more important than the richness of the fabric itself. In fact, simplicity and appropriateness in dress were extolled repeatedly in women's periodicals. The "perfect agreement" of one's dress and the occa-

sion was considered "success" in dress.[3] A poorly made dress, however, was "beneath contempt": one was advised to ignore not only the unsatisfactory garment but also the person inside it.[4] Exceptional construction, as well as the materials and personal flair of both the maker and the wearer, played a crucial role in distinguishing a woman's social status through her clothing.[5]

Men's ready-made clothing became available early in the nineteenth century. In 1815, for example, William Stead, who operated a clothing store in Albany, New York, advertised "all kinds of ready made clothing such as dress coats, coatees, vests, pantaloons, fine shirts."[6] In Cincinnati, David Evans opened his tailor's shop on Second Street in 1825, offering men's ready-to-wear clothing made in the "neatest manner, on the shortest notice and in the most fashionable style." Frock coats and greatcoats could be purchased for $4.00 to $4.50; pantaloons and vests, for a dollar.[7]

The advent of women's ready-made clothing lagged well behind men's wear. In the early decades of the nineteenth century, the items available to women included mantillas, cloaks, and shawls—articles of clothing that were basically unfitted. The complex creation of fashionable dress, designed to fit an individual woman's body like a second skin, was left to dressmakers. Such clothing was impossible to mass-produce not only because of the complexity of the fit but also because styles changed so frequently. Throughout the 1860s, cloaks and corsets were virtually the only ready-to-wear items a woman could buy. Although a wider assortment of ready-made women's garments became available in the second half of the century, the entire range of women's dress could not be purchased until 1910.[8]

If a woman was talented with the needle, she could make her own clothing; if she was not, her lack of ability was obvious in the poor fit. In that case, she faced the unfavorable prospect that both she and her dress would be "ignored." Many nineteenth-century women, however, made and remade their own clothing, often using old garments as patterns, unless their size or the fashions had changed sufficiently to make their previous wardrobe unusable. In fact, drafting systems for both professional dressmakers and amateur seamstresses were available in the early nineteenth century.[9] Mass-produced, sized paper patterns were introduced in the 1860s; by 1871, the Butterick Company was producing twenty-three thousand patterns daily and sold more than six million that year alone.[10] Even so, most women lacked the requisite skills to make their own wardrobes. These women kept a multitude of dressmakers busy throughout the nineteenth and early twentieth centuries.

The Importance of Fashionable Dress

Nineteenth-century women were highly motivated to dress well and to have their dresses fit them well. An individual's appearance, including his or her dress, was regarded as an index of character. In society's eyes, a well-dressed lady was not only socially but also morally superior to a poorly dressed, working-class woman whose position required her to move about in the public world. The very nature of fashionable dress—its restrictive construction and its obvious cost, both in materials and in labor—presumed leisure. By definition, a fashionable woman did not work; fashion implied pleasure and self-indulgence.

More important, in accordance with the ideals of the separate sphere, woman's moral superiority, by which she elevated her family, was indicated in her dress, as well as her demeanor. Poorly made clothing, reflecting both taste and financial status, affected one's reputation.[11] Dress revealed in an instant the "refinement" or the "vulgarity" of a person one might be meeting for the first time.[12] In Sarah Josepha Hale's words, "[D]ress and personal appearance . . . are important things. Character is displayed, yes! moral taste and goodness, or their perversion, are indicated in dress."[13]

Women were indoctrinated from an early age with the social and moral importance of dressing both themselves and their families well. Regardless of wealth, a woman of character was expected to clothe herself and her family respectably—that is, in a fashionable manner. Those who did not care properly for their appearance were pronounced "deficient" in important qualities such as good character.[14] In his 1865 book,

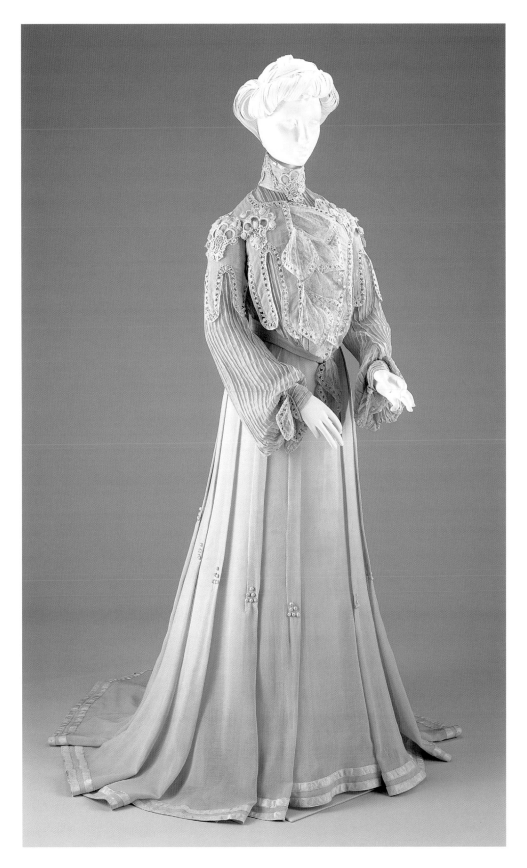

The H. & S. Pogue
Company (founded
1863); *Afternoon Dress,*
1902–1903; wool, silk;
Label: Pogue CINCIN-
NATI; Gift of H. & S.
Pogue Co. thru Mrs.
Fred Rice, 1963.15a,b.

Habits of Good Society, William Dean Howells stated, "Indifference and consequent inattention to dress often show pedantry, self-righteousness, or indolence." Howells described the moral effects of dress on both the wearers and those around them at each social level: "Amongst the rich and great, the love of dress promotes some degree of exertion and display of taste in themselves, and fosters ingenuity and industry in inferiors; in the middle classes it engenders contrivance, diligence, neatness of hand; among the humbler it has its good effects."[15]

Although such inspiring qualities were ascribed to dressing well in the Victorian era, the ideals they represented were still considered true and relevant after the turn of the twentieth century. In 1906, the editorial page of the *Ladies' Home Journal* contained an article titled "Where Women Err in Dress." The writer declared, "After all, our clothes, like our eyes, our voice, even our words, are but the messengers which our soul sends out to speak for it to the world, and it is, indeed, a poor sort of a woman who allows the meanest of these servants to slander or belittle her to her friend and sex."[16]

Both desire and social pressure created an enormous need for fashionable, custom-made garments. Women's periodicals and books on dress and etiquette explained in detail how to dress correctly and fashionably both in public and at home. S. A. Frost's *The Art of Dressing Well*, published in 1870, was touted as "A Complete Guide to Economy, Style and Propriety of Costume, containing full information on all points relating to ladies' and gentlemen's dress, at all times, places and seasons." The author thoroughly outlined appropriate attire and accessories for ladies for breakfast, marketing, shopping, promenade, visiting, receiving calls, church, croquet, skating, picnicking, traveling, stormy weather, and every other possible occasion.[17]

A wealthy or upper-middle-class woman's wardrobe contained a number of required garments. In the morning, before she dressed, she would take her breakfast and relax with her most intimate family members in a less structured gown that went by many names, including *wrapper*, *morning* or *breakfast gown*, or *robes de chambre*. If she was to spend the day at home supervising her domestic servants or even participating in the household work herself, she might wear a cotton gown that was less elaborate and possibly unboned, to allow her to move more freely. In the afternoon, when she might be receiving visitors or going out of the house to make calls herself, a highly structured dress, generally with a high neck and long sleeves for modesty, was required. Evening events required the most elaborate and highly ornamented gowns; different styles were required for dinners, balls, or public events such as the theater or the opera. Special functions often required a new gown; different seasons, of course, called for wardrobes appropriate to the climate and a woman's social calendar. In short, although the need for fashionable dress was dependent on seasonal demands, competent dressmakers were almost never at a loss for work.

A "Natural" Occupation

Dressmaking was seemingly a "natural" occupation for women. In the nineteenth century, learning to sew was a necessity for a young girl, who was expected first to assist

—BACK OF FROCK
FIG. 1.

Magazines such as *Harper's Bazar* were a primary source of fashion information, providing illustrations, as well as detailed descriptions of the latest styles, particularly for women and children. *Harper's Bazar* (February 1898); *Public Library of Cincinnati and Hamilton County.*

her mother in the household duties, and then to marry and manage her own household. These basic sewing skills, acquired at an early age, enabled almost all women to execute the functional requirements of plain sewing, including the seaming and hemming of sheets, table linens, simple garments, undergarments, and textile furnishings, as well as the simpler, unfitted pieces of men's clothing, such as shirts.

In wealthy families, this type of menial, utilitarian work was performed by seamstresses. Often, poor, working-class women seamstresses made little money and occupied very low status for the unskilled work they performed. In 1854, a writer for *Godey's Lady's Book* related that a widow supporting two children by sewing seams of a garment precut by a tailor was paid 7 cents for simple shirts, 12 cents for simple trousers, and 30 cents for cloth jackets. The most she could earn by doing this work for a full day and half the night was 25 cents. Yet her monthly rent for a single room could be as much as $3. These meager earnings barely sustained her and her children; in addition, the labor was harmful to her health.[18]

Women who sewed were severely

limited if they possessed no more than basic sewing skills.[19] The increasing intricacy of the cut of fashionable dress in the mid- to late nineteenth century strained the abilities of amateur seamstresses and increased the demand for professional dressmakers. *The Workwoman's Guide*, published in 1838, detailed the construction and maintenance of nearly every conceivable item used in the nineteenth-century household. It included explicit instructions for making garments of all types, household linens, upholstery, and bed furnishings, and explained in detail how to clean various materials, to knit, and to plait straw for bonnet making. The manual, however, "strongly recommended to all those who can afford it, to have their best dresses invariably made by a mantua-maker, as those which are cut out at home seldom fit so comfortably, or look so well, as when made by persons in constant practice."[20] In other words, making fashionable clothing was a job best left to a professional.

Traditionally, dressmakers used the pin to form method to fit a dress, a technique that probably originated in the eighteenth century. In this method, the fabric was draped and pinned directly onto the customer's body while she was wearing the appropriate undergarments.[21] Early nineteenth-century styles, which were quite simple in cut—a neoclassically styled high-waisted or empire bodice with a long, unfitted skirt—were easily constructed by amateurs and professionals alike.

Later in the century, however, fashions changed more rapidly and became increasingly complex. Dressmakers and fashionable women kept abreast of these changes through periodicals such as *Godey's Lady's Book*, *Harper's Bazar*, and *Peterson's Magazine*, which were distributed widely throughout the United States, even in remote areas. *Godey's* included monthly, hand-colored fashion plates with verbal descriptions of trimmings, appropriate fabrics, and popular colors; in *Harper's Bazar*, first published in 1867, engraved fashion plates reached a new height of detail and elegance (see page 47). These plates, however, provided only two-dimensional illustrations of fashionable dress. They did not show the viewer how to cut the garment, nor the shape or number of required pieces.

As early as 1853, *Godey's* began to supplement fashion illustrations with simple diagrams that were reduced in size to fit into the magazine. Full-size patterns were soon developed, but they were not sized: the reader was told ambiguously that the pattern would fit "a lady of middle height and youthful proportion."[22] These patterns were intended for the amateur's use but did not provide the subscriber with the technical expertise needed to fit a dress well. Accurate fitting to the individual's size and shape still had to be done by the laborious "pin-to-form" method.

Indeed, professional dressmakers possessed the skills required to cut a sheath, so to speak, for a complex curved form—the fashionable female body. To be successful, a dressmaker first needed a thorough understanding of the current fashionable styles—styles that were constantly changing. Illustrated in two dimensions, they had to be superimposed onto a three-dimensional form, the human body. A thorough understanding of anatomy was helpful but was not the only key to success. Many fashionable styles had no relation at all to the true shape of the human body; in fact, they attempted

RIGHT: Kate R. Cregmile (active 1891–1923); *Evening Dress,* 1900–1902; silk, linen; Label: Cregmile Cincinnati, O.; Gift of Mrs. Christian R. Holmes, 1920.123, 124.

LEFT: Anna Dunlevy (active 1889–1913); *Evening Dress,* 1902–1903; silk, sequins; Label: Dunlevy CINCINNATI, OHIO.; Gift in memory of Elizabeth Blake Shaffer, 1993.104a,b (see pages 113 and 185).

to re-form the body as often as the styles changed. In addition, the dressmaker was not dealing with a static form. A woman needed to be able to move and assume a variety of positions (although limited) within this sheath. Also, her body, although ideally symmetrical, often was not: one shoulder might be higher than the other, one breast larger or smaller. A client's body also might change from one fitting to the next through gain or loss of weight, by a change of stance from the original fitting, or even because the client was wearing a different corset. Furthermore, each body the dressmaker encountered had different proportions. Only a dressmaker with extensive experience could construct a fashionable, well-fitted garment.[23]

Dressmakers were highly skilled not only in the technical aspects of sewing, cutting, and fitting garments but also in the creative aspects. They were "designers as well as craftswomen, artists as well as artisans."[24] Both their technical and their artistic skills were held in high esteem, and their earnings were significantly higher than those of their seamstress sisters.

Although some middle-class women made their own clothing, they sometimes relied on professionally cut garments as patterns. A fashionable dress purchased from a dressmaker was a precious commodity. It served as a guide in understanding, cutting, and assembling a garment's many pieces for the woman who purchased it, for family members, and sometimes for friends as it was passed from hand to hand. The copied cut and fit, however, never approximated the precision that a professional dressmaker was able to attain.[25]

Because few personal accounts of making garments at home have survived, it is difficult to know how common this activity was and how women of modest means arranged to have their clothing cut, fitted, and sewn by dressmakers. The 1861 journal of Amanda Wilson, who lived at 118 Richmond Street in Cincinnati, suggests the amount of sewing that even an upper-middle-class woman was required to perform. Amanda, whose husband Obed was editor-in-chief of publications and later co-owner of the Winthrop B. Smith Company, had no financial worries. In fact, the Wilsons later purchased a home in the wealthy suburb of Clifton, employed a succession of German maids, enjoyed a five-month tour of Europe in 1869, and spent their latter years traveling throughout Europe and Asia. Yet Amanda mentioned sewing ninety-nine times in her journal over the course of one year. She also referred to buying ready-made articles of clothing and having dresses fitted by a Miss Leveer, a Cincinnati dressmaker. Like most women able to have their dresses made professionally, Amanda still performed a large quantity of "plain" sewing, including stitching her husband's shirts and the household linens by hand.[26]

The diaries of Hannah Ditzler Alspaugh also provide a glimpse into this world. Hannah Ditzler apparently gained her expertise at sewing from her mother, who made the family's clothing. Hannah, whose fabric scrapbooks date from 1867 to 1913, meticulously recounted her efforts at both dressmaking and remaking dresses herself. She also described garments made by local dressmakers in her hometown of Naperville, Illinois. In all, Hannah mentioned thirty-three people who assisted her in creating and re-creating her wardrobe throughout her life.

For a middle-class woman who did not regularly patronize a dressmaker, having a custom garment made was a momentous occasion. Hannah, who made much of her own clothing, engaged dressmakers only occasionally, and primarily for remaking gowns. The most expensive garment she described in her diaries, her wedding gown, was made in 1903 by a Mrs. Pagel.[27] Women like Hannah, with limited means, chose carefully which dresses would be constructed by a dressmaker; usually, they were garments for significant occasions. The cost of construction by a dressmaker significantly increased the price of an already costly venture: the fabric itself was a considerable investment.

Although a particularly talented woman might achieve the status of dressmaker with her mother's instruction as her only training, many women learned the trade by becoming apprentices. Much like male apprentices in artisanal trades, dressmaking apprentices were bound to their mistresses for a fixed length of time. They boarded with their employers and labored without wages, a privilege for which their parents sometimes paid a cash premium. In the worst cases, they were used as domestic servants and errand girls, and never truly learned the trade lest they should create even further competition in an already highly competitive field. In the best of circumstances, however, aspiring modistes learned the trade along with the reading, writing, and bookkeeping skills that would enable them to establish their own successful

ventures.[28] In March 1891, the *Ladies' Home Journal* admonished women interested in becoming dressmakers to receive proper training: "In these days of exact fit, desired style and accurate finishings, it will not do for one just to 'pick the trade up.' There are certain laws to be learned, and from a good teacher that can only be taught by beginning at the foundation. In a word, technical education is necessary in order to become a successful dressmaker."[29]

The apprentice system began to break down as early as the 1840s. Tradeswomen found it less and less cost-effective to take in boarders and spend their time instructing while trying to maintain a thriving business. In 1848, the *New York Tribune* complained that dressmakers kept apprentices "sewing and learning nothing until the very day that their apprenticeship expired."[30] The apprenticeship system, however, was never abandoned completely. Even in the early twentieth century, aspiring dressmakers still climbed the ladder of experience from finisher to fitter under the guidance of a dressmaker acting as mentor.

In the latter half of the nineteenth century, schools were founded to teach women trade skills, including dressmaking. *Harper's Bazar* featured an article in 1890 titled "Domestic Training for Girls," which included an illustration of a sewing class.[31] In 1891, in the article "Women's Chances as Bread Winners: Women as Dressmakers," Emma M. Hooper reported, "Every large city has schools for teaching certain systems or charts, but I know of only one such school where every rudiment of the business is taught, from hand-sewing, hemming, over-casting, blind-stitching, etc., up

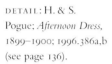 DETAIL: H. & S. Pogue; *Afternoon Dress*, 1899–1900; 1996.386a,b (see page 136).

through cutting-out, measuring, basting, fitting, draping, buttonholes, machine-stitching, trimming and entirely finishing a suit. Any woman going through this course cannot fail to do her work correctly."[32] Hooper strongly encouraged those who had the money to board for three months in the city to attend such a school—a venture that would cost about one hundred dollars. Some schools provided board for their pupils and advertised that they would secure positions for their best students.

As early as 1872, M. Holzer advertised instruction in the art of dress cutting and dressmaking in her rooms at Number 22 West Seventh Street in Cincinnati. Other dressmaking schools in the city at the turn

of the century included the Social Service Sewing School at 421 East Third Street, the Davaillon School of Designing of Ladies' Garments at 809 Race Street, and Kramer's Cutting School, listed in 1906 at 811 Clark Street. Several individuals advertised their services as dressmaking teachers in the city directories.

In fact, the study of dressmaking became popular not only for women who needed to earn an income but also for society ladies who wished to dabble in the "art." In a "Social and Personal" column from March 1902, the *Cincinnati Times-Star* advertised a dressmaking class for upper-class ladies. In 1910, simpler styles allowed the amateur to fashion more easily her own garments rather than relying on the custom dressmaker, and publications on home dressmaking flourished.

Dressmaking was assumed to be a natural occupation for women as an extension of their domestic duties, but this was not always the case. Although women's work traditionally included sewing, producing items for market sale was considered men's work. Well into the seventeenth century, tailors, organized in guilds, created fashionable garments for both sexes. The earliest milliners, whose title originated with the sixteenth- and seventeenth-century purveyors of fancy goods in Milan, also were male. Dressmaking was not firmly established as a female pursuit until the eighteenth century.[33]

The increased concerns regarding sexual propriety in the Victorian era undoubtedly promoted this conversion of the trade from male to female. Construction of a garment by a dressmaker required numerous consultations and fittings, during which the client's measurements were taken while she wore only her undergarments. Whether the dressmaker was using the "pin to form" method or one of the drafting systems devised mid-century to simplify the process, taking measurements and fitting a dress to a woman's body required some degree of intimate contact.

A man's presence in the fitting room was highly improper. When Charles Frederick Worth first began to make dresses in Paris in the 1850s, he was derided as the "man-milliner." High society was outraged at the idea of "men seeing ladies in a state of undress, and actually fitting garments on them, touching their bodies, ordering them to move around and parade up and down in various stages of déshabillé."[34] His salon was

rumored to be a brothel. Worth's house was not legitimized until 1860, when he was appointed dressmaker to the Empress Eugénie of France.

Dressmaking as a Woman's Trade

In the context of the separate sphere ideology, women who became dressmakers—in other words, wage earners—were clearly stepping outside their sphere. At the same time, however, a widow or spinster without a family had very few choices of means for supporting herself. If she wished to be regarded as "proper," she was restricted to the traditional female roles: governess, domestic servant, cook, seamstress, or dressmaker. Domestic work was disdained as subservient. Sewing was women's work and was therefore deemed respectable, although seamstresses were paid so poorly that they could barely survive. Caroline Dall summed up the situation clearly in 1859, when she stated, "The command of society . . . is 'Marry, stitch, die or do worse,'" referring to the possibility of becoming so desperate as to resort to prostitution, a fate worse than death.[35] Dressmaking, however, offered the potential for advancement and the opportunity to become an independent entrepreneur. The dressmaker who established her own business challenged women's proper place but did so within the confines of a "proper" feminine pursuit.

Dressmakers as wage earners and purveyors of fashionable dress were perceived in various ways. Often the subject of popular nineteenth-century fiction, they were generally portrayed in novels and short stories either as victims or as villains. As victims, they were pathetic figures who had been forced into their present, seemingly demeaning occupation. Perhaps the cause was the loss of their father's fortune, or a regrettable choice of husband, who revealed himself to be a drunkard and a gambler. Whatever the cause, these unfortunate women were reluctant breadwinners who did not enter the commercial world of their own volition: although downtrodden, they still were considered respectable.[36] Oftentimes, it was marriage, regarded as the only proper state for a woman, that acted as a savior.

As villains, dressmakers were depicted as overdressing and foisting extravagant attire on their clients. Eliza Farrar, writing in the *Young Lady's Friend* in 1837, appealed to her readers not to bend to their dressmakers' every suggestion. The fictional dressmaker Mrs. Randall, portrayed in the 1849 novel *Caroline Tracy* as a woman "with large ears," was also described as "vulgarly dressed," with "larger ornaments" and "gew gaws strung about her." The obvious and immediate Victorian assumption in the novel, based on her disagreeable appearance alone, was that Mrs. Randall was a woman of poor taste, who undoubtedly treated her workers unfairly, and was involved in numerous unsavory activities, including intemperance and prostitution.[37]

Fashionable apparel was often linked to females' general ill-health. Dress reformers chastised dressmakers for promoting clothing that limited women's movements, restricted their breathing, and deformed their internal organs. Feminists railed against fashionable attire as a symbol of oppression and social subordination.

Others lamented the hours and dollars frittered away in dressmaking and millinery shops, where women "deprived of meaningful intellectual and vocational pursuits"[38]

found matching the perfect fabric with the perfect trimming their most important decision of the day. It was feared that upstanding young wives would become delinquent in their duties at home and spend beyond their husbands' means if lured consistently into the dressmaker's shop.

Breaking the prescribed bounds between the private and the public sphere, upstanding tradeswomen were frowned upon and portrayed as madams, "public women," and prostitutes. In other words, independent businesswomen were either victims of circumstances beyond their control or despicable characters. These women presented to Victorian society a "frightening specter of female autonomy."[39]

It was precisely this idea of "female autonomy" that attracted many ambitious women to the dressmaking trade. At first glance, women in the sewing trades appear to have been conformists who accepted the prevailing sexual division of the labor market and acknowledged traditional women's work as proper. They represented a dichotomy, however: although appearing to conform, they also challenged traditional gender roles as independent businesswomen. They had "one foot in the male world of profit-seeking, but the other firmly planted in a world of tradition and female culture."[40] Dressmakers stepped into the man's sphere by selling goods and services in the marketplace, ignoring the dictates of their "proper place," but they did so within a female culture. Few men dared to trespass into this world, and women did not have to compete with the male sex.

While feminists fought for equal employment opportunities and portrayed women as victims of a segmented labor market, women actually helped in some cases to shape this division of labor. Dressmaking was one area from which men were barred.[41] It was female territory that provided them with a *desired* separate sphere, in which they worked with and for women. They had control and enjoyed the supportive female relationships they valued so deeply.

Women entered dressmaking for a number of reasons, one of which was the lack of male competition; also, for a young apprentice, the prospect of proprietorship was quite attractive. It meant economic independence, something that most women in the nineteenth century never tasted. Although dressmakers were disparaged in fictional literature, in reality, once established in the dressmaking trade, they performed skilled work that commanded respect within their communities and produced relatively high wages. The trade offered the "potential to overcome women's dependent status and to provide female aspirants with the sort of independence sought by male craftworkers."[42]

The small business*man* has always captured the American imagination. He is the underdog who, against all odds, turns his small, home-based venture into a successful business. It is the epitome of the American dream. The small business*woman*, however, is an elusive character who has not commanded the same attention until recently. Yet in the nineteenth century, an impressive number of women were entrepreneurs in their own right. It is curious, in a way, that so many women chose this path. The probability of failure was quite high. Most dressmaking establishments lasted only two or three years; only women with exceptional

talent were able to weather the seasonal slumps and the fierce competition. Their capital was severely limited, as was their credit. Yet hundreds of thousands of women chose this path. What was their motivation?

Most dressmakers were not intent on social change. For the most part, they did not participate in unionizing, as did factory workers, nor were they social reformers. They were not generally involved with the feminists, a group that was one of their harshest critics. They did not benefit from the educational, organizational, and occupational gains enjoyed by upper-middle-class women as a result of the women's rights movement. In general, they worked out of economic necessity. For these women, the choice of entrepreneurship over wage earning gave them a chance for economic independence. Establishing their own business freed them from dependence on a male.[43] By the latter part of the nineteenth century, even women whose social position required them to work were hungry for independence and sought it out despite great economic risk.

Some women took this risk as an avenue to avoid marriage. Although many women entered the dressmaking trade as widows, especially in the wake of the Civil War, and others as "legitimate" spinsters who had no other means of support, some clearly *chose* not to marry. Perhaps inspired by their upper-middle-class sisters, who were clamoring for educational and occupational opportunities for their own intellectual stimulation, these women may have taken a similar path that afforded them freedom and intellectual stimulation of their own. In "Talks with Women," a regular column in *Demorest's Monthly Magazine*, one successful dressmaker described her attitude toward marriage: "The fact is, when women have once tasted the charm of an honorable independence achieved by themselves it is very difficult to persuade them to marry."[44] Author Caroline Woods, in her 1867 fictionalized autobiography *Diary of a Milliner,* stated, "I am left a widow with the necessity upon me of getting my own living." At this point she addressed her deceased husband: "I did love you dearly, Will; but I will own to one decided objection to married life. I was often obliged to go one way when I wished to go another . . . business will be independence."[45] Clearly, businesswomen of the nineteenth century, including dressmakers, were quite unlike many other women of their time, who awaited or even depended on marriage for their "rescue" and sole means of financial support. Successful, single dressmakers enjoyed independence and a freedom of their own making.

Census statistics support the fact that most dressmakers were unmarried, but there were some who enjoyed the married state. Marriage for a businesswoman could offer both advantages and disadvantages. A supportive husband who admired his wife's independent spirit might simply stay out of the business and allow her to manage her own concerns. Others actually contributed physical labor, managerial assistance, or the advantage of greater credit, which was generally offered to males but not to females.[46] Although unmarried women clearly depended on their income as a sole means of support, married women may have entered the trade simply because they enjoyed the work. Others may have used it to boost the family income and, thereby, as

an avenue to achieve middle-class status for their families.[47]

Much criticism was directed at women of "sufficient means" who worked. Such women, it was believed, usurped opportunities and thereby injured "their poorer sisters," who *had* to work. Claire Alix, in a letter dated June 1887, to the editor of *Ladies' Home Journal,* defended her way of life. Having married a poor man whose profession enabled him to provide only the necessities of life, Claire hoped that her income would allow them to purchase a home of their own. Although she never stated her type of employment, she assured the readers that being employed outside the home did not cause her to neglect her duties to her husband in any way. She believed firmly in her "right" to pursue her dream of owning a home by working outside of it.[48]

Marriage also could have a detrimental effect on a woman's business. Matrimony often resulted in some lack of independence, and marriage to the wrong man could spell financial disaster. "An inventory of husbands' occupations reveals employments whose remuneration was modest at best, unpredictable at worst: piano tuner, glass-cutter, salesman, roofer, artist. Linked to spouses with less than certain prospects, these women were not in business merely because they 'liked it.'"[49]

Legally, married women were aided by the Married Women's Property Act. Passed in 1855 as a comprehensive statute in Massachusetts, the law granted married women the right to own and control their own property independent of their husbands. Similar laws were enacted in Michigan (1855), Iowa (1870), Ohio (1871), Wisconsin

The H. & S. Pogue Co. (founded 1863) *Wedding Dress* (1898); silk; Label: The H. & S. Pogue Co. COSTUMES CIN-CINNATI, O.; Gift of Natalie Gates Morrison and Muriel Gates Richards, 1973.503.a,b.

(1872), Minnesota (1878), and Indiana (1879). These laws enabled married women to protect their assets from a ne'er-do-well spouse, who might gamble away their hard-earned profits. Although the business*man* may have viewed marriage as an incentive to greater endeavors, marriage for the business-*woman* was an uncertain venture that might ruin her.

Dressmaking was attractive to many women, married or single, because it offered both a flexible schedule and the possibility of working at home. Only the most successful dressmakers established a salon in the fashionable part of town; many combined home and shop. For working mothers with small children, the ability to stay at home and still earn an income was ideal. Older children could provide supervised care of younger siblings and assist in the work, once they were old enough to learn the trade.

It was not unusual for dressmakers to work as a family group. Many businesses were made up of teams of sisters or mothers and daughters. The Tirocchi sisters, Anna and Laura, were successful dressmakers in Providence, Rhode Island, who lived with Laura's husband and son. The family house served as the office for Dr. Louis J. Cella, Laura's husband, the Tirocchi sisters' dress-making shop, and their home. Laura Tirocchi Cella must have found it very con-venient to watch over her young son and attend to her husband's needs, with the dressmaking shop housed in the same building.[50] Working at home also may have allayed some women's fears about the impropriety of working in a more public arena, as well as eliminating the costly over-head of a separate establishment.

Compared with men's wages, working

women's compensation was consistently dismal. Although there certainly were exceptions, the great majority of dress-makers did not live a life of luxury and ease. In comparison with women in other occu-pations, however, particularly those that involved sewing, dressmakers earned the highest wages. In contrast to other working women, nearly half of the dressmakers earned a living wage—an amount on which a self-supporting woman could survive. In 1888, the Bureau of Labor submitted the report *Working Women in Large Cities*, which examined the number of working women in various occupations and their marital status, place of birth, and wages. The study concluded that dressmakers living in Cincinnati earned, on average, a yearly income of $417, whereas their annual living expenses, including rent, meals, clothing, and other expenditures, averaged $399.67. If the statistics are correct for both income and expenses, only $17.33 of income was not spent before it was earned. In contrast to other wage earners, however, dressmakers did earn enough to cover expenses. "[O]nly a third of boot and shoe workers, a fifth of ladies' garment workers, 13 percent of pant, shirt, and cap makers, 18 percent of printers, 11 percent of bookmakers, and 9 percent of paper box makers enjoyed a 'living wage.'"[51]

The highest salaries in the dressmaking trade were earned by fitters, forewomen, and the proprietors themselves. At midcentury, most earned $7 to $15 per week; by 1900, earnings rose to $15 to $25. It must be noted that dressmaking was seasonal to some degree, and modistes needed to earn enough to sustain themselves through the off-seasons.

Dressmaking offered more than monetary rewards to those who pursued it as a career; it also conferred status. Dressmakers, as well as those who observed them, thought themselves superior to wage earners. In an 1870 column titled "Talks With Women," Jennie June contrasted the demeanor and carriage of a seamstress and a dressmaker, both of whom were observed by two women out shopping. The seamstress stole away "with the bundle of sewing concealed under her shawl" and a "downcast appearance"; obviously, she was ashamed of her need to work. In contrast, the dressmaker was described as gay, tall, "elegantly-formed . . . dressed in rich black silk, with lace ruffle and diamond ear-rings." She was said to "live like a princess," making $50 per week.[52]

Dressmakers earned their genteel status through their work with "fine things" and their association with ladies of the upper and middle classes. Close, regular contact with the upper classes offered them the opportunity to develop poise and social ease beyond their social standing. They were also skilled workers, whose artistic abilities were praised in women's magazines of the period, and highly respected by their customers. In 1891, Emma M. Hooper called dressmaking a noble art. She urged any reader who might be considering such a career "not [to] remain a dressmaker, but aim at becoming an artist in the profession."[53]

Dressmakers, even those who rose from the ranks of the working class, dressed fashionably. Dressing well was a requirement of the job; a raggedly dressed modiste would hardly inspire confidence in prospective customers, and upper-class women certainly would not feel comfortable being fitted by unkempt employees.[54] In an article titled "The Dressmaker's Life Story," Amelia Des

Moulins, a young Parisian seamstress who came to New York City in 1899, recounted the regular thievery of cloth practiced by dressmakers for whom she worked, which enabled them to afford their fashionable attire: "Our proprietress would always exaggerate the amount of material needed and then, in cutting out, would be able to reserve some for herself. Often she got as much as two yards. These pieces she slipped into a drawer, of which she had the key. It did not take long, therefore, to get enough to make herself a new skirt or a waist."[55]

The Workings of the Salon

Most dressmaking establishments were humble affairs. As mentioned earlier, many dressmakers did not keep separate shops at all but worked from their homes or went out by day, sewing for weeks at a time in a particular household. In the case of the highly successful Tirocchi sisters, whose house doubled as their salon, the business occupied a considerable portion of the house—all of the second floor and part of the third. Customers entered at the front door and were ushered past the formal parlor and up a flight of stairs. The showroom/billiard room on the second floor was arranged artistically with sumptuous fabrics, giving customers an opportunity to view the available stock of fabrics and trims. Husbands who accompanied their wives on the buying trip could wait here as well. The two fitting rooms were comfortably furnished; here, the customers discussed their orders and had their fittings. The second floor also housed an office, where the bookkeeping was maintained, and an area in which the Tirocchis could meet with salesmen. The third floor held the workrooms and storage for both stock and dress forms. Between 1915 and 1931, the Tirocchis employed a total of twelve to sixteen women. They were a particularly successful team, and the elegance and spaciousness of their salon reflected their success.[56]

The most successful and fashionable dressmakers of the period presided over ornate establishments that rivaled the most elegantly appointed dry goods and department stores. Most dressmakers, however, probably managed to contrive only a humble showroom and a screened-off workroom. Located either in their home or in rooms in commercial buildings in the heart of the downtown retail district, most entrepreneurs employed two to four seamstresses at most.[57]

Unless a dressmaker worked entirely on her own, each dressmaking establishment, no matter how small, utilized two labor forces: "one highly skilled, amply compensated, and relatively permanent; the other less skilled, poorly paid, and temporary."[58] As in every occupation, dressmaking had its own hierarchy. Beginning as apprentices, aspiring dressmakers paid their dues by performing menial tasks such as sewing straight seams, organizing stock, and running errands. If they persevered, they graduated to the level of finishers or trimmers. In this position, they did fine hand sewing, finished seams, and applied trim, such as endless yards of lace and thousands of beads on a single garment. At last, they achieved the rank of fitter, sometimes called the cutter. The fitter, technically the most skilled worker in the shop, was responsible for fitting the garment to the client's body. If a woman succeeded in completing an apprenticeship, she clearly possessed considerable skill and often opted

to establish her own business.

Seen in this light, the lowly apprentices, often characterized as mistreated and maligned, enjoyed the promise of fulfilling their ambitions if they remained steadfast.[59] An apprentice's reward came at great cost, however—a cost that was often too great for the truly destitute. She might spend as little as three months or as long as two years working for a dressmaker for little or no pay. Whereas some modistes actually taught their apprentices the ins and outs of the business, many only feigned to do so, letting the young women go, with little more knowledge than they had originally possessed.

Good and bad employers can be found in any trade, and dressmaking was no exception. But high wages, excellent working conditions, ample food, and a regular workday probably were the exception rather than the norm. Pay for seamstresses in a shop was low, and the promised wages often failed to materialize. Many seamstresses worked in cramped quarters with inadequate ventilation and poor lighting, and many young women died of consumption after working daily under these conditions. The typical workday was ten hours, reduced to nine by the early twentieth century, but violations were common. The ten-hour day was often extended by an additional five or six hours to accommodate seasonal demands. This demand derived as much from the patron as from the proprietor herself.

Dressmakers were vulnerable to their clients' whims in regard to both pay and timing. Often, the dressmakers suffered along with their employees when attempting to satisfy demanding customers who ordered gowns at the last minute and

Salon of Béchoff-David in Paris, 1911. Only the most successful American dressmakers could provide such elegant surroundings for their clients. When competition with department stores became intense, however, dressmakers were encouraged in trade journals to create more elaborate settings for showing their latest designs. *Vogue* (October 1911). *Public Library of Cincinnati and Hamilton County.*

then refused to pay for them.[60] The seasonal aspect of the trade often offset the overtime earned during busy periods. The length of the season varied from year to year and from city to city. Dressmakers faced a potential lack of income particularly in the summer months, when the wealthy literally abandoned the cities for the countryside or for fashionable spas and resorts.[61]

The relationship between the modiste and her clients, like that between the dressmaker and her workers, certainly varied from shop to shop. Dressmakers attracted their clientele primarily by word of mouth.

Because dressmaking shops were often located in a home or sequestered in commercial buildings, they were not obvious to the casual passerby. Few dressmakers opted to purchase advertising space in the newspapers, local periodicals, or city directories. They and their clients were walking billboards, testaments to the finery they could create.

Dressmakers held a unique position in the community. In more rural areas, their shops served as a bridge to fashion in a period when styles were imported from Europe. They provided women with an opportunity for socialization outside the normal structure of formal calls and visits. In a small town, there might be only one dress-making establishment; it was not only a place of business but also a venue for establishing the network of relationships so highly valued by women in the nineteenth century.[62]

In the city, however, competition was fierce. Thousands of women were vying for a share of the market, hoping that their craftsmanship and artistry might woo the most prominent into their fold of clients. A wealthy client, once acquired, could attract other well-to-do customers if she was satisfied enough to recommend the dressmaker to others. Dressmakers sought to provide their customers with the finest in fashionable attire, a commodity that intimated a very personal relationship. The numerous fittings and consultations involved a level of intimacy that ready-to-wear clothing did not. Even after the rise of ready-made garments at the turn of the twentieth century, when shopping became a more public event, women continued to patronize custom dressmakers. Not only did they obtain an original design, unavailable in mass production, but they also received personal attention, privacy, and individualized service that could not be obtained in any other setting. Carrie Taylor, a dressmaker of Bowling Green, Kentucky, went to unusual lengths to accommodate her clients. Out-of-town customers frequently stayed overnight at the Taylor home, receiving regal treatment while their gowns were being fitted and completed.[63]

A genuine intimacy often developed between dressmaker and client. Much like today's hairdresser or bartender, who takes on the role of *ad hoc* psychologist, customers often unburdened themselves to their dressmaker. In *Suggestions for Dressmakers*, published in 1896, Catherine Broughton advised her readers that a dressmaker "is supposed to have a brain large enough to remember all the foibles and fads of all her customers, and a heart sensitive and loving enough to bathe each one in sympathy for all the troubles and trials to the unbosoming of which the fitting of a dress somehow leads."[64] These tradeswomen were expected to provide "emotional labor": listening sympathetically to their customers' troubles was part of their job.

Yet despite the genuine intimacy of the interaction, it was ultimately a business relationship between two unequal parties. Dressmaking brought together women from very different social milieus, and the highly personal nature of this relationship did not preclude conflict. The awareness of class differences was expressed clearly by clients who remarked that they had sent for "my little Irish dressmaker" or reported that "our Anna made it for me."[65] Wealthy clients were keenly aware of the social distance between themselves and their dressmaker, a working-class woman.

Dressmakers, on the other hand, viewed themselves in many ways as having risen above their social origins. They were independent, fashionably dressed businesswomen who took great pride in their work. In some cases, they attempted to assert their respectability by advertising their "ladylike demeanor" or stating that, in fact, they were distressed gentlewomen who formerly had been in "excellent circumstances" but were forced to work because of some unfortunate turn of events. Some dressmakers accepted

Mary Cassatt (1844–
1926), United States;
The Fitting (ca. 1891);
drypoint and color
aquatint (sixth state),
14¾ x 10¹/₁₆ in. (37.5 x
25.5 cm); Gift of Her-
bert Greer French,
1940.158.

their subservient role passively, whereas others demanded the respect they thought due them in accordance with the value of the artistic and skillful commodities they provided.[66] But even within the dressmaking trade itself, proprietors ranked each other by the wealth and social prominence of the clients to whom they catered.

Dressmakers were expected to accommodate their clients' schedules, whims, and demands. Although women who patronized custom dressmakers did so because they valued the individual style and the personal attention given to every detail of the garment, often they were unforgiving about the time required for such a production. Dressmakers juggled orders from several and perhaps many women at one time, depending on the size of their shop. Clients often expected immediate service that fit *their* agendas, notwithstanding the dressmakers' own demanding schedules. One client of the Tirocchi sisters wrote to inform Anna and Laura that she would appear for a fitting at a particular time on the following day, assuming that they would be available. Another breezily announced, "I have decided to have my clothes made this month instead of April." The customer's time and social schedule took precedence over those of the dressmaker because of the client's social position.[67]

Yet even while dressmakers were constantly reminded of their social position, both by their clients and by society at large, they exerted a psychological authority over their customers. They were the arbiters of fashion in their community; many women depended on their dressmaker to present them not only with the most fashionable styles but also with clothing that would be flattering and becoming. A wealthy woman with no sense of style was essentially at the mercy of her dressmaker, who could provide either correct or absurd advice. Most dressmakers, however, certainly sought to please their customers; if they did not do so, they faced immediate ruin.

Dressmakers, however, were not wholly responsible for the creation of fashions: styles were dictated largely by Parisian couturiers. American dressmakers followed widely accepted standards that were obtainable through the fashion plates of women's fashion magazines, available to fashion makers and consumers alike. Fashion news traveled fast, and little time elapsed between the presentation of new styles in Europe and their adoption in America. Many dressmakers, even those in rural areas, traveled to New York regularly to keep abreast of the current styles. The wealthiest and most prestigious modistes journeyed to Europe annually or biannually to view, sketch, and purchase stylish garments, in order to copy the cut and to buy sumptuous fabrics and trimmings. Sometimes these trips were financed by, and taken in the company of, a wealthy client who wished to take advantage of any advice her dressmaker might provide before purchasing fabrics. Mrs. (A. H.) Carrie Taylor of Bowling Green, Kentucky, who catered to the best trade from 1878 to 1917, bought fabrics, buttons, and trim in both Europe and New York; in a period of twenty-four hours, she would purchase fabrics valued at over one hundred thousand dollars.[68]

In some cases, the design of the dresses was left entirely to the dressmaker's discretion, but customers could play a significant part. Most often, they were not passive recipients, and in some cases they were even co-creators. The wealthiest and most prestigious dressmakers kept a stock of fashionable fabrics and trim on hand; the Tirocchi sisters decorated their showroom with bolts of fabric and yards of trimmings from which potential clients could choose.[69] Still, it was not uncommon for a customer to purchase fabric at the local dry goods store and trim at the fancy goods shop before coming to the dressmaker's salon.

Customers could be both a help and a hindrance to the process. Full of praise when the finished product was a perfect fit and full of criticism when it was not just right, customers could make a dressmaker's life quite uncomfortable. Letters from the Tirocchi sisters' shop offer a unique glimpse of dressmaker-client relationships that range from hostile to affectionate. Dissatisfied clients alleged that the work was unsatisfactory; they criticized the cut, the color, and the fit, saying that the dress was "impossible for me to wear as it is," that "neither dress was carefully finished," and that the flaws were so obvious "I can't understand why you could not have seen [them]." At the same time, others offered high praise for both the work and the service rendered. One satisfied customer, vacationing in Florida, sent Anna Tirocchi a gift along with her thank-you note. Still others offered compliments from their wealthy acquaintances as praise; one went so far as to say that her friends thought her gown had been purchased in Paris.[70]

Dressmakers, much like today's hairdressers or plastic surgeons, were expected in some cases to remake the client who was stout or plain into a picture-perfect fashion plate. Seamstress Amelia Des Moulins recounts the story of a stout woman who entered the shop and insisted that her waist measurement was twenty-four inches, an obvious understatement. With her corset laced tightly to the stated measurement, a gown was made, but the client soon returned it, with the complaint that it did not fit. "Soon she was in the hands of the tighteners, gasping and perspiring. When the corsets were well pulled in the dress fitted like a glove, but the poor lady's face was the color of blood and she could hardly speak. . . . The poor lady staggered away trying to look comfortable. I don't believe she could wear that dress, tho. . . . "[71]

The most common source of tension between client and dressmaker was cost: fashionable dress was expensive. The ability and willingness of a wealthy or upper-middle-class woman to bow to constant changes in fashion trends, as well as the number of garments theoretically required for each particular time of day or social event, created an enormous financial burden. Periodicals of the time are filled with articles that present the "facts" of dress versus the cost. "How to Dress Well and Cheaply," "Some Facts about the Cost of Dressing a Woman," and "Dressing on $50 to $200 a Year" are titles of a few of the articles that advised women on the cost of dress, how to dress well on a limited budget, and the potential savings in making one's own clothing.[72] In "Dressing on $50 to $200 a Year," Emma M. Hooper stated, "[T]here must be a great deal of planning if the sum is to cover the necessary outlay for the year."[73] The sum of $200 per year enabled the middle-class woman, to whom this article was directed, to hire a dressmaker, and then only for making "two best suits."

In another article, "The Most Feminine of All Problems: To Dress Well at a Reasonable Cost," the author offered a system for calculating the proportion of one's annual income that might comfortably be spent on dress. Fifteen percent was judged reasonable: if one's yearly income was $3000, then $450 could be spent on clothing.[74] In *Habits of Good Society* (1865), William Dean Howells complained that it was difficult to establish any rule of thumb as to how much to spend on one's dress. He did suggest, however, "For married women of rank, five hundred a year ought to be the maximum; a hundred a year the minimum." He tempered this advice by saying that station and fortune ultimately must be the deciding factors, but called two thousand a year for a lady of rank "a monstrous sum!" and exclaimed it was "a monstrous sin to spend it!"[75]

Compared with ready-made clothing, custom garments were quite expensive. In the latter years of the nineteenth century, when ready-made clothing for women was just beginning to appear, it was advertised regularly in periodicals. In 1896, the National Cloak Company offered dresses for $7.00 and cloaks for $3.50. In 1897, "stylish costumes made to order" by Montgomery Ward and Company in Chicago were advertised for $9.25. In contrast, Mrs. H. A. Du Villard, a customer of the Tirocchi sisters, ran up an account totaling $668.50 in 1921, "about sixty percent of what a male factory worker earned in that year. The Tirocchis' work for Dorothy Newton's June 1923 wedding came to $1797, a sum substantially higher than most Rhode Island working-class families then lived on for a year."[76] Carrie Taylor's prices "ranged from $48 for a white silk net [dress] with silver and chenille

66

appliqué to $80 for a black taffeta robe embroidered and trimmed in black cluny lace."[77] Emma M. Hooper advised would-be dressmakers on the moderate prices they might ask for their work: $12 for a woolen dress and $12 to $15, or perhaps as much as $30, for a silk dress or evening gown.[78]

Few actual receipts or accounts from dressmakers have survived. However, several receipts found in the collection of the Cincinnati Historical Society Library from the H. & S. Pogue Company for items sold to a Mrs. W. B. Ludlow indicate costs for various fabrics and related sewing items between 1881 and 1886: 10 yards of dress goods cost $11.00, 8 yards of net, $20.00, and 18 yards of silk, $22.50. Mrs. Ludlow's receipts included mostly dress-related items such as ready-made bows, lace, ribbon, buttons, needles, thread, elastic, and a wide variety of fabrics. Without fail, the most costly items charged to her account were dress fabrics.

Prices in custom shops were often negotiated by client and craftswoman. A price was set for each individual garment based on the cost of the fabric, the intricacy of the cut, and the handwork required. Prices ranged widely and seemed to be regulated only by what the local market would bear. Sometimes preferential treatment and prices were negotiated for a particularly loyal client. Customers occasionally attempted to dictate prices: in 1861, First Lady Mary Todd Lincoln ordered a bonnet of a specific shade of purple to be made within three days. She insisted that the milliner not ask more than $5, a price well below current market levels. Thrift obviously motivated women in all walks of life.[79]

Whatever the established price, it was the dressmaker who was usually at a disadvantage. Dressmakers were fully expected to extend credit to their customers; clients were billed monthly or sometimes only twice a year. Often, they were tardy in paying their bills, a practice that could ruin a dressmaker's credit and her ability to pay her help. Eventually, it could cause her business to fail altogether. In 1861, the *Bureau County Republican* newspaper in Bureau County, Illinois, ran a typical advertisement from a Mrs. H. A. Starkweather, who "earnestly requests that all Persons, indebted to her will call and settle at their earliest Convenience, as she wishes to leave for New York the first of March."[80] Mrs. Starkweather apparently was going on a buying trip and needed to assess her capital. Edward Bok, in his 1901 article "Women as 'Poor Pay,'" recounted the plight of a dressmaker "on the verge of nervous prostration." According to Bok, she received the "most lavish orders from the 'best people,' whose overflowing purses could meet the cost of what they had chosen without the least effort"; yet they had not paid. A friend advised her to give up her establishment because her "reputation as an honorable woman of business [was] in danger." Another fashionable dressmaker committed suicide by throwing herself in front of a New York elevated train. She had over $15,000 worth of outstanding accounts that she could not collect.[81]

The Tirocchis, too, met with difficulties in collecting overdue accounts. Some clients "forgot"; others, when faced with the bill, recited a list of financial difficulties. One client, whose bill for $678 was sent on October 6, 1916, did not remit payment until the following February. Payments, even when received, might be for the amount the client felt was "fair" rather than for the price negotiated when the order was placed.[82]

Dressmakers whose clients did not pay promptly found themselves in a difficult position. Some, like Mrs. Starkweather, ran advertisements that actually mentioned the names of customers with past due accounts as a means to embarrass them publicly. This tactic could backfire, however: dressmakers who offended their clients by being too aggressive in attempting to collect what was due them could drive a wealthy customer to another dressmaker's door, and possibly take other wealthy customers with her.

Bok stated that the average American woman had "a very poor pay reputation among tradespeople in the matter of paying her bills."[83] Many women were simply unwilling to pay or perhaps were thoughtless in the slow payment of their bills, but others may have been powerless to settle their accounts. In many cases, the purse strings rested in the hands of the woman's husband, who may simply have refused to pay. Economic tensions between husband and wife in regard to her extravagance in dress, whether real or imagined, could play a significant role in a dressmaker's life. Urban men who worked all day saw their wives, who did not work, spending their money—throwing it to dressmakers, who sometimes were viewed as extortionists insisting that shorter hems were fashionable one day and

longer hems the next.[84] Ultimately, both the dressmaker and the fashionable woman, for all their efforts, were dependent on a male. Despite their vast social and economic differences, they did not differ greatly in that respect.

The typical American dressmaker was a single (either a spinster or a widow), native-born, Caucasian woman of working-class status. But she was much more than these statistics tell us. Whether because of dire economic need or a fascination with the work, she saw in dressmaking an opportunity to move beyond her social class and to escape her presumed dependence on the male sex. Independent and ambitious, she sought to reach beyond the constraints with which society wished to bind her.

Neither fully dependent nor fully independent, these entrepreneurs challenged women's sanctioned role, but they did so in a unique way. With one foot in the man's sphere, they expanded their own. They associated regularly with women far above their own social level, dressed and conducted themselves with the poise and decorum of upper-class women, and traveled regularly far beyond their sphere to New York and Europe to maintain their business viability. Dressmakers, unlike many of their wage-earning sisters, broadened their scope in a distinctively progressive way and at the same time created unique garments of great beauty.

Cincinnati: A Historical Perspective

SO SPOKE an anonymous traveler on a visit to Cincinnati from New York in 1830. Such high praise of the city was heard often, particularly in the early years of the nineteenth century. Cincinnati, named for the Society of the Cincinnati, an organization of Revolutionary War officers, was situated on the banks of the Ohio River. Unlike its sister settlements of Columbia to the south and North Bend to the west, Losantiville (as it was originally called) sat above the flatland immediately across from the mouth of the Licking River, an important artery flowing out of the developing territory of Kentucky. The advantages of location and natural topography had made this area attractive to Native Americans long before white settlers discovered it, and these characteristics allowed for its unparalleled growth in the early 1800s. The flatland stretched approximately 800 feet back from the river; at that point, it rose sharply to a 4.5-square-mile plateau. The lower plain protected the site from the flooding that the neighboring settlements of North Bend and Columbia suffered regularly.

This strategic location across from the Licking River, as well as the tendency not to flood, made Losantiville the clear choice for the erection of Fort Washington in 1789. The Fort provided security for its settlers and stimulated trade in the ensuing years. On January 12, 1790, General Arthur St. Clair, governor of the Northwest Territory, arrived to inspect Fort Washington and subsequently changed the settlement's name to Cincinnati. In 1802, Cincinnati was incorporated as a town with a population of 2,500 inhabitants.

In the 1780s, southwest Ohio lay at the edge of the Northwest Territory, America's newest frontier. Since 1774, settlers had been streaming across the Allegheny Mountains into Kentucky. Despite resistance from Native American tribes in the area, white settlers pushed north of the Ohio River, flooding into southwestern Ohio and Indiana, and across the plains into Illinois and beyond. Thousands of eager residents of eastern seaboard states saw wealth and opportunity in these western lands. So began the rise of Cincinnati from a collection of rude log houses in the late eigh-

Middleton, Wallace & Company, Cincinnati, nineteenth century, United States; *Cincinnati, from a Point West of Covington, Ky.*, 1856; color lithograph, 16I × 26M in. (42.6 × 68.2 cm); Bequest of Herbert Greer French, 1943.652.

teenth century to one of the nation's largest and most important cities in the mid-nineteenth century.

Cincinnati was located strategically on the Ohio River, which connected seaboard cities and states with the interior of the new nation. It was, without a doubt, the river that catapulted her into such high standing. Overland travel was rough and slow; the river was a natural avenue for farmers and manufacturers, providing quick and easy access downstream to Louisville, and (by way of the Mississippi) St. Louis and New Orleans. Upstream, it reached markets as far north as Pittsburgh. In 1811, Robert Fulton's and Robert Livingston's steamboat, the *Orleans*, arrived in Cincinnati. The effects were immediate and dramatic: within fifteen years, upstream shipping costs equalized with downstream rates. By the mid-1820s,

one or two steamers a day were stopping at Cincinnati's public landing. By 1830, Cincinnati was the economic leader of the West. It quickly became the distribution center for large parts of Ohio, Indiana, Kentucky, Illinois, and Missouri, as well as many southern areas.

The steamboat not only facilitated trade through Cincinnati but also provided one of its earliest and most important industries; consequently, the city became the nation's second most important center for steamboat construction. This industry stimulated other types of manufacturing in the city, including foundries, machine shops, and woodworking industries. Cincinnati, with the development of the steamboat, was able to exploit the river more completely than ever imagined by the city's founders.

Cincinnati's wealth on the river was not

her only asset. It was complemented by rich farmland, which already supported more than 150 thousand settlers by 1820. These farmers produced a variety of commodities including flour, bacon, lard, pork, whiskey, butter, beef, feathers, and linseed oil. Well-built roads that radiated from Cincinnati to neighboring towns, including Dayton, Columbia, Lebanon, Hamilton, Lawrence-burg, and North Bend, provided farmers the means for marketing their goods, in addition to the ready market within Cincinnati itself. City founders also provided additional water routes in the form of canals in an effort to attract more farmers to the area. A series of canals was built between 1825 and 1843, connecting Cincinnati with markets south to Louisville and north to Columbus, Toledo, Cleveland, and the Great Lakes. These canals provided shipping lanes for flour, hams, hogs, and grain; like the river, they established Cincinnati as the pivotal shipping center to all points east, north, south, and west. Gradually, the city's wealth of agricultural products and ever-increasing commercial activity also fueled its growth as a major manufacturing center.

As early as 1806, Cincinnati boasted a variety of artisans plying their trades, including joiners and cabinetmakers, brick-layers, blacksmiths, shoemakers, saddlers, bakers, tanners, and tinsmiths, as well as bookbinders, hatters, tailors, printers, and brewers.[2] Flour milling and pork processing were long-standing agricultural industries in the area; in the 1820s, these were joined by the production of cotton cloth, machine tools, and engines. By 1826, Cincinnati's industries produced almost $1,850,000 worth of goods, and the city's population had increased to 16,000. By 1830, Cincinnati

had ceased to be a frontier town; the inhabitants were no longer fending off Indian raids and scrabbling to meet basic survival needs. Because of its agricultural richness, its vigorous commercial activity on the readily accessible waterways, and its ever-increasing industrial base, Cincinnati had become an important western river town of great promise. It was already being called "The Queen City of the West."

From 1830 to 1860, Cincinnati's industrial development accelerated and redefined the city. The business most responsible for this change was pork packing, an important industry from the city's earliest days. In the 1820s, aided by the steamboat as a faster and cheaper mode of transportation, Cincinnati's pork packers greatly expanded their markets. By 1835, Cincinnati had become the nation's largest pork exporter, and by 1850, it was the largest in the world, employing more than 2,400 workers. Cincinnati's association with pork packing, however, led not only to prosperity but also to ridicule: the city was familiarly known as Porkopolis. In any case, the success of this industry fostered the rise of other industries that utilized pork by-products, including tanning, soap manufacturing, and the production of brushes.

During these years, Cincinnati was America's boomtown. Immigrants streamed into the city from northern Europe, particularly Germany in the 1830s, and Ireland in the late 1840s. The population grew faster than that in any other American city. This extraordinary growth increased the demand for both goods and services, which stimulated growth even further, and the city became the nation's second largest industrial center. Cincinnatians and their leaders soon came to believe that their city was destined for greatness. In fact, in 1841, one leader, Jacob Scott, predicted that "within one hundred years from this time, Cincinnati will be the greatest city in America; and by the year of our Lord two thousand, the greatest city in the world."[3]

Although Cincinnati was known most widely for its meat-packing industry, in 1855, this actually accounted for only about 15 percent of the city's local manufacturing base. Other industries had developed as well. By 1850, Cincinnati had forty-four iron and metalworking foundries producing stoves, iron railings, steam engines, and boilers. The Eagle Iron Works, established in 1829, was the second largest foundry of its kind in the nation. Eagle made an array of items for the home, including teakettles, pulleys, spittoons, and tailors' shears.

In 1841, five shipyards in Cincinnati employed 306 workers in manufacturing steamboat engines. The city was second only to Pittsburgh as a center for steamboat manufacturing and repair. In addition, the availability of fine woods allowed the development of an important furniture-making industry: cherry, walnut, maple, sycamore, and poplar harvested from the surrounding countryside served as raw materials for local cabinetmakers and chairmakers, who produced $515,600 worth of goods in the 1840s. By the middle of the nineteenth century, Cincinnati-made furniture graced the parlors and dining rooms in homes across the Midwest and the South.

The manufacture of ready-made clothing ("slops"), particularly for farmers, slaves, and sailors, expanded during this period. In 1859, the clothing trade was the largest business in the city; forty-eight wholesale establishments and eighty-six retail houses employed 7,080 seamstresses and produced $15 million worth of clothing a year. Although Cincinnati lost its leading position in clothing production after the Civil War, it remained second only to New York City in clothing production as late as the 1880s.[4]

In thirty years, Cincinnati had built upon her strengths as a river town and a center of transportation to become a booming industrial center. Both the industry and the resulting influx of people transformed Cincinnati's size and appearance. Impressed with Cincinnati's grandeur, Horace Greeley praised the city in 1850:

It requires no keenness of observation to perceive that Cincinnati is destined to become the focus and mart for the grandest circle of manufacturing thrift on this continent. Her delightful climate; her unequaled and ever-increasing facilities for cheap and rapid commercial intercourse with all parts of the country and the world; her enterprising and energetic population; her own elastic and exulting youth; are all elements which predict and insure her electric progress to giant greatness. I doubt if there is another spot on earth where food, fuel, cotton, timber, iron, can all be concentrated so cheaply—that is, at so moderate a cost of human labor in producing and bringing them together—as here. Such fatness of soil, such a wealth of mineral treasure—coal, iron, salt, and the finest clays for all purposes of use—and all cropping out from the steep, facile banks of placid, though not sluggish navigable rivers. How many Californians could equal, in permanent worth, this valley of the Ohio![5]

This tribute to Cincinnati, as recorded

by historian Charles Cist in 1851, seemed to predict a glorious future, but by midcentury, the city had reached its zenith. The 1850 census described the Queen City of the West as the nation's sixth largest city, the third largest manufacturing center, and the fastest-growing urban center. In the 1850s, Cincinnati grew by 40 percent. Yet other cities in the midwest were expanding at an equal or faster rate: St. Louis added 83,000 new residents to reach Cincinnati's population of 161,000, and Chicago exploded from a town of 30,000 to a city of 109,260. Cincinnati was being surpassed and would never again hold such an advantage over her midwestern sister cities.

The steam engine had spurred Cincinnati's growth by its adaptation to river travel. Just as great numbers of settlers were pouring into the Ohio River valley, the development of the steamboat allowed Cincinnati to exploit the river's commercial opportunities. Thanks to the steam engine and the area's agricultural richness, Cincinnati had emerged in the early nineteenth century as a commercial and industrial city with a diversified economy. But just as steam had empowered the city, so did it contribute to her decline. When the steam engine was adapted to overland travel in the form of the steam locomotive, Cincinnati was not ready. At the same time, the vast lands of the Mississippi River valley were being exploited, and Cincinnati's era of rapid growth came to an end.[6]

Early attempts at incorporating railways into the Cincinnati area began in the 1830s. The first successful Cincinnati-based rail company was the Little Miami Railroad, established in 1836. This line connected Cincinnati to Springfield, with a connecting line to Lake Erie. In 1846, the Cincinnati and Hamilton Railroad was chartered; later it was extended to Dayton, Ohio, where it joined another line to the north. Between 1850 and 1860, more than $100 million was spent on building rail lines in Ohio, making it the state with the most track in the country. Despite these early efforts, however, Ohio railways generally failed to generate significant profits. Some of the lines actually worked to the detriment of Cincinnati's commercial success, allowing neighboring cities such as Louisville and Indianapolis to profit by funneling off goods and services.

Although Cincinnati's growth continued, the rate of growth slowed. Economic development in the latter half of the nineteenth century was characterized by diversity of industry. Boot and shoe manufacturing became increasingly important; hides generated from the pork industry were converted into all types of leather goods including boots, shoes, and saddles. By 1890, only Massachusetts produced more footwear than Cincinnati. The machine tool industries, which initially had been spurred by steamboat manufacture, also diversified; consequently, Cincinnati became the nation's largest supplier of machine tools and safes, and a leading producer of hardware and stoves. Cincinnati's carriage and wagon industry grew explosively in the 1870s, after the establishment of large steam-powered factories; by 1880, Cincinnati was the nation's largest manufacturer of carriages. Although Cincinnati had a reputation as a major publishing center by the early 1840s, competition from eastern companies forced local firms into production of specialized items such as textbooks, magazines, greeting cards, and playing cards. Long-standing

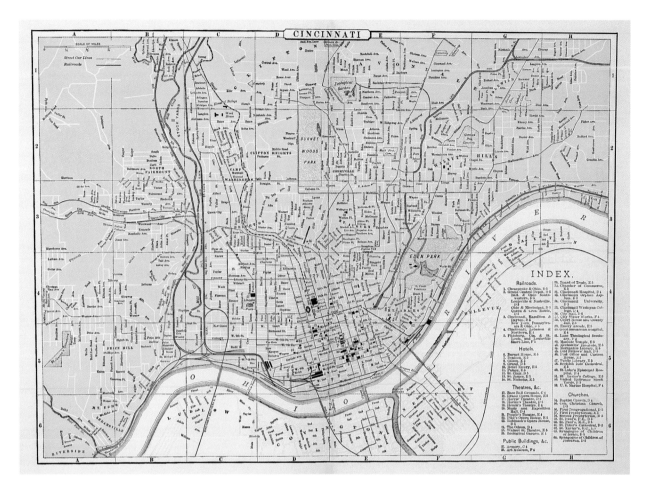

Map of Cincinnati, 1894; *Mary R. Schiff Library, Cincinnati Art Museum.*

industries such as soap, ready-made clothing, furniture, and the distillation of beer and whiskey remained important. In addition, small industries that accounted individually for less than 2 percent of the city's manufactured products together made up about 40 percent of the total dollar volume of manufacturing. Cincinnati was a leader in many of these smaller industries, including plug tobacco, glycerin, coffins, and harnesses. This broad diversification enabled the city to weather later recessions and depressions, and to continue a slow but steady growth to wealth.

In 1860, the city's entire population of 161,000 resided in a basin area covering less than six square miles. On average, 30 thou-

sand persons inhabited each square mile, making Cincinnati one of the most densely populated cities in the nation. The city's natural topography, with steep hills to the north, east, and west, and the river to the south, prevented the growing population from moving beyond these natural borders. The basin was a jumble of residences, warehouses, factories, and shops.

By the second half of the century, Cincinnati's population was looking for a way to escape living in the river basin. Two major developments in the late 1860s and early 1870s provided some relief. One was the completion, in 1867, of the Suspension Bridge, built by John A. Roebling. The bridge, spanning the Ohio River, connected

Cincinnati with its counterpart, Covington, Kentucky, just across the river.

The second and most effective breakthrough, however, occurred in 1872, when the Mount Auburn Incline opened. The Incline used steam-powered engines and cables to raise and lower platforms carrying people, horse-drawn wagons or carriages, and even electric streetcars to the top of the hillside. By 1876, three additional inclines were built, which provided residents, for the first time, with cheap and convenient transportation from the basin to the surrounding hilltops. At the top of each incline, streetcar and railway lines branched out, providing access to burgeoning neighborhoods. In the years following, lavish establishments known as "hilltop houses," consisting of a hotel or pavilion adjoining an amusement park, were popular attractions, where people congregated to enjoy the view, the food, dancing, fireworks, and the unpolluted atmosphere.

Cincinnati's wealthiest residents had escaped the congestion, the smoky industrial valley, and the less affluent inhabitants as early as the 1830s and 1840s, creating communities on the surrounding hills. The inclines provided access to these communities for the middle class, leaving the least privileged in the basin. Cincinnati's suburbs were called "its crowning glory."[7]

For a long time, the city was confined to the great basin made by the surrounding hills. "These bold elevations seemed impassable barriers. . . . [T]here were few who anticipated the time when these beetling cliffs would be scaled; when population, . . . having surmounted Nature's parapets, would spread over the swelling lands, and build cottages and palaces, churches and school-houses, and set itself to the work of converting a rough, broken country into a region of such loveliness, that the most favored might covet there a home."[8]

Development of these communities affected the city's structure dramatically. Neighborhoods sprang up around Cincinnati in concentric rings, creating a new type of city. The exodus was profound; by 1890, more than 100,000 persons lived in dozens of communities in the surrounding areas of Hamilton County and northern Kentucky.

Each community developed differently, with distinctive characteristics. Wealthy, upper-class citizens who had moved to the hills in earlier years had built mansions surrounded by acres of woods, which provided a quiet retreat from the city squalor. The "incomparable mountain suburb of Clifton"[9] became the enclave of wealthy industrialists such as Henry Probasco and George Schoenberger, whose mansions were compared with European castles. In contrast, solid, middle-class neighborhoods sprang up along the streetcar lines in Pleasant Ridge, Kennedy Heights, and Westwood. College Hill developed a distinctive intellectual identity with the establishment of the Farmers College and the Ohio Female College. Avondale attracted wealthy industrialists and, in the 1890s, became a destination for German Jews. Both Avondale and Walnut Hills contained small settlements of African Americans. Glendale, situated on the rail line, was planned specifically to provide an avenue for those who commuted into the city each day.

This diffusion of the city's population across the river and onto the surrounding hillsides coincided with the concentration of manufacturing concerns in the Mill Creek Valley and the Norwood Trough. The basin or city center was freed to accommodate commercial concerns such as offices, department stores, and banks.[10]

A Cultural Perspective

As Cincinnati's growth slowed in the latter half of the nineteenth century, local leaders succeeded in diversifying the city's industry, thereby solidifying its economic future. But they also hoped to create a new image for the city—one not based on Cincinnati as the nation's largest and therefore leading city. They worked to create a city of culture and tradition, a beautiful and livable place. In 1898, in *Picturesque Cincinnati*, O. A. and G. A. Kraemer assured their readers that "[T]he Queen City is pre-eminently an artistic and cultural center. Cosmopolitan as well as metropolitan."[11]

The cultural advancement that began in Cincinnati in the 1870s was as phenomenal as the city's commercial advances in the first half of the century. Parks, playgrounds, a music hall, an art museum, expositions, and even a professional baseball team provided Cincinnatians with new sources of civic pride. In 1871, Henry Probasco gave the city a fountain in honor of his deceased brother-in-law, Tyler Davidson. The fountain, designed by Bavarian artist August von Kreling, portrayed the blessings of water. The "Genius of Water" stood atop the thirty-eight-foot cast bronze structure. Water fell from her fingertips onto sculpted figures, depicting the importance of water in quenching thirst and fire, for bathing, and for watering crops. The fountain was erected

at the city's center on Fifth Street; its unveiling was attended by more than twenty thousand persons. It soon became the city's symbol, around which citizens could rally.

The city's appearance, long neglected and spoiled by billowing coal dust and manufacturing by-products, was in desperate need of green spaces. Many parks were established, including Burnet Woods in Clifton, and Eden Park in East Walnut Hills. In 1875, the Cincinnati Zoological Gardens opened, providing residents with another sort of park that included a curious menagerie that grew rapidly in size, scope, and popularity.

In the 1870s, a series of expositions and festivals were initiated, which demonstrated the city's ability to combine commerce with culture. In 1838, the first of a series of eighteen exhibitions of home products and works of art had been organized by the Ohio Mechanics Institute; this series was not interrupted until the outbreak of the Civil War. In 1870, however, the Ohio Mechanics Institute joined with the city's Chamber of Commerce and the Board of Trade to launch a grand industrial fair, which was larger than any held before the war. The fair included machinery, much of which was manufactured in Cincinnati and displayed in the "Power Hall," as well as horticultural and art exhibits.

Fourteen such fairs were held in subsequent years, culminating in the 1888 Centennial Exposition of the Ohio Valley and Central States. This extensive industrial and arts exposition celebrated the centennial of the city's settlement, and its grandeur could not be matched. Machinery Hall, three blocks long, was built over the Miami Canal

Cincinnati Exposition Building as seen from the canal with a gondola in the foreground, 1888; *Public Library of Cincinnati and Hamilton County.*

(now Central Parkway). Gondolas were imported from Venice and transported visitors along the canal. This exposition could not be surpassed, and no more of its kind were ever held.

As the expositions continued year after year, they included more pageantry and less mechanics. The Tyler-Davidson Fountain was dedicated at the conclusion of the 1871 exposition. In 1875, the parade that opened the exposition was five miles long. By the end of the decade, exhibitors from across the country crowded the city.

The grand exposition of 1870 was accompanied by the opening of the Saengerfest Hall. The *saengerfest*, a festival of German choral societies, was first held in Cincinnati in 1849. The event brought together groups from Cincinnati, Louisville, Kentucky, and Madison, Indiana, and attracted many visitors to the area. Out of this tradition grew the annual May Festival, as it had come to be called by May 1873. The conductor, Theodore Thomas, spurred on by the interest and prodding of the socially prominent Maria Longworth

Nichols, directed the festival, overseeing the performances of thirty-six musical societies. The huge success of this festival led to another *saengerfest* in 1875, and generated for the festival support for the construction of a permanent home with better acoustics. Consequently, Music Hall was built in 1878, in time for the third festival. The May Festival continued as a musical tradition, bringing international fame to Cincinnati as the region's leading musical center.

The late 1870s also saw the birth of the Aesthetic Movement in America, for which the 1876 Philadelphia Centennial Exhibition was a catalyst. The organizers of the exhibition "initiated calls for the integration of culture and commerce in the United States,"[12] a phenomenon that already seemed to be afoot in Cincinnati. Inspired and awed by the ceramics exhibited by Japan at the Centennial Exhibition, Maria Longworth Nichols established her own pottery works in 1880, just four years later. The Rookwood Pottery, whose doors did not close until 1967, was the largest, longest lasting, and most important art pottery studio in the country during the late nineteenth and early twentieth centuries.[13]

Many of the individuals instrumental in establishing the Zoological Park and the May Festival also helped to found the Cincinnati Art Museum. In 1877, a dynamic group of women founded the Women's Art Museum Association of Cincinnati; their mission was to establish a museum in the Queen City. They hoped to model it after the South Kensington Museum in England, which emphasized the role of the decorative arts in making the connection between art and industrial development. In 1882, the city provided the Association with twenty acres of land in Eden Park. From atop the hill, the museum commanded a superb view of the city and the river. On May 17, 1886, the "Art Palace of the West" opened to the public as a showcase of the decorative arts. It quickly expanded its scope to include painting, sculpture, antiquities, and treasures from around the world, which formed the basis of its present rich collection.

Adjoining the Art Museum, and dedicated in 1887, was the Art Academy of Cincinnati, which provided a training ground for the city's young artists. The Academy actually began in 1869; in that year, Joseph Longworth and Thomas S. Noble organized the school in a rented building at Third and Main Streets, and called it the McMicken School of Design. By 1873, with more than 300 students, the Academy offered courses in drawing, oil painting, engraving, and lithography.

In the following year, woodcarving and sculpture were added to the curriculum, with the intention of supporting the integration of art and industry through formal training in the industrial or decorative arts. The 1887 faculty of the academy boasted numerous artists of note, including landscape painter L. H. Meakin, and designer and woodcarver Benn Pitman. Pitman's work included the fifty-by-sixty-foot cherrywood organ screen for Music Hall. Other illustrious faculty members were J. H. Sharp, who taught from 1892 to 1902, and specialized in painting Native Americans, and sculptor Clement Barnhorn, who was part of the faculty from 1898 to 1935.

Frank Duveneck (1848-1919) brought international attention to the Art Academy. A native of Covington, Kentucky, Duveneck studied in Munich from 1871 to 1873. He returned to Cincinnati, where he taught evening classes at the Ohio Mechanics Institute. Duveneck then traveled, worked, and taught extensively in Europe, but in 1889 returned again to Cincinnati and became a teacher at the Art Museum and in his private studio. In 1900, he joined the faculty of the Academy, where he taught until his death in 1919.

Cincinnati's burst of energy to create cultural institutions in the 1870s enriched the residents' lives. The city no longer had a reputation only as a manufacturing and commercial center; it was a place rich in culture. With the establishment of the Cincinnati Art Museum, the May Festival, and the Art Academy of Cincinnati, its history of native-son artists, the presence of the Rookwood Pottery, and the many other institutions dating from the late nineteenth century, Cincinnati's cultural heritage was in place for future generations to nurture and enjoy.

Cincinnati's Dressmakers

FROM THE EARLIEST YEARS of Cincinnati's settlements, fashion and being fashionable were part and parcel of life in the Queen City. Cincinnati's citizens, who migrated from the eastern seaboard, brought with them the refinements of the East. The city, strategically located on one of the most important waterways of the period, was a major boomtown on the western frontier; there was no limit to the potential for shipping from the East the "conveniences and luxuries of every clime and soil" that Cincinnatians may have desired.[1]

In 1825, William Greene, a young barrister with an eye toward earning $3,000 per year or more, came from Rhode Island to Cincinnati, but he needed to convince his fiancée, Abby Lyman of Massachusetts, that Cincinnati was worthy of her. In his letters, he compared Cincinnati to Providence and Boston, describing the "enormous blocks of brick buildings, wide, straight and elegantly paved streets, genteel carriages and fine equipages." He marveled at the "existence of an *Eastern* City in the heart of a comparative wilderness." Greene assured Miss Lyman

that "the people . . . are dashing in their fineries and rolling in luxury. . . . [Y]ou will find elegance of manners and refinement of conversation."[2] Greene must have convinced his bride-to-be that Cincinnati was refined enough to offer her the luxuries to which she was accustomed, because they lived in the city until the middle of the nineteenth century.

Another visitor, Frances Milton Trollope, was not so complimentary when she came to Cincinnati in 1828. An Englishwoman, Trollope recorded her impressions of America in *The Domestic Manners of Americans*, published in 1832. During her travels in this country, she spent a great deal of time in Cincinnati. Trollope described Cincinnati society as having a "total and universal want of manners, both in males and females," with none of "the little elegancies and refinements" enjoyed by the middle classes of Europe.[3] Viewing Cincinnati women as shallow, judging each other only by their exteriors—their dress and appearance, she accused them, in their attempts to imitate fashionable women of the East Coast, of overreaching their models in both show and

Ehrgott & Forbringer, Cincinnati, nineteenth century, United States; *Edmund Dexter's Residence* (ca. 1861–1869); color lithograph, 15I x 20G in. (40.0 x 51.4 cm); Gift of Mrs. William H. Chatfield, 1936.23.

Set at the southwest corner of Fourth and Walnut Streets, the Edmund Dexter residence was in the heart of fashionable Cincinnati. Ladies of the mid- to late 1850s promenade along the street in their finery.

gaudiness. It was said that she formed this poor impression of Cincinnati women because she was never "admitted" into the best society, arriving as she did with no letters of introduction and not dressed in the "approved fashion."[4]

In fact, not just Cincinnatians were criticized for gaudy, extreme taste in clothing. Other European visitors agreed with Mrs. Trollope that American women in general outdid their European sisters in elaborate dress. In 1850, novelist Maria McIntosh observed that foreigners were appalled by the ostentatious display of finery. English writer John Robert Godley remarked in his *Letters from America* in 1844, "I do not think I ever saw so large a proportion of highly dressed men and women. The Parisian fashions of the day are carried out to their extreme . . . "; noted actress Frances Kemble

Butler commented in her 1835 book, *Journal of a Residence in America*, that American women "never walk on the streets but in the most showy and extreme toilet."[5]

American women, including Cincinnatians, were intent on dressing well, perhaps in an attempt to dispel any European notions that all Americans were frontier people without any refinements whatsoever. From east to west, American women in all walks of life attempted to dress as fashionably as they could. Lucy Larcom, nineteenth-century women's rights activist and mill worker, recounted that all the mill girls subscribed to *Godey's Lady's Book*. Factory workers and teachers whose wages barely sustained them scrimped on necessities to acquire more fashionable clothing. Dress reformer Abba Woolson complained in 1873, "The feminine mind is occupied by clothes—and nothing but." "Dress has become primary, woman secondary," wrote reformer Celia Burleigh. She stated that if you asked a friend to describe a social affair from the previous night, the friend would describe what the men said and did, and what the women wore.[6]

Despite the belief that dress and morality went hand in hand, ministers, dress reformers, feminist activists, fashion correspondents, and etiquette writers all railed against American women's obsession with dress.[7] As late as 1901, the *Ladies' Home Journal* complained about the grip fashion had on women: "We are all hypnotized by some evil magician whose spell we cannot break."[8]

Dressmakers, whether viewed as villains who fueled the fire or merely as service providers who profited from this obsession, were an all-important link in bridging the gap between Paris, the absolute arbiter of fashion in the nineteenth century, and women across America. They established their businesses wherever there were women who desired fashionable dress. From New York City to small towns in Iowa and beyond, dressmakers provided a vital service.

By 1850, Cincinnati had grown from a frontier settlement to a commercial center with a population of 115,000. The city supported both a healthy middle class and a wealthy upper class. The men of early founding families such as the Baums, the Kilgours, the Schoenbergers, the Straders, the Longworths, and the Lytles accumulated great wealth as steamboat and railroad magnates, ironmasters, bankers, and lawyers. The women of these families had ample means at their disposal for maintaining a fashionable wardrobe. In fact, as evidenced by costumes

in the collection of the Cincinnati Art Museum, local women were purchasing couture gowns from the most highly regarded designers in New York, London, and Paris as early as the 1860s. They patronized the salons of Charles Frederick Worth, Vignon, Jacques Doucet, Emile Pingat, John Redfern, Ernest Raudnitz, and Lucile.

There was a steady stream of social events to which these women could wear their finery. The theater was a popular amusement in the early years; more than 140 performances of various Shakespearean plays were staged by troupes that traveled between New York and New Orleans in the first two decades of Cincinnati's history—as many as in Detroit, St. Louis, and Lexington combined. Cincinnatians entertained themselves at the Burnet House and at the St. Nicholas, Grand, Emery, and Palace hotels, all of which were known for excellent service, as well as popular entertainment. Opera became an important social event in 1857, when Pike's Opera House was built. Other popular theaters were the Grand Opera House, the Columbia, and Robinson's Opera House; both the Odeon Theater and Heuck's Opera House were touted as establishments patronized by the rich and famous.

Dinner parties, dances, cotillions, and balls of all sorts were common events. "Assemblies," a series of balls that were supported by subscription, were held each winter. The Bachelor's Ball, the Buckeye Ball, and the Military Ball were all annual events. Mrs. Trollope herself included a magnificent ballroom on the third floor of the Bazaar she built in 1829, with its elaborate arabesque windows and gas-illuminated walls designed to resemble the Alhambra mosque. Matinees, the term for dances held in the middle of the day, also became popular. The organizers would close the shutters, light the gas, and proceed with the event as if it were a fashionable evening assembly. Bal-masques, or costume balls, were the rage as well; guests wore elaborate costumes, sometimes created by Parisian couturiers.

The May Festival, established in 1873, became a biennial event of great importance to the city's elite. Organized at the urging of Maria Longworth Nichols, daughter of wealthy Cincinnatian Nicholas Longworth, the May Festival gained the support of the most prominent men and women in the city. The Festival itself, an incomparably elaborate event, was accompanied by various social gatherings and balls. In the 1870s, Cincinnati's most prominent women had new gowns made for the event each time it was staged.

Eliza Potter's 1859 autobiography, *A Hairdresser's Experience in High Life*, provides a unique view of Cincinnati's social life in the mid-nineteenth century. Eliza Potter, an African-American hairdresser, migrated westward from New York to various points, including Cincinnati, where she combed and dressed the hair of many "wretched slaves to fashion."[9] She divided Cincinnati fashionables into four distinct circles: the old aristocracy, the moneyed aristocracy, the church aristocracy, and the school aristocracy; the latter referred to those who sent their daughters to a particular finishing school in hope of gaining entrée into a loftier social circle.

Potter worked in Cincinnati for several years, dressing hair from eight in the morning until six in the evening except on ball nights, when she was busy as late as eleven. In one chapter, she described instances in which she dressed Cincinnati women's hair for balls, weddings, and other special events, and related the surprise of women from eastern cities at the elegance of the local social events. Potter advised one fashionable woman from New York that she might like to purchase an elegant headdress for an event she was attending at the Burnet House: "She laughed at me, and said if she was in New York she would, but did not think it worth while to take so much trouble for a party in Cincinnati. The next day . . . she was very much mortified, and told me if she had known the Cincinnati ladies dressed so well, she would have bought the head-dress."[10]

Potter regularly followed the city's fashionable women to summer resorts. In the 1820s and 1830s, Cincinnatians chose rather modest retreats just north and south of the city, such as Yellow Springs and Big Bone Lick, where they sought the leisurely pleasure of clear air in a rural setting. By the middle of the century, however, as the city's wealth increased, members of the elite began to travel to the fashionable eastern resorts, Newport and Saratoga. These places were not only a retreat from the unhealthy air of the city and daily cares, but they also offered women the opportunity to display their fashionable attire among the elite social circles of the East. Potter, who spent many summers dressing hair at both Newport and Saratoga, observed women who first traveled to Europe to supply themselves with a Parisian wardrobe so as to "return to Saratoga with a glittering display in August." A woman Potter identified only as Mrs. W was known to travel with as many as fifty

An opening at the Cincinnati Art Museum was an opportunity for Cincinnati women to display their elegant dress. This 1893 illustration from *Harper's Weekly* illustrates Cincinnati socialites on the main staircase; *Public Library of Cincinnati and Hamilton County.*

trunks containing 150 costumes just for the summer resort season, where she "made five toilets a day."[11]

The debutante season was yet another reason for fashionable women to order new gowns from their dressmakers. The coming-out of young women at age sixteen or seventeen was an annual rite that introduced them to society. The elaborate social functions surrounding this event required countless new costumes for the debutante and her close relations. Debutantes were the guests of honor at both dances or balls organized specifically for

them by their parents and a series of subscription balls. Afternoon receptions or teas were customary, as were "numberless theatre parties."[12] In short, the debutante season created an enormous need for the dressmaker's skills. In the 1912-1913 debutante season, twenty-six debutantes were listed in *Mrs. Devereux's Blue Book of Cincinnati*. If each debutante needed eight new evening gowns and four new afternoon dresses—a conservative estimate—to be dressed appropriately for her coming-out, at least 312 new costumes would have been required for the debutantes alone in that season. This estimate does not take into account new gowns that may have been required for the debutante's mother, grandmother, aunts, sisters, and acquaintances, who also would be attending not only their own debutante's events but also those of other prominent families. Weddings were another occasion that required new gowns. Also, in the 1912-1913 season, Mrs. Devereux reported no fewer than forty-five marriages, which called for wedding gowns, as well as bridesmaid's dresses and garments for other members of the wedding party.

Beside the many social occasions or momentous life events that called for a visit to the dressmaker, a fashionable woman was expected to dress in style at any event she might attend. Although a new dress was not required every time she stepped out of the house, a woman needed an updated wardrobe when styles changed. Women in Cincinnati were involved in many activities beyond the required visiting or shopping, which took them out of the home regularly. As women's clubs grew popular in the late nineteenth century, Cincinnati women founded their own groups, including the Ladies' Musical Club, the Ladies' Junior Musical Club, the Monday Musical Club, the College Club, the Woman's Art Club, the Cincinnati Woman's Club, the Riding Club, the Mount Auburn Literary Club, and the Cincinnati Pottery Club. Many women in Cincinnati also were involved in philanthropic organizations, such as the Maternity Society, the Women's Art Museum Association, the Cincinnati Orchestra Association Company, and a variety of church-sponsored organizations.

Motivated as they were to dress well not only for show but also for moral and ideo-

logical reasons, women feared the criticisms of society column editors such as Clara and Marion Devereux. The society column of the *Cincinnati Enquirer* chronicled the dinners, teas, balls, weddings, and travels of the city's prominent citizens. Debutantes, known as "rosebuds" to Marion Devereux, were not truly debutantes unless the society editor called them by that title. Women of prominence hoped they might be portrayed favorably and feared they might be described as wearing "the [familiar] gown which has graced so many occasions"—a devastatingly sarcastic remark that reminded women not to wear the same dress too many times.[13]

It is not surprising, then, that the business section of the 1897 Cincinnati City Directory listed 1,553 women working as independent dressmakers. This statistic, without doubt, represents only a small percentage of the women actually working in this occupation. Many dressmakers never listed themselves in the business section of the city directories under the "Dressmakers" heading; one would have to scour the hundreds of thousands of individual listings to determine a more accurate count. Even federal census records are unreliable. Women were assumed to be homemakers, and their "occupations" were recorded as such. In some cases, the women themselves chose not to divulge their working status, so that they did not appear as anything other than respectable housewives. If no residents were home at a particular address when the enumerator called, he might just as easily have obtained his information from the neighbors—a questionable source at best. Many dressmakers advertised only by word of mouth; those who did not list themselves in the business section of the directory were

84

Number of Dressmakers Working in Cincinnati, 1850–1930, as listed in the City Directory								
1850	1860	1877	1885	1897	1906	1915	1925	1930
71*	74*	482	825	1,553	1,144	933	422	326

*Figures include both milliners and dressmakers, who were listed together in these years.

satisfied with the brisk trade that walked in the door. Indeed, "the Gilded Age *was* the golden age for the dressmaker."[14] There was no lack of work in this period, when fashionable styles changed rapidly and women were engrossed in the acquisition of stylish dress.

Although relatively few dressmakers were listed in the city directories in the late 1870s, these figures probably were skewed by the fact that fewer women "advertised" in these earlier years. "Dressmakers" as an occupational category was first listed in the business section of the Cincinnati directories in 1875, combined with "Milliners." (Prior to this date, dressmakers were noted as such only in the individual listings.) In 1875, 466 dressmaking and millinery establishments were listed. In 1877, dressmakers were listed as a separate category; 482 were recorded for that year. By 1885, this number had increased by 71 percent to 825. After 1897, the peak year for dressmaking establishments in Cincinnati, the number of dressmakers, at least as indicated in the directories, began to decline—slowly at first, then precipitously in 1900. In 1899, 1,460 dressmakers were listed; in 1900, only 1,243. By 1915, when ready-made garments for women were becoming readily available, fewer than 1,000 dressmakers were recorded. By 1925, the number had decreased to 422.

The prolific production of Cincinnati

dressmakers is evident in more than eighty surviving garments that belong to the costume and textile collection of the Cincinnati Art Museum, as well as those in various museum collections across the country. The Cincinnati collection represents the work of twenty-nine individual designers and seven retail establishments and custom salons in department stores, dating from 1877 to 1922.

This "golden age" of dressmaking before the advent of the ready-to-wear industry coincided with what is referred to as the Golden Age of Cincinnati. In the last quarter of the nineteenth century, the arts flourished in the Queen City. Cincinnati artists such as Henry Farney, Frank Duveneck, John H. Twachtman, Elizabeth Nourse, and Edward Potthast all attained national recognition. Equally important was the rise to prominence of the decorative arts in the form of acclaimed silver design by Edward Kinsey and by Duhme & Company, as well as the superb metalwork of Maria Longworth Storer and E. T. Hurley, who reflected the spirit of the Arts and Crafts Movement in their work. Major furniture makers, including Mitchell & Rammelsberg and woodcarvers Henry and William Fry, and Benn Pitman catapulted Cincinnati into the limelight as a major producer of Aesthetic Movement designs. Cincinnati also boasted more art pottery works than any other city in the United States. The famed

Rookwood Pottery Company won international recognition at world's fairs in competition with Europe's best.

In the midst of this surge of artistic and creative energies, Cincinnati's dressmakers were creating no less superb examples of fashionable dress. Cincinnati's wealthiest women, who patronized the Parisian salons of Worth, Doucet, Vignon, and others, also regularly sought out the services of local dressmakers.

In the late 1870s, Mrs. Joseph C. Thoms (née Mary Swift) traveled to Paris and was fitted for a reception gown by Worth. The Swifts lived on a farm on Reading Road, north of the city, and had made their fortune through banking and the pork business. In 1870, Mary Swift married Joseph Clark Thoms, a wealthy Cincinnati attorney and real estate investor; this union joined together two of Cincinnati's most prominent families. After their marriage, the Thoms resided in Mount Auburn, one of the most fashionable areas in the city at the time.

The gown Mary Swift Thoms purchased from Worth (see page 86) follows the fashion of the day in the combination of several colors and textures in one garment. Blue satin forms the panniers that Worth revived in the late 1870s, as well as a divided overskirt, much in the style of the eighteenth century. The overskirt is pulled back over the hips to form both a low bustling of fabric at the back and the train. The exposed selvedges of the floral silk, which forms the draped underskirt in the front, are a signature conceit of the House of Worth, indicating the luxury of utilizing the full width of the fabric in a single element of the garment. The day bodice, worn for receiving

guests, has a low-cut neckline but appropriately modest three-quarter-length sleeves. The cuirass-style bodice, fitting tight and low over the hips, had become popular in the middle of the decade and continued to be worn into the early 1880s.

The most distinctive fact about this dress, however, is that Mrs. Thoms brought extra yardage of the floral silk when she returned to Cincinnati. She took this to Selina Cadwallader, a Cincinnati dressmaker, and had the evening bodice on page 87 made to be worn with the same skirt. Perhaps this was Mrs. Thoms's method for saving a bit of money, or perhaps she did not have time to wait for Worth to construct the second bodice. In any case, neither Mrs. Thoms nor any of Cincinnati's other elite women seemed to have any compunction about patronizing Cincinnati's own dressmakers as readily as they patronized Parisian couturiers.

Selina Hetherington Cadwallader was not a typical dressmaker. An Irish immigrant, she married Morris Cadwallader in Cincinnati on March 31, 1862, at the St. John Episcopal Church at Seventh and Plum Streets. Morris Cadwallader, originally from Henrietta, New York, seemed unsettled in his business interests. In his late thirties, when he married Selina, he had worked in the post office and as an attorney. His credit was first reviewed by R. G. Dun and Company (later Dun and Bradstreet) in early 1866, after he and another gentleman had bought out a boot and shoe retailer. By November of that same year, the partnership already had dissolved, and Cadwallader was trying to sell the business to pursue other interests.[15] In 1871, the city directory listed Morris Cadwallader as a farmer. Most likely,

DETAIL: Cadwallader *Reception Dress: Evening Bodice*, 1877–1878; 1986.1200b.

Selina Cadwallader made the evening bodice for Mrs. Joseph C. Thoms to coordinate with the skirt made by Charles Frederick Worth, Paris.

OPPOSITE: Charles Frederick Worth (1826–1895), England (worked in Paris); *Reception Dress: Day Bodice and Skirt,* 1877–1878; silk; Label: Worth 7. RUE DE LA PAIX, PARIS; Gift of Mrs. Murat Halstead Davidson, 1986.1200a,c.

he had recognized the wealth that could be accrued in the pork business and was probably raising hogs, a lucrative venture in Cincinnati. Despite his erratic career changes, upon his death in 1880, Morris Cadwallader left his wife and three children an estate appraised at approximately $110,000, to be divided between them—a significant sum roughly equivalent to $1,837,000 today.[16]

The Cadwalladers lived at 49 East Fourth Street, in the heart of the most fashionable area of downtown Cincinnati. East Fourth Street was the city's shopping and social center; here, the H. & S. Pogue Company, established in 1863, sold dry goods, millinery, and other fancy goods, such as dressmaking fabrics and trims. Also, the Mabley & Carew Company, another high-end retailer, was located on the corner of Fifth and Vine Streets. The John Shillito Company was nearby on Race Street. Duhme & Company, at the corner of Fourth and Walnut, catered to discriminating customers who wished to purchase fine china, jewelry, and silver. A. B. Closson's, Jr. and Company on West Fourth Street sold the paintings of local artists Frank Duveneck, Henry Farney, and Joseph Sharp.

Throughout their marriage, Selina was not sitting idly at home. She was not only raising her three children, Jessie, Mary, and Selina (or Lena, as she was called), but she also operated a boarding house and a dressmaking business at the same time. Boarding houses, in the nineteenth century, often became semipermanent residences for wealthy families. Prominent women who did not wish to be bothered by the daily cares of running a household found life in a respectable boarding house a way of maintaining fashionable idleness. Therefore, managing a boarding house, like dressmaking, was a respectable economic opportunity for women of that period. Married women who ran boarding houses could "stay at home," in their proper place, while rubbing elbows daily with the fashionable and the elite. One of Selina Cadwallader's most renowned boarders was French dancing master M. Charles Ernst, a well-loved figure in Cincinnati society for over thirty years.

Selina operated her dressmaking business from 1870 to 1886. Her concern was listed, separate from her husband's affairs, in the Dun and Company ledgers, beginning in May 1871. The comments were generally short and succinct; she was described as "industrious & energetic," and was said to pay her bills promptly. In 1873, her business was reported as "first class" but small overall and making little more than a living. Interestingly, after her husband's death in 1880, the reports on "Madame S. Cadwallader," as she was then called, suddenly became glowing. The amount of her inheritance was reported twice, in 1881 and in 1882, and mentioned again obliquely in 1884. Her assets in 1881 were valued between $30,000 and $35,000. In June 1881, the Dun and Company credit reporter described Selina's concern as follows: "She has been in this business many years [and] always done a large business and made money. Her trade is all first class & consequently she gets good prices. She is what is termed [an] authority of fashion here. Is regarded as an honorable lady in every respect. Stands well with the trade & Bank in general. Has ample means for her business, safe for all wants." She was listed as a "safe credit risk" in April 1884.[17]

Certainly, Selina's inheritance provided

her with more cash to pour into the business and a fund on which to rely in case of misfortune. But the change in the credit reporter's language also occurred, without doubt, because her husband, whose business affairs always seemed somewhat impermanent, was no longer a concern. In this way, Selina was like many other dressmakers whose husbands only hindered their progress with unprofitable or unsavory lifestyles.

Despite Morris Cadwallader's varied occupations, the family was profitable. The large inheritance left to Selina and her children upon her husband's death suggests that they were living well even while Morris was alive. Selina certainly was busy with three children and a successful boarding house, as well as her dressmaking business. In 1880, the year her husband died, the census listed her as a widow living with her three daughters. Perhaps a bit overwhelmed, Selina was well off enough to hire a servant, Mary Renther, who also lived in the household.

With her daughters Jessie, age fourteen, and Mary, age ten, as potential helpers, Selina was perhaps one of those dressmakers who did the work because she loved it. She had a ready clientele within easy reach; perhaps many clients were her boarders. On Fourth Street, in the fashionable shopping district, Selina's salon was easily accessible; still other clients undoubtedly came because of her reputation.

Mary Swift readily entrusted her expensive French floral silk to Selina's skillful hands. Selina's workmanship inside the evening bodice she created for Mrs. Thoms is expert. All the finishing was completed by hand: The buttonholes are hand-worked, and each seam edge is whipstitched by

is actually made up of three parts: the bodice, the skirt, and a chemisette or dickey. The opaque chemisette, made to be worn under the bodice, gave the wearer the option of greater modesty by covering the upper chest and back for occasions when this was required. Even without the chemisette, the gown is designed in a modest manner: a sheer embroidered net covers the upper chest and is framed with a white lace ruffle, which succeeds in suggesting a low décolletage. The gown is styled fashionably in the deep tones popular in the period. The bodice is just long enough to warrant a crenellated edge that allows it to fit easily over the top of the hips. The skirt is beautifully asymmetrical, with an inset of red checkered damask trimmed with satin ribbons.

Selina Cadwallader died of uterine cancer in October 1886, at age 50. She left a will that valued her personal belongings at $50,000 and her real estate at $70,000. The dispersal of her estate to her daughters included seventy shares in the Cincinnati, Lebanon and Northern Railroad, as well as dresses and dress goods appraised at over $2,300. She is buried in Spring Grove Cemetery, where Cincinnati's elite have been laid to rest since 1858, with her sister, Mary Ann Hetherington, her husband, Morris, and one of their children, Charles, who died at the age of ten months.

Selina was a typical dressmaker in that she was Caucasian and worked after she was widowed, supporting herself through dressmaking. She was atypical in that she started her business as a married woman, also ran a boarding house, and was wealthy enough to hire a servant and leave a sizable legacy to her heirs. Selina also was particularly

LEFT: Selina Cadwallader (active 1870–1886); *Tea Gown,* 1877–1878; silk; Label: S. Cadwallader. CINCINNATI, OHIO.; Bequest of Katherine V. Gano Estate, 1945.53.

RIGHT: Selina Cadwallader (active 1870–1886); *Reception Dress,* 1877; silk, linen; Label: Mrs. S. Cadwallader CINCINNATI, OHIO.; Gift of Mr. Benjamin Miller, 1946.18a,b.

Selina Cadwallader
(active 1870–1886);
Reception Dress, 1886;

silk, cotton; Label: S.
Cadwallader CINCIN-
NATI—OHIO—;

Gift of Wilmar
Antiques c/o Mr.
Maurice Oshry,
1971.550a–c.

successful, remaining in business for sixteen years—a significant accomplishment in a field in which few survived more than two or three years.

Mary J. Bannon, like Selina Cadwallader, was an Irish immigrant who was quite successful in Cincinnati. Bannon initially may have operated her dressmaking business out of her home in the city's West End. She first appeared in the city directory in 1872, living at 88 Longworth, downtown, between Fifth and Sixth Streets, just two blocks north of fashionable Fourth Street. Mary resided with Thomas Bannon, her nephew, who worked as a japanner, and her sister Maggie, who may have helped her with the business from time to time. Mary, like many dressmakers of the period, never married; in 1872, she was listed in the directory with no occupation. In 1873, the directory recorded her occupation in the individual listings as "dressmaker." In 1875, Mary made her appearance in the business section under the new "Milliners and Dressmakers" heading at the Longworth address. In 1877, however, she took up residence at 270 West Eighth Street and continued to work out of her home. Just one year later, in 1878, she had become successful enough to move her business from her home to 120 West Fourth Street, down the street from Selina Cadwallader's establishment.

It seems, however, that Mary's stay on fashionable Fourth Street was short-lived; by 1880, her business was located at 251 West Seventh Street, with her residence still at West Eighth Street. Perhaps she found Fourth Street beyond her means. Nevertheless, Mary's prominent clientele followed her to West Seventh Street and to the various addresses in the West End, where she both

lived and worked until 1898, the year she died. At that time, she was living at 2233 Burnet Avenue in the fashionable Mount Auburn neighborhood. Her business address, still in the West End, was 518 West Ninth Street. As with many dressmakers, Bannon's residential and business addresses changed frequently. Financial constraints and family obligations often precipitated these moves from one address to another, often within the same neighborhood.

Mary Bannon was listed most often in the city directory as a dressmaker. Occasionally, however, when her stated occupation reflected the caliber of her clientele, she was listed as a modiste. It was not uncommon for dressmakers to concoct a French-sounding name or to call themselves "Madame," or adopt the title "modiste" to associate themselves more closely with French couturiers. Mary Bannon, however, had no need to manufacture such an impression. She served some of the wealthiest women in Cincinnati, including Mrs. George K. Schoenberger (née Ella Beatty). The Schoenbergers lived in a palatial home in the wealthy suburb of Clifton. Set on one of the hills surrounding the downtown area, Clifton was home to many of Cincinnati's most prominent families, who were able, early on, to build colossal residences above the city. The Schoenbergers' home, Scarlet Oaks, was considered at that time to be one of the most magnificent private residences in Ohio. George K. Schoenberger amassed his fortune in the iron business. His philanthropic efforts included public service on the Cincinnati Chamber of Commerce, trusteeship of Spring Grove Cemetery, and service as a major benefactor of the Cincinnati Orphan Asylum.

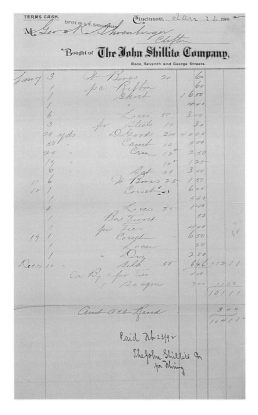

Mrs. George K. Schoenberger patronized the John Shillito Company in January 1892 and spent a total of $104.11 on dress fabrics, corsets, ribbon, and various other clothing-related dry goods. The receipt notes that the purchased items were "for delivery." *Cincinnati Historical Society Library.*

Receipt for the making of a brocade jacket for $12 by Mary J. Bannon for Mrs. George K. Schoenberger, February 1, 1892. *Cincinnati Historical Society Library.*

No stranger to the finest retailers in Cincinnati, Mrs. Schoenberger spent $248 on fabrics, trimmings, millinery, and ready-made garments between January 2 and February 1, 1892. These purchases included waists (blouses) from Mabley & Carew; various fabrics, veils, and gloves from the H. & S. Pogue Company; fabrics from Le Boutillier & Simpson Company; corsets, laces, ribbons, and a ready-made skirt from the John Shillito Company; as well as items from Cincinnati's renowned silversmiths, Duhme & Company.

A single receipt from the same year reveals that Ella Schoenberger hired Mary Bannon to make her a brocade jacket and paid her $12 for her labor. Mrs. Schoenberger also paid Mary a total of $22 for various fabrics and trims, including four yards of lining fabric, various ornaments, ribbons, and jet edgings. Perhaps these were the lining and trim for the brocade jacket or other costumes that Bannon was making for Mrs. Schoenberger. Although these payments seem small in relation to the time Bannon probably spent making the jacket, they are placed in perspective by receipts from the same year for two seamstresses who performed general sewing tasks for Schoenberger. They indicate the great discrepancy in wages between the dressmaker and the seamstress. Seamstress Minnie Hoffsess received $18.00 for twelve days of sewing, and Mary Southard was paid $3.90 for making six nightgowns—garments that most likely were entirely hand-sewn, hand-embroidered, and trimmed with lace inserts or edgings.

Mary Bannon is one of only three Cincinnati dressmakers whose credit was reviewed by R. G. Dun and Company. The

94

Mary J. Bannon (active
1873–1898), *Evening
Dress,* 1893-1894; silk;
Label: Bannon
CINCINNATI; Gift of
Mrs. Clifford R.
Wright, 1966.1311a,b.

This evening dress
created by Mary J.
Bannon uses unusual
crescent shapes of
fabric on the bodice
and sleeves to create
volume.

first entry regarding Bannon, however, immediately expands our vision of her world. In September 1880, the Dun and Company ledgers showed that Bannon was "at present on her way home from NY [New York] where she has been making purchase[s] for fall business."[19] Like many dressmakers, Mary Bannon found it necessary to make seasonal trips to New York, and often to Europe, to purchase the best fabrics and trims for her clients and to view firsthand the newest styles. As indicated by the Schoenberger receipt and the credit ledgers, Bannon was able to carry "a stock of fine goods"[20] in her shop—a luxury available only to those dressmakers successful enough to have amassed sufficient capital. The Dun and Company reporters are conservative in their estimations of Bannon, referring to her as industrious, honest, energetic, and "worthy of some confidence." She was said to do a "moderate business," had a "fair balance in Bank," and in 1884 was "thought to be worth about $2,000 to $3,000." The ledgers also note that the only drawback to Bannon's credit was that her customers were slow to pay, a problem experienced by most dressmakers.[21] Upon her death in 1898, Mary Bannon left the majority of her estate, worth over $5,300, to her nephew Thomas Bannon. Mary Bannon's career as dressmaker to an elite clientele had lasted a noteworthy twenty-five years.

The Cincinnati collection contains only one gown bearing Mary Bannon's label. This white ribbed silk dress (opposite) trimmed with sheer silk and brocaded and satin ribbons, was worn by Mrs. Perin Langdon (née Eleanor West), who also had gowns created by M. A. Ryan, another Cincinnati dressmaker. Two garments

designed by Bannon, however, are part of the collection of the Kentucky Historical Society. Both gowns were worn by Olivia Procter Benedict (1868-1959), granddaughter of William Procter, one of the founders of the Procter and Gamble Company. Olivia married the Reverend Cleveland Benedict, who served for eighteen years as rector at Christ Church in Glendale, Ohio.

Anna Dunlevy was one of Cincinnati's most successful dressmakers, whose reputation reached far beyond the Queen City. Like Selina Cadwallader and Mary J. Bannon, Anna was an Irish immigrant who came to America in 1865 at age fourteen. She first appeared in the 1884 city directory as a saleslady at Le Boutillier and Simpson, a high-end fancy goods retailer located at 102, 104, and 106 West Fourth Street. By this time, Anna was already married to Patrick Dunlevy, a laborer, also born in Ireland. According to the 1880 census records, the Dunlevys had five children, ranging in age from thirteen to two years.

Anna continued to work in retail until 1887, but by 1889, she had begun to make dresses in the family's flat at 299 Central Avenue. Her position at Le Boutillier, working with expensive fabrics and fancy goods, and dealing with the elite customers who patronized the store, provided invaluable experience. In any case, Anna's step into entrepreneurship was fortunate, because Patrick Dunlevy drowned accidentally in 1894, in the Ohio River.

We can only speculate whether Patrick was the love of Anna's life or whether their marriage was an uneasy union. His drowning easily could have been caused by an accident on the job, or by too much

Advertisement for Le Boutillier and Simpson Company, a high-end fancy goods retailer, for whom Anna Dunlevy worked as a saleslady from 1884 to 1887; *Williams' Cincinnati Directory*, 1892. *Cincinnati Historical Society Library.*

drink and carousing on the river's edge. Life could not have been easy for the Dunlevys. Patrick's wages as a laborer would not have stretched far, with (by 1894) six children to feed. Anna's work as a saleslady and dressmaker was surely needed to make ends meet. Their family was squeezed into the flat on Central Avenue, along with Anna's dressmaking business. This was probably not the life of opportunity Anna and Patrick had envisioned when they immigrated from Ireland.

Nevertheless, in 1894, Anna was left a widow at age forty-three, with six children to support. According to census records, she could neither read nor write. Yet in a few years, Anna managed to create a thriving business. In 1892, she moved her business out of her home, still on Central Avenue, to rooms on the tenth floor of the Neave Building, a commercial and office building

at the corner of Race and Fourth Streets. In 1895, Anna, who employed at least twelve women, spent the time and money to have them photographed professionally by a Cincinnati photographer at Dayton's Studio. She remained in business in the Neave Building until 1913, working a total of twenty-four years.

The earliest sample of Anna's work in the collection dates to 1894, and was made for the trousseau of Mrs. John Boulton of Walton, Kentucky. Walton, once the home of the governor's mansion, was just twenty miles from Cincinnati, an easy journey on the L & N railroad line. In the 1890s, Cincinnati was the largest city in the region, and many women came from neighboring towns and cities to shop. For Mrs. Boulton, Anna created a fashionable gown of olive green and pink changeable silk, with large leg-of-mutton sleeves (see pages 98 and 99).

Anna Dunlevy's seamstresses, photographed at Dayton's Studio in Cincinnati, 1895. Amanda Clara Kebler, who is on the far left in the back row, had recently been divorced when this photo was taken. A petite woman less than five feet tall, she was highly talented and became a fine seamstress in a year's time.

The Neave Building, at the corner of Fourth and Race Streets, where Anna Dunlevy had her salon from 1892 to 1913, and where Josephine M. Kasselmann worked from 1913 to 1919, before moving to Race Street. The dressmaking team of Mary Donegan and Katherine Willging also had their salon in the Neave Building. *Cincinnati Historical Society Library.*

MME. BOWMAN,
❧ ❧ Modiste ❧ ❧
122 West Seventh Street.

MISS K. R. CREGMILE,
❧ ❧ Modiste ❧ ❧
15 Garfield Place.

DUNLEVY,
❧ ❧ ❧ Robes ❧ ❧ ❧
1003 Neave Building.

Anna Dunlevy and Kate R. Cregmile advertised in the *Cincinnati Society Address Book* of 1898. *Public Library of Cincinnati and Hamilton County.*

Anna Dunlevy (active
1889–1913); *Afternoon
Dress,* 1894; silk, beads,
metallic thread; Label:
Dunlevy, NEAVE
BLDG. CINCINNATI,
O.; Gift of Lolita
Harper, 2000.78a,b.

Most notable from this period is Anna's creation of a wedding dress and trousseau for Ida Caldwell McFaddin, the daughter of wealthy railroad and coal magnate James Lewis Caldwell of Huntington, West Virginia. The trip to Cincinnati took only three hours by train, and the Caldwells often came to the city to shop. At age twenty-two, Ida met W. P. H. McFaddin, a handsome widower, who had made his own fortune as a Texas rancher. They were married in 1894, in Huntington, and soon after returned to McFaddin's home in Beaumont, Texas. The Dunlevy gown, worn by Ida in the photograph on page 100, features the huge balloon sleeves of the period. With an eye for elegant detail, Dunlevy chose to scallop the hem edge of the skirt and train, which must have taken many painstaking hours of hand sewing to complete.

Ida Caldwell McFaddin was so pleased with Anna Dunlevy's work that she continued throughout her life to order gowns from Anna exclusively. She traveled by train from Beaumont to Cincinnati, where she ordered fashionable gowns from Madame Dunlevy, as she referred to Anna. Ida would stay in Cincinnati for several days en route to Huntington, New York, or Washington, D.C., and select both designs and fabrics that Anna had brought back from her buying trips in Europe.

Ida's daughter, Mamie, later recounted her own excitement when the new dresses arrived from Madame Dunlevy. "She sent one dress in each box, and I can remember how thrilled I was when the box came, to see the beautiful dress[es]. They were really . . . very different and very unusual; they were . . . works of art."[22]

Like all dressmakers of the period, Anna

DETAIL: Dunlevy *Afternoon Dress,* 1894; 2000.78a,b.

Elaborate trimmings of ribbon, beaded braid, and gathered chiffon ornament the bodice of this dress created by Anna Dunlevy for the trousseau of Mrs. John Boulton of Walton, Kentucky. Cincinnati provided many services unavailable in outlying areas, including fine dressmakers. Clients came from as far away as Texas for Madame Dunlevy's unique designs.

Ida Caldwell McFaddin
was married in this
Dunlevy design in 1894,
in Huntington, West
Virginia. Mrs. McFaddin
continued to patronize
Madame Dunlevy after
she and her husband,
W. P. H. McFaddin,
returned to his home in
Beaumont, Texas. *Photo
courtesy of McFaddin-
Ward House, Beaumont,
Texas.*

Dunlevy followed the trends of the day.
Paris was still the absolute arbiter of style
and remained so until the 1930s. Good
dressmakers were certain to be vigilant to
provide their clients with the newest fashions as soon as they appeared in Parisian
salons. Anna, whose success allowed her to
travel to Europe regularly to purchase fabrics, obviously kept her finger on the pulse
of fashion. She was well aware of the current
styles, and there is nothing conservative
about her designs.

Anna cut the blue faille gown on the
page opposite in the more severe and vertically oriented mode of the turn of the century. The bodice is full in the popular
monobosom style. The skirt is cut to fit the
hips, and flares out only below the knee.
Anna chose to emphasize this vertical silhouette with multiple rows of vertical pleats
that are not perfectly straight but waver
slightly as they stand off the surface of the
gown. These wavering lines travel the length

Anna Dunlevy (active 1889–1913); *Day Dress,* 1900–1901; silk, cotton; Label: Dunlevy CINCINNATI, OHIO.; Gift of Mrs. J. C. Boyd Jr., 1971.97a,b.

of the sleeves and partially down the skirt, complemented by vertically placed elliptical lace appliqués. To contrast this strong vertical line, Dunlevy "capped" the gown with a spreading lace yoke, a riotous combination of zigzags, meandering ribbons, and medallions. Together, these elements form a visually arresting pattern; the gown comes alive with movement.

Another dress from this period, shown at right, illustrates Anna's eye for unusual fabrics and, again, her ability to combine seemingly incongruous patterns and colors into a harmonious whole. The dress itself is cut from linen woven into a sheer cloth. In this case, the fabric has a tan cast, probably its original unbleached or undyed shade. Sections of the dress—the lower sleeve, the yoke of the bodice, and a large curved inset on the skirt—are brocaded with a pattern of small and large dots in a variegated black-and-tan yarn. The brocade is overlaid with a delicate floral print in red, green, yellow, and brown. The edges of the brocaded and printed sections are outlined with a decorative off-white lace band, and lace insets run vertically on the sleeves, bodice, and skirt. As though this were not enough to stir the eye, Dunlevy lined the gown with a bold salmon-colored taffeta that succeeds in pulling together the varied elements of the dress. A "corsage" of twisted salmon and yellow ribbons on the bodice was Dunlevy's final bravado on this both visually complex and pleasing piece.

Two Dunlevy dresses (opposite page) illustrate the fuller upper sleeves and skirts popular between 1905 and 1908. Such elegant gowns would have been worn at home for receiving guests or for evening events, such as dinner parties or excursions to the

Anna Dunlevy (active 1889–1913); *Afternoon Dress,* 1900–1901; linen, silk; Label: Dunlevy CINCINNATI,
OHIO.; Gift of Mrs. John V. Campbell, 1940.1076a,b.

LEFT: Anna Dunlevy (active 1889–1913); *Afternoon Dress,* 1906; silk, cotton; Gift of Anna E. Winston, 1954.414a,b.

RIGHT: Anna Dunlevy (active 1889–1913); *Afternoon Dress,* 1905–1906; silk, cotton, linen; Label: Dunlevy CINCINNATI, OHIO.; Gift of Mrs. J. C. Boyd Jr. 1971.93a,b.

Both dresses employ suspenderlike bands on the bodice called *bretelles,* a design device that served visually to widen the shoulder line and make the waist appear smaller.

theater. Low, bare necklines were considered inappropriate in America for such occasions, but these gowns utilize lace and sheer silks to approximate the low-cut gowns worn comfortably by European women. In each of these gowns, Dunlevy has employed a version of the *bretelle,* suspenderlike bands on the bodice. The *bretelles* appear to broaden the shoulders, causing the waist to appear smaller than it actually is, much like the balloon sleeves of the mid-1890s.[23] Dunlevy made each gown unique by altering the form of the sleeve, the shape of the *bretelle,* and the delicate, handworked details.

The blue taffeta dress was worn by Annie May Morris, daughter of Robert Thomas Morris and Anne Wise Froome. Her brother, Robert Froome Morris, was a prominent attorney and vice mayor of Cincinnati; her father was the president of the R. T. Morris Printing Company. Annie's grandfather, Samuel Froome, developed the town of Winton Place, now a neighborhood within the city limits. Annie married Maurice Alvin Long of Middletown, Ohio, in 1905; this dress was probably part of her trousseau.

The red velvet dress was created for Anna E. Winston, the daughter of prominent Kentucky attorney Albert G. Winston. When this dress was added to the collection, a note pinned to it read, "This chiffon velvet gown is the Master Production of Miss Dunlevy of Cincinnati Ohio . . . for Anna E. Winston. . . . It was the realization of a girlhood dream." Obviously, Miss Winston had long anticipated owning a gown made by Anna Dunlevy. Perhaps as a girl she had visited Madame Dunlevy's salon with her mother and imagined herself in one of the gowns

ABOVE, DETAIL:
Dunlevy *Wedding Dress,*
1909; 1968.116;

Cincinnatian Bessie
Louise Bradley wore
this gown for her marriage to Monte Jay
Goble Sr. in 1909.

OPPOSITE, LEFT:
Celia Steinau (active
1900–1917); *Wedding
Dress,* 1908; silk, cotton;
Label: Steinau
CINCINNATI.; Gift of
Mrs. Ralph Grossman,
1969.533.

The wedding dress on
the left was created by
Celia Steinau and
worn by Ruth Grossman for her marriage
to Joseph Schild on
December 1, 1908.

OPPOSITE, RIGHT:
Anna Dunlevy (active
1889–1913); *Wedding
Dress,* 1909; silk, linen;
Label: Dunlevy
CINCINNATI,
OHIO.; Gift of Miss
Mary N. Goble,
1968.116.

she had seen there. The dress, constructed of deep-red silk velvet, is beautifully appliquéd and hand-embroidered with red silk flowers and ribbon edgings. Anna Winston must have worn this delicate piece with great pride.

Anna Dunlevy used hand-embroidery as an embellishment on more than one gown. She also employed it on Bessie Louise Bradley's wedding dress for her marriage to Monte Jay Goble Sr., in 1909. The wedding dress on pages 104 and 105 has an empire waistline, sheer lace yoke, and straight skirt. The shaped panel that surrounds the yoke is both edged and embellished with a white-on-white floral embroidery pattern. The same pattern appears on the vertical panel at the center front of the skirt.

Similar in design and use of embroidery is a wedding gown created by Cincinnati dressmaker Celia Steinau for Ruth Grossman for her marriage to Joseph Schild on December 1, 1908 (see page 105). Steinau, a dressmaker of German descent, lived with her sister Eva at various addresses in the West End. It was Eva, in fact, who established the dressmaking business that Celia inherited in 1907. Eva had been making dresses for twenty-four years, from 1882 to 1906. Celia's occupation in the directories is inconsistent. First listed as a dressmaker in 1900, from 1901 to 1906 she is recorded with no occupation, but it is almost certain that she worked with or for her sister. In 1907, one year after Eva disappeared from the business directory, Celia was listed as a dressmaker working in the Andrews Building at the southeast corner of Fifth and Race Streets. She continued making dresses until 1917.

Celia's creation for Ruth Grossman has

an elaborately embroidered panel that covers the bosom. A central bow motif with tendrils that twine among flowers is repeated on the distinctive medallions that grace the gown from shoulder to thigh. Cotton net edged with silk is threaded through slits in the embroidered medallions, ending with plaited silk fringe at the hem. The sheer net sleeves are graced with the same device, and fringe falls delicately over the hand at the wrist.

Like Eva and Celia Steinau, many dressmakers worked in family groups. Margaret Kavaney, her mother Catherine, and her sister Nellie formed an amazingly long-lived and successful business. Margaret first appeared in the city directory as a dressmaker in 1881; she was listed as living on Cinnamon Street in O'Bryonville, an Irish neighborhood just southwest of fashionable Hyde Park. At that time, she was living with her parents. Catherine McBride and Edward Kavaney had immigrated from Ireland in 1865, when Margaret was just five years old. Catherine, known as Katie, also was listed as a dressmaker in 1885. This mother-daughter team later appeared at various addresses in the same neighborhood under a variety of names: Maggie, Maggie A., Katie G., and Miss M. Margaret's father, Edward Kavaney apparently died in 1893. Beginning that year, Catherine, age fifty-eight at her husband's death, was no longer listed as a dressmaker, probably for propriety's sake alone, although Margaret continued the business in their home.

By 1898, Nellie, Margaret's younger sister, had become part of the business; she and Margaret continued making dresses until their deaths in 1928 and 1929, respectively. Neither sister ever married. The

Kavaneys' career as dressmakers occupied their lives for the forty-eight years between 1881 and 1929. During that time, they moved from O'Bryonville to various addresses on Madison Road, Edwards Road, Menlo Avenue, Burch Avenue, and Eastside Avenue in Hyde Park. Their creative designs took them on a journey from the structured and bustled gowns of the 1880s to the revealing, simple shapes of the 1920s.

The life work of these three industrious and independent women is represented by a single evening gown that has survived from the mid-1890s, a superb and elegant example of design in that period. The gown shown on page 108 is cut from a costly chiné, or warp-printed fabric. Such a fabric is created by printing a pattern on the warp threads, and sometimes on weft threads, before it is woven into cloth. During the weaving process, the threads stretch and shift slightly, causing the print to blur. The French word *chiné* refers to this blurred effect in the fabric. Chiné designs were very popular as dress fabric in the 1890s—a fact probably related to the Impressionist style of painting.

The unembellished, gored skirt is constructed of a crisp silk taffeta cut to fall in a fashionably perfect triangle. It fits neatly over the hips, with fullness pleated in at the center back. The bodice, however, is highly ornamented. The large balloon sleeves typical of the period have been gathered in three places. The central area of the bodice is overlaid with gathered sheer silk embroidered with arabesques. Satin bands form a slimming V-shape that extends below the waist; these bands are embellished elaborately with gold sequins and encrusted with seed beads along the edge. The Kavaneys

chose green velvet to form a "bow corsage" at the neckline and a faux belt at the waist.

Like many other Cincinnati dressmakers, the Kavaneys situated themselves in an upscale neighborhood, where they could easily serve upper-class women. This single example of their work comes from the estate of Mrs. W. H. Chatfield (née Elizabeth Wolcott Henry) and was worn by her mother-in-law, Mrs. Albert Hayden Chatfield (née Helen Fletcher Huntington). Albert Chatfield was president of the family business, Chatfield & Woods Company, a paper manufacturer, as well as a director of the Cincinnati Equitable Fire Insurance Company. A patron of music and the arts, Chatfield served on the Executive Committee for the Cincinnati Symphony Orchestra, was a leader in supporting the May Festivals and the Cincinnati Art Museum, and was a trustee of Rookwood Pottery in the early twentieth century. Helen Chatfield, one of the founding members of the Cincinnati Symphony Orchestra in 1896, served as a trustee and as honorary president of the Symphony's Women's Committee. The Chatfields lived in East Walnut Hills, as did the Kavaneys; thus, the Chatfields found it convenient to patronize Margaret, Nellie, and Catherine.

Much like the Kavaneys, Martha, Virginia, and Cordelia Wischmeier worked together as dressmakers. The three lived downtown at 47 Kossuth in the West End. They began creating gowns in 1880, when Virginia, age twenty-six, was first listed in the city directory as a dressmaker. Cordelia followed in 1881 at twenty-three years of age. Martha, their mother, a German immigrant, was always listed as a widow or as keeping house rather than as a dressmaker.

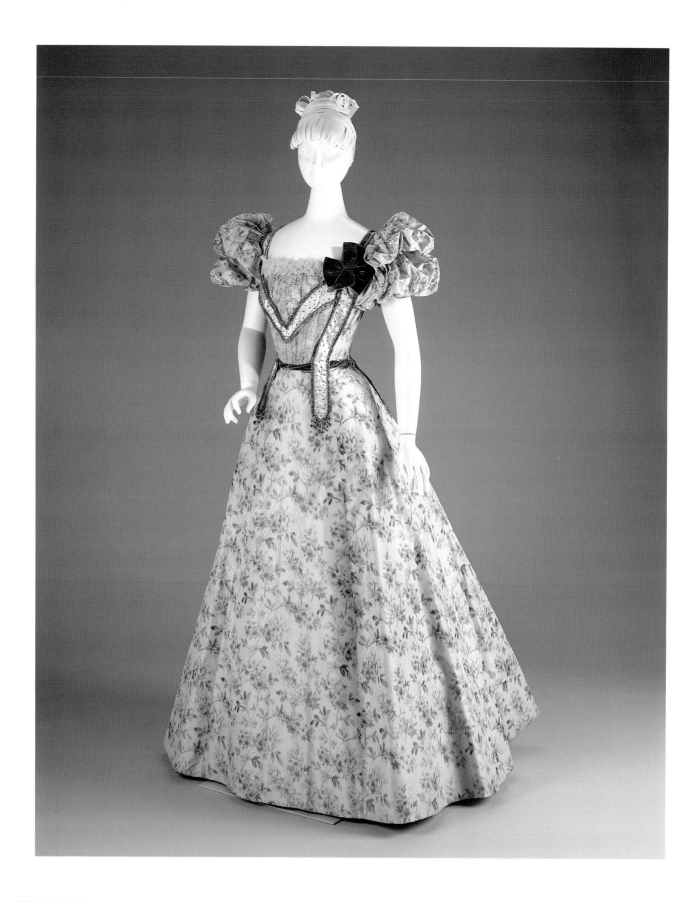

DETAIL: Kavaney
Evening Dress, ca. 1897;
1973.587a,b.

OPPOSITE: Margaret
Kavaney (active 1881–
1929); *Evening Dress,*
ca. 1897; silk, beads,
sequins, metallic braid;
Label: M. Kavaney E.
WALNUT HILLS.
CINCINNATI, O.;
Gift of Estate of Eliza-
beth W. H. Chatfield,
1973.587a,b.

Yet for the one surviving garment created by the Wischmeiers (see page 110), the donor attribution indicates that it was made by Martha Wischmeier as a wedding gown for Cordelia. In fact, Cordelia, who was married on March 8, 1882, appeared in the directory for only a single year. Her choice to marry, as was true of many women of that period, was also a decision to leave the business world. Virginia worked only until 1884; perhaps she, too, opted for marriage.

Although the Wischmeiers were in business for only four years, they represent a familiar pattern in dressmakers' lives. Women who lacked a male to support them often took on this task quite successfully. But when the opportunity for marriage presented itself, most women chose to abandon their public life and assume the responsibilities demanded by their "proper" sphere.

Kate R. Cregmile's experience was similar to that of the Kavaneys. From 1891 to 1923, she conducted her business from her home. Throughout her thirty-two years of dressmaking, she lived and worked at 251 West Seventh Street—the same address occupied by Mary J. Bannon in 1880, and again from 1882 to 1890. Cregmile then moved to 15 Garfield Place (see page 97), just three doors down from Mrs. Myrick's dressmaking parlor at Number 18 (see page 144). From 1900 to 1923, she was located at 706 Ridgeway Avenue in Avondale.

In 1900, Kate Cregmile was a single woman living with her widowed mother, three sisters, two nieces, and two nephews. By 1910, the extended family group had dwindled to one sister, two nieces, and a nephew, but as a unit, they had managed to purchase the house on Ridgeway Avenue and to hire a cook and a servant. The 1920

Martha Wischmeier
(active 1880–1884);
Wedding Dress, 1882;
silk; Gift of Mrs.
August Greiwe,
1964.48.

This wedding dress was
worn by Cordelia
Wischmeier, who was
married on March 8,
1882. It was made by
her mother, Martha
Wischmeier. Both
Cordelia and her sister
Virginia worked as
dressmakers alongside
their mother from 1880
to 1884. Cordelia left
the business after she
married.

census confirms that Kate was not alone in
her dressmaking business: Her sister, Laura
C. Smith, is listed as a dressmaker, as is
Gypsy Post, a niece. Morton S. Post, Kate's
nephew, is listed as a cloth buyer. It is interesting to speculate about Kate Cregmile's
possible connections to fabric manufacturers, both in America and abroad, through
her nephew. Perhaps this is how she man-

aged to acquire for her clients the exceptional fabrics we see in her work.

The satin and velvet reception dress
made for Nannie Robinson Maeder (opposite) illustrates the exceptional quality of
Kate Cregmile's work in the early 1890s,
when styles were in transition. The long,
slim silhouette of the 1880s walking suit is
paired with the expansive leg-of-mutton

Kate R. Cregmile
(active 1891–1923);
Reception Dress, 1891–
1892; silk; Gift of Mrs.
Robert S. Alter,
1963.542a,b.

Kate R. Cregmile
(active 1891–1923);
Wedding Dress, 1900;
silk, linen; Label: Creg-
mile Cincinnati, O.;
Gift of Mr. and Mrs.
John J. Strader Jr.,
1967.440a,b.

This wedding gown is
completely hand-
stitched and was worn
by Jean Abbot for her
marriage to Whiteman
E. Smith.

sleeves that became so popular by the mid-
1890s. The styling also represents a transition
in inspiration, drawn both from the Pre-
Raphaelite styles of the 1880s, derived from
medieval dress, and from elements of the
Tudor and Cavalier periods that influenced
fashion in the 1890s. The center front lacing,
the keyhole effect at the neckline, and the
crenellated hem are all historical elements
revived in late nineteenth-century dress.
Cregmile's combination of dark and golden
browns, with a silk floral damask fabric in
soft yellows and peaches, makes a luxuri-
ously elegant statement.

Kate Cregmile, like many Cincinnati
dressmakers, attracted a fine clientele. Two
gowns that date to the very early years of
the twentieth century were made for prominent Cincinnati women. Jean Abbot, the
daughter of George Morton Abbott, wore a
Cregmile design for her marriage to White-
men E. Smith in 1900. The gown, at left, is a
remarkable confection of ruched and gathered sheer silk crepe, completely stitched by
hand.

Cregmile also designed an evening gown
(opposite) for Mrs. Christian R. Holmes.
Mrs. Holmes (née Bettie Fleischmann) was
one of three children born to Charles and
Henrietta Fleischmann, whose fortune was
made in the yeast and distilling business. In
1892, she married Danish-born Christian R.
Holmes, one of the city's leading physicians
at the turn of the century. An ardent philanthropist, Holmes crusaded tirelessly for a
modern hospital and a better medical
school in the city. His dreams finally were
realized in 1912, when the newly opened
General Hospital was heralded in a *New York
Times* headline as "The Finest Hospital in
the World in Cincinnati." He was also

Kate R. Cregmile
(active 1891–1923);
Evening Dress, 1900-
1902; silk, linen; Label:
Cregmile Cincinnati,
O.; Gift of Mrs. Chris-
tian R. Holmes,
1920.123, 124.

instrumental in the establishment of the Medical College at the University of Cincinnati. After his death in 1920, Mrs. Holmes financed the construction of the Christian R. Holmes Hospital in memory of her husband.

The gown worn by Mrs. Holmes makes a dramatic statement through the combination of contrasting colors and fabrics. Tape lace twists and turns in a floral pattern between spider-weblike connections of pale brown cotton thread, forming the bodice, the sleeves, and the upper portion of the skirt. This is paired with a yellow panne velvet with a jagged edging of appliquéd black lace, a striking combination that must have turned many heads when Mrs. Holmes entered the room.

Prominent women who patronized dressmakers often utilized more than one. Depending on their taste, they might find that one dressmaker was particularly talented at creating stunning evening gowns, whereas another specialized in fashionable tea gowns. Margaret Kavaney and Adelaide Martien shared a client in the 1890s. Adelaide Martien, whose label refers to her as "Madame Martien," had no need to create a French mystique to attract a fine clientele: she was born in France. Other Cincinnati dressmakers, such as the Kavaneys, Kate Cregmile, and Anna Dunlevy, may have viewed Martien as formidable competition. Being French gave her the *cachet* of having learned her trade from the masters, and she readily attracted at least two of Cincinnati's wealthiest women.

Adelaide Martien came to the United States in 1870, at age twenty-three, with her husband August. They had two daughters, Adelaide and Mary or Marie, both born in

Ohio. Adelaide first began dressmaking in Cincinnati in 1880, in her home at 71 West Seventh Street. The census for that year revealed that seventeen-year-old Delia O'Brien, a "nonrelative," also lived in the household. Obviously of Irish descent, Delia was probably a housekeeper or a caretaker for the Martiens' children.

Adelaide's dressmaking business continued until 1918, at various downtown addresses, including 71 West Seventh Street, 317 Walnut, 627 Broadway, 510 Lock, and 20 Lansing Place. From 1889 to 1894, she lived and worked at 59 East Fourth Street, just ten blocks from Selina Cadwallader's place of business in the 1870s and 1880s. Unlike many dressmakers, Adelaide never became a widow; she and August were last recorded living at 20 Concord Place with their daughter Marie and her husband, Frederick O'Neal, a baker. Adelaide died in June 1925 at age seventy-eight.

During her thirty-eight years as a dressmaker in Cincinnati, Adelaide Martien was patronized by both Mrs. Albert Hayden Chatfield and Mrs. Nathaniel Henchman Davis (née Jeanette A. Skinner). In 1887, Jeanette Skinner married Davis, who had graduated from Yale with William Howard Taft in 1878, and returned to Cincinnati to practice law. At the time of his death in 1910, Davis was president of the Central Trust and Safe Deposit Company, the first institution of its kind established in Cincinnati and one of the first west of New York. The Davis homestead was located on Grandin Road in Hyde Park.

Martien's 1889-1890 evening gown designed for Mrs. Davis (opposite, left) is constructed of silk damask brocaded with floral bouquets in soft pinks and greens, a

LEFT: Adelaide Martien (active 1880–1918); *Evening Dress,* 1889-1890; silk; Label: Madame Martien CINCINNATI, O.; Gift of Mrs. Chase H. Davis, 1958.51.

RIGHT: Adelaide Martien; *Walking Suit,* ca. 1890; silk, beads; Label: Madame Martien CINCINNATI, O.; Gift of Estate of Elizabeth W. H. Chatfield, 1973.590a,b.

Born in France, Adelaide Martien was probably considered stiff competition by her counterparts in Cincinnati because of her presumed association with Parisian couturiers. She was patronized by two of the city's wealthiest women, Mrs. Chase H. Davis and Mrs. Albert Hayden Chatfield. The evening dress was designed for Mrs. Davis.

fabric inspired by eighteenth-century dress silks. Martien chose to accentuate the green in the brocade with an eye-catching ribbon to form a faux belt with dangling tails.

At the same time that Adelaide was completing her work for Mrs. Davis, she also made a walking suit for Helen Chatfield. According to an 1888 issue of *Godey's Lady's Book*, walking suits were the latest novelty in Paris. For this suit, Martien chose tan, a very utilitarian color, in silk faille. It would have been far less likely to show the dust and dirt that Mrs. Chatfield would encounter when she was out walking. Martien took this functional garment and ornamented it elegantly with panels of dark-gray velvet, embellished with hand-applied, steel-cut beads in an elaborate design. Even the decorative buttons, the cuffs, and the stand-up collar have been graced with Adelaide's fine handwork (see page 115, right).

Elizabeth Galvin was another dressmaker who might have felt the need to compete with Adelaide Martien's French *cachet*. Her billing statements advertised that she made "*Robes et Manteaux*" (dresses and cloaks). The labels in her garments read Miss E. Galvin Robes. She even advertised herself in the city directory as an Artistic Dress and Cloak Maker. Galvin's salon at 133 West Seventh Street was only blocks from Madame Martien's establishment. For a woman in a highly competitive field such as dressmaking, anything that might attract potentially wealthy clients was worth trying.

Like Selina Cadwallader and Mary Bannon, Elizabeth Galvin underwent a credit review by Dun and Company. The ledgers provide some historical data. Miss Galvin, a single woman, originally was in business in New York City for several years.

Elizabeth Galvin (active 1880–1895); *Wedding Dress,* 1890-1891; silk; Label: Miss E. Galvin ROBES 133 WEST 7TH STREET CINCINNATI OHIO.; Gift of Mary T. Verkamp, 1977.176.

OPPOSITE, DETAIL: Elizabeth Galvin *Wedding Dress,* 1890-1891; 1977.176.

Then she was "engaged by 'J. Shillito & Co'" of Cincinnati for two years and earned about $2,000 per year.[24] Perhaps Galvin, lured by the prospect of being an employee rather than dealing with the stress of entrepreneurship, worked as a buyer of fine dress fabrics for the Cincinnati department store or reported on the latest styles for the store's custom salon. Having saved $2,500 from her salary, however, Galvin opened her own concern in 1880, at the West Seventh Street address in partnership with a Miss Kate Higgins, as Galvin and Higgins. The partnership was brief, however; beginning the following year, Galvin was listed without Kate. According to the credit reports, "Mrs H" and Miss Galvin "did not agree," and the partnership was dissolved.[25]

From 1882 to 1890, a Julia Galvin was listed as living at the same address as Elizabeth. Julia was recorded as having no occupation for all of these years except for 1885, when she was listed as a dressmaker. Perhaps Julia was Elizabeth's mother, sister, or niece, who worked with her for those eight years. Elizabeth herself carried on until 1895. She was successful; according to her credit reviewer, "she had a g[oo]d class of custom & all the work she can attend to." Galvin was considered industrious and honest, and was thought to pay her bills promptly.[26]

Though little is known about "Miss E.," one thing is clear: she, too, served Cincinnati's social elite. A single remaining receipt from May 1888 indicates that Mrs. James E. Murdoch was one of Elizabeth Galvin's customers. James Murdoch, a celebrated actor in both the United States and Europe, was best known for his work in *School for Scandal* and his portrayal of Hamlet. In the mid-

Receipt for one mantle, five dresses, and ribbon, totaling $166.29, from Elizabeth Galvin for purchases made by Mrs. James Murdoch, May 30, 1888. *Cincinnati Historical Society Library.*

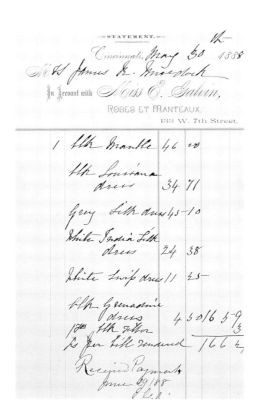

nineteenth century, Murdoch was ranked with Edwin Forrest and Junius Brutus Booth as one of America's greatest actors. He frequently visited Cincinnati and eventually purchased a farm in Loveland, a northern suburb. Murdoch also established a residence on Reading Road near Oak Street, where he died in May 1893.

In 1888, Mrs. Murdoch paid Elizabeth Galvin $46.00 for a black mantle, $45.10 for a gray silk dress, and $24.38 for a white India silk dress, among other items. Her bill totaled $166.29. Luckily for Elizabeth Galvin, Mrs. Murdoch paid her bill promptly, almost exactly one month later, on June 29.

Alma Heimbach, who operated a dressmaking business in Cincinnati from 1885 to 1907, was patronized by Mrs. Herbert L. Brenneman (née Eunice Swift), sister to Mrs. Joseph Clark Thoms (née Mary Swift), for whom Selina Cadwallader had worked. Heimbach's work is represented by a tan velvet gown (above and opposite) highly ornamented with lace and beading. Eunice Swift Brenneman wore this gown to the weddings of her two daughters, Martha, in 1902, and Helen, in 1904.

Like many other Cincinnati dressmakers, Alma Heimbach worked out of her home at various addresses on McMillan Street in Mount Auburn. She moved her concern to

DETAIL: Heimbach
Afternoon Dress, 1902;
1975.52a,b.

Alma Heimbach
(active 1885–1907);
Afternoon Dress, 1902;
silk, linen, beads; Label:
A. Heimbach
CINCINNATI, O.;
Gift of Mrs. George
Eustis and William B.
Stone, 1975.52a,b.

34 East McMillan after the death of her husband, George Brainard Heimbach, in 1897. In 1900, the census recorded her as living with her daughter Laura, a nephew, and a servant at this address. Alma Heimbach died in 1933.

Although research has yielded bits of information about many of the dressmakers represented in the Cincinnati collection, others remain virtually anonymous save for the labels in the garments they created. An evening gown worn by a member of the prominent Straus family has a small printed label bearing the name "Johnson, Cincinnati, O." Such a common name, with no first initial or street address, does not yield enough information even to begin a search. The gown (opposite page, left) is constructed of a rich lavender satin damask, with large paisley motifs composed of small flowers in two shades of pale green. Johnson probably created the dress in the early to mid-1890s, when the leg-of-mutton sleeve was popular. But as styles changed and the large sleeves fell out of favor, Johnson's client returned and asked if the sleeves could be made smaller, so that the dress would remain fashionable. Johnson succeeded in tacking down the fashion fabric and compressing the sleeves, so that, in its present state, the dress dates to 1897. Like many middle-class women who remade their dresses as styles changed, wealthy women were interested in prolonging the life of a favorite dress in order to avoid the expense of a new garment.

Mary Z. Carey, M. A. Ryan, Mary Donegan, and Katherine Willging are other Cincinnati dressmakers whose lives have been difficult to document. Because of spelling mistakes, typographical errors, and incomplete, insufficient, and incorrect information taken by census enumerators, directory publishers, and vital statistic recorders, it is difficult and sometimes impossible to research these women. Through a simple oversight, for example, Nellie and Margaret Kavaney, who died in 1928 and 1929, respectively, were listed in the city directory until 1932.

M. Z. Carey's address at 8 Curtis Street appears on the label in the wedding dress (opposite page, right) she created in the mid- to late 1890s. She can be traced at this address in the 1894 and 1895 city directories. In 1897, Mary Z. Carey, dressmaker, was listed as living at 37 West Twelfth Street; between 1898 and 1904, her address changed five times. The only census that possibly records Mary Z. Carey appeared in 1900, when a Mary Sylpha Carey was found living with her two daughters at 37 West Twelfth Street. Her occupation was listed as "dressmaker," yet no Mary S. or Mary Sylpha Carey can be found in the city directories.

Not surprisingly, the name Ryan was even more common than Johnson in the late nineteenth- and early twentieth-century in Cincinnati. Countless Marys, Maggies, Margarets, Mamies, and Mauds with the last name of Ryan were listed as dressmakers in the city directories. The most likely prospect is a Mary A., sometimes listed as M. A. and Mrs. M. A., the widow of James M., who appeared in the directories on West Seventh Street, East Seventh Street, East Ninth Street, and West Fourth Street throughout the 1890s and until 1909. Her listings varied in the early 1890s, but after she became a widow, probably in 1896, she was listed consistently as M. A. Ryan. This makes perfect sense, because once her husband, her main means of support, was gone, she had to fend

Johnson (active 1890s);
Evening Dress, 1896–
1897; silk, linen, beads,
metallic net; Label:
Johnson, Cincinnati,
O.; Gift of Mrs. Stanley
M. Straus, 1967.113a,b.

The sleeves of this
evening dress were
altered to make the
dress fashionable even
after the large leg-of-
mutton sleeve became
outdated. The gown
probably was originally
constructed in the
early to mid-1890s.

M. Z. Carey (active
1894–1904); *Wedding
Dress,* ca. 1896; silk;
Label: M. Z. Carey 8
CURTIS ST. CINCIN-
NATI OH.; Anony-
mous Gift, 986.800a,b.

This dress created by
M. Z. Carey is beau-
tiful in its simplicity
and exemplifies the
extremes of the leg-of-
mutton sleeve in the
mid-1890s.

122

DETAIL: M. A. Ryan *Evening Dress*, 1900–1901; 1966.1310a,b.

ABOVE, LEFT: M. A. Ryan (active 1896–1909); *Evening Dress*, 1907–1908; silk, cotton; Label: Ryan CINCINNATI; Gift of Mrs. Alvin H. Knoll, 1973.376a,b.

RIGHT: M. A. Ryan (active 1896–1909); *Evening Dress*, 1900–1901; silk, cotton; Label: Ryan CINCINNATI; Gift of Mrs. Clifford R. Wright, 1966.1310a,b.

for herself. With no other records to substantiate this finding or to provide additional information, however, M. A. Ryan remains somewhat of a mystery.

Even so, Ryan's work is exquisite. Each surviving piece is constructed primarily of lace and is both elegant and feminine. Ryan designed an evening dress (above, right) for Mrs. Perin Langdon (née Eleanor West). Perin Langdon was director of the First National Bank and managing head of the Langdon branch of the National Biscuit Company, later Nabisco. The dress is embellished around the neckline with delicate fabric flowers, a device used almost as a trademark by the celebrated English

couturier Lucile. Perhaps Ryan was inspired to use fabric flowers as a design element by fashion plates of Lucile's work. Using layers of sheer fabrics, white lace over pale lavender chiffon, Ryan created a softly feminine dress of subtle color.

She also designed the graceful gown on the opposite page constructed of machine-made cotton lace inset with medallions and bands of embroidered cotton. The neckline and sleeves are ornamented with fabric flowers covered with a sparkling gold net. The net coordinates with the gold metallic lace from which the sleeves and the center front bodice are cut.

The label in the evening gown made for

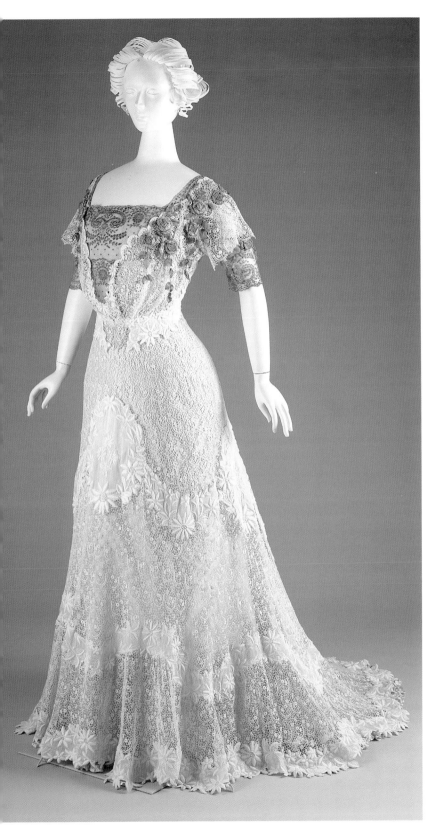

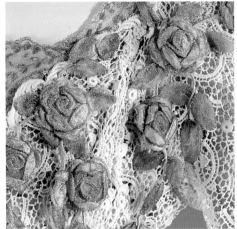

DETAIL: M. A. Ryan
Evening Dress, 1909;
1965.119.

The delicate fabric
flowers that ornament
the bodice of this
gown are covered with
gold metallic net.

M. A. Ryan (active
1896–1909); *Evening
Dress,* 1909; cotton, silk,
metallic net, metallic
lace; Label: Ryan
CINCINNATI; Gift of
Mrs. Richard P. Field,
1965.119.

124

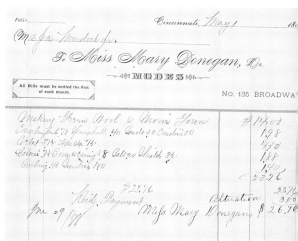

Receipt for various
articles of clothing,
including the making
of a green wool gown
for $14, by Miss Mary
Donegan for Mrs.
James Murdoch, May
1, 1888. *Cincinnati His-
torical Society Library.*

Mary Donegan (active
1880–1895); Katherine
Willging (active 1889–
1897); *Evening Dress,*
1898–1901; silk; Label:
Donegan & Willging.
NEAVE BUILDING.
Cincinnati.; Gift of
Mrs. Chase H. Davis,
1958.45.

OPPOSITE: Estelle T.
Hart (active 1912–
1916); *Dress,* ca. 1915;
linen, silk; Label: Estelle
T. Hart CINCINNATI,
O.; Gift of Benjamin
Miller, 1948.59.

Mrs. Chase H. Davis (opposite page) reads "Donegan & Willging. NEAVE BUILD-ING. Cincinnati." Mary A. and Lizzie E. Donegan were listed consistently in the city directories as dressmakers from 1880 to 1897. In 1897, Mary Donegan worked in the Neave Building, where Anna Dunlevy also had her salon. The receipt on page 124, dated 1881, is evidence that Mary Donegan, like Elizabeth Galvin, was patronized by Mrs. James E. Murdoch. Katherine or Katie Willging appeared in both the census and the city directories as a dressmaker living on Belvedere Street in Norwood, Ohio, but the names Donegan and Willging never appear together, nor at the same address. Yet the garment produced by Donegan and Willging is a stunning ball gown from the turn of the century.

Even Cincinnati dressmakers working in the 1910s and 1920s, when one might expect to find information more readily, are lost. The dress at left, created by Estelle T. Hart, in 1915, is a masterful example of style in that period. Hart's use of sheer white organdy trimmed starkly with black velvet ribbon may perhaps be a response to prevailing fashions, which were affected by the shortage of dyestuffs in America during World War I. Between 1915 and 1918, the British blockade of German ports prevented the importation of dyestuffs from Germany. Lacking colored dyes, fabric design houses began to produce a variety of fabrics printed with stripes, checks, and other motifs in black and white. Fashion illustrations featured garments created from expanses of white fabrics trimmed sparingly in black.[27] Obviously, even Cincinnati's dressmakers were affected by the war effort, or at least

126

LEFT: Josephine M.
Kasselman (active 1913–
1933); *Wedding Dress,*
1917; silk, linen, beads,
metallic thread; Label:
Josephine 911 NEAVE
BLDG. CINCINNATI;
Gift of Mr. William
Schreiber, 1967.1172.

CENTER: Josephine M.
Kasselman (active 1913–
1933); *Wedding Dress
and Train,* 1921; silk,
linen, beads; Label:
Josephine 411 RACE
ST. CINCINNATI;
Gift of Mrs. Clifford
R. Wright,
1966.1313a,b.

RIGHT: Josephine M.
Kasselman (active 1913–
1933); *Evening Dress,*
1917–1920; silk, cotton,
metallic cloth; Label:
Josephine 911 NEAVE
BLDG. CINCINNATI;
Gift of Mrs. William
Vollmer, 1985.18.

Wealthy Cincinnatians,
including Marjory
Langdon, Eunice
Thoms Resor, and
Helen Rentschler
Waldon, patronized
Josephine, who was
well-known regionally
for her exceptional
designs.

Belle and Huggins (active early twentieth century); *Evening Dress,* 1916–1918; silk, beads, sequins; Gift of Caroline and Herbert Marcus, 1972.435.

The Duchesse lace train of Adele Werk Oskamp's gown on page 126, right; 1985.18.

followed the fashionable trend created by the shortage of colored dyes.

Estelle Hart graciously provided her full name on her label. Her appearance in the city directory, from 1912 to 1916, tells us that she worked in the Perin Building at the northwest corner of Fifth and Race Streets downtown, and lived on Zumstein Avenue in Hyde Park. All other possible sources of information yielded nothing, however.

Similarly, research on the dressmaking pair Belle and Huggins yielded no information except that Belle and Huggins were the maiden names of the wives of the Proctor and Gamble Company's founders. This is an interesting coincidence, but it seems unlikely that members of those families would have been making custom dresses in 1916, when their fortunes had been amassed in the middle of the nineteenth century. Even so, the dress (upper left), ornamented with plush pansies and long, beaded tassels is a charming example of the styles in the mid-1910s.

Josephine, whose surviving work dates from 1915 to 1921, provides us with two different addresses on her labels: 411 Race Street and 911 in the Neave Building. Because only her first name appears on her labels, Josephine's trail was elusive but not impossible to follow. Josephine M. Kasselman's shop, according to the city directories, was located at 104 West Fourth Street (probably the Neave Building location) from 1913 to 1919. By 1920, she had moved to 411 Race Street and remained in business there until 1933.

The caliber of Josephine's clientele and her work shows that she was both successful and innovative. Josephine was patronized by wealthy Cincinnatians, including Mrs.

128

Josephine M. Kas-
selman (active 1913–
1933); *Afternoon Dress*,
1918–1920; silk, cotton;
Label: Josephine 411
RACE ST. CINCIN-
NATI; Gift in memory
of Helen Rentschler
Waldon, 1991.237.

Clifford R. Wright (née Marjory Langdon),
Mrs. Robert L. Resor (née Eunice Swift
Thoms), and Mrs. Sidney D. Waldon (née
Helen Rentschler). Josephine seemed to
love asymmetry. Her gowns are elegant
examples of drapery and layering with sheer
fabrics. The garments are studies in pattern
played against transparency, and texture
played against density.

Of ten garments in the collection
designed by Josephine, three are wedding
gowns, two of which appear on page 126.
She created Ruth Willey's for her marriage
to William Schreiber in 1917 and Marjory
Langdon's for her marriage to Clifford R.
Wright in 1921. A third gown (page 126)
appears to be a wedding dress but is not; it
was worn by Mrs. William J. P. Oskamp (née
Adele Regina Werk). The daughter of
Michael Werk and Pauline La Feuille, Adele
married William Oskamp in 1878. They
built a house in Westwood, a suburb west of
Cincinnati, on Harrison Avenue. Wiladele, as
they named the house, was a showplace, and
the Oskamps entertained often and lavishly.
This gown, with its impressive train of
Duchesse lace that falls from the shoulders,
must have rivaled the elegance of the
Oskamp's home.

Helen Rentschler was a native of
Hamilton, Ohio, a city twenty miles north
of Cincinnati. She, too, purchased a
Josephine design (left) before her 1928 marriage to Sidney Waldon. Rentschler surely
made the trip to Cincinnati because of the
dressmaker's fine reputation, which is still
recalled today. Here, Josephine has combined
a dense machine-made lace with a sheer,
gray crepe in a dramatic asymmetrical drape.
This light, airy piece, with a cummerbund
around the hips, relates more closely to the

Josephine M. Kasselman (active 1913–1933); *Evening Dress,* 1916–1918; silk, cotton, beads; Label: Josephine CINCINNATI; Gift of Mrs. Murat Halstead Davidson, 1986.1156.

This elegant beaded evening dress was worn by the donor's mother, Mrs. Robert L. Resor.

A tag denoting the client's name, "Resor," was sewn into the slip of the black beaded evening dress at left, 1986.1156.

fashions of the 1920s than to 1910 styles. Josephine was a very forward-looking designer whose work was justifiably renowned.

Like other Cincinnati dressmakers, Josephine also created gowns for the prominent women of the Thoms family. She designed the elegant black net and satin beaded dress above for Mrs. Robert L. Resor (née Eunice Swift Thoms). A rather conservative design for Josephine, it is elaborately embellished with faceted, iridescent and steel-cut beads surrounding metallic

threads in a medallion motif. The tag sewn into the slip confirms that the gown was made for Mrs. Resor and notes that she desired an "open back."

Dressmakers such as Estelle Hart and Josephine, working in the 1910s, faced a new challenge. Not only were they competing against one another for clientele, but the specter of ready-made clothing was rising. Like the Tirocchi sisters in Providence, these women were forced to adopt new attitudes and methods of working. Many women whose wardrobes previously had consisted

exclusively of custom garments now began
to purchase ready-made gowns from department stores. Anna and Laura Tirocchi
adapted by carrying ready-made garments in
their shop to augment their custom trade
and maintain their client base.

One Cincinnati dressmaker who weathered this transition successfully was Minnie
K. Kaufman, whose amazingly long career
started in 1882. Kaufman was first listed in
the city directory as a twenty-one-year-old
dressmaker working out of her home at 666
Queen City Avenue in Fairmount. By 1893,
Kaufman had moved her business out of her
home to Walnut Street, in the heart of
downtown Cincinnati; in 1897, she reestab-
lished her salon at 621 Walnut, where she
remained for the next twenty-six years. In
1924, she moved her salon to Room 47 in
the Electric Building at 9 West Fourth
Street, and continued in business there until
1944. Minnie Kaufman died just three years
later, at age eighty-six.

Although Minnie worked for a total of
sixty-two years, only two of her garments
have made their way into the Cincinnati
collection. One is a beautiful suit—a skirt,
blouse, and jacket ensemble—of silk poplin
(opposite). The sleeves of the blouse are cut
from a double layer of soft silk net and end
in a ruffle at the wrist. The blouse is hand-
embroidered in off-white silk twist in a
flowing floral design. The styling of the suit
accurately represents the blending of the
feminine with the independent nature of
the "new woman" of the twentieth century.

Kaufman, who never married, lived in
the mid-1880s with her older brother Jacob,
who was a hog buyer for F. A. Laidley &
Company. The Laidley family, who lived
across the river in Covington, Kentucky, had

Minnie K. Kaufman
*Suit: Bodice, Skirt, and
Jacket*, 1914–1917;
1954.459a–c.

This serviceable but
elegant suit represents
the new attire of the
"modern" woman of
the 1910s.

Minnie K. Kaufman
(active 1882–1944);
Suit: Bodice and Skirt,
1914–1917; silk; Label:
Minnie Kaufman
CINCINNATI; Gift of
J. Wallace Taylor,
1954.459a,c.

When the jacket is
removed, the suit's
more feminine design
elements, the net
sleeves and the silk floss
embroidery, are
revealed.

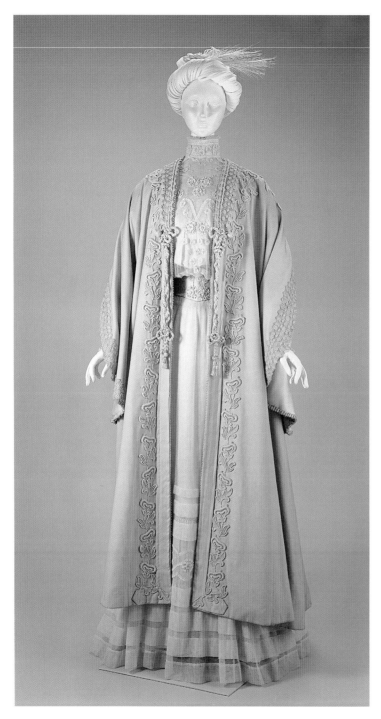

Minnie K. Kaufman
(active 188–1944);
Evening Coat, 1907–
1910; wool, silk; Label:
Minnie Kaufman
CINCINNATI;

Gift of Bernard
Moorman and Dr.
Donald Nash, 2002.25.

made their fortune in the pork business, like many Cincinnatians. The Laidleys undoubtedly knew of and respected Minnie's work as a dressmaker. By 1900, she was no longer living with Jacob but with her younger brother George, in another part of town, but the connection with the Laidleys remained. Between 1907 and 1910, Kaufman created a woman's coat for a member of the Laidley family. It is likely that, over the years, she created many other garments for the Laidley women.

Kaufman, a spinster, lived from 1900 to 1944, when she finally closed her business, with her brother George, his wife Anna, and their two sons, at 2526 Montrose Avenue, and later on Homestead Avenue in Fairmount. Listed in the 1910 census as a "dressmaker" with her "own business," she seems to have been a remarkably independent and successful woman. She must have had a number of seamstresses working for her, including Katherine Willging, who served as Kaufman's forelady from 1901 to 1923, after closing her own salon in 1897.

Cincinnati dressmaker Clara Becht's experience provides an unusual glimpse into the apprentice system late in the age of custom dressmakers. Becht worked her way up through the system in the traditional manner. She got her start at the early age of twelve or thirteen as a runner for a Cincinnati dressmaker. It was her duty, early each morning, to pick up various notions, fabrics, trims, and findings that had been ordered from local dry goods establishments. After approximately one year in service, Becht was entrusted with the delivery of finished garments and often worked until eight in the evening. She spent several years as an apprentice, learning all facets of the trade:

Clara Becht (active
190–1919); *Evening
Dress,* 1919–1921; silk,
sequins; Label: Clara
Becht CINCINNATI,
O.; Gift of Mrs. Henry
M. Goodyear, 1991.123.

Hannah Taylor Shipley
graduated from Smith
College in 1921, then
married Henry
Goodyear one year
later. The donor wore
this sequined evening
dress prior to her
marriage.

134

The Perin Building at
the northwest corner
of Fifth and Race
Streets, where both
Estelle T. Hart and
Clara Becht established
their dressmaking
salons in the early
twentieth century.
*Cincinnati Historical
Society Library.*

designing, draping, drafting patterns, cutting,
and assembling a garment on a dressmaker's
dummy padded to replicate the client's
measurements. She learned the art of
applying trims, from the simplest to the
most elaborate.[28]

Clara Becht's training proved invaluable.
The dress she created for Mrs. Henry
Goodyear, née Hannah Taylor Shipley,
(opposite page) is a beautiful example of her
work. Henry Goodyear, a physician, came to
Cincinnati in 1919, and inherited Dr. Christian Holmes's practice. Hannah Shipley, a
1921 graduate of Smith College, married
Goodyear just one year later. Although she

did not debut herself, the soon-to-be Mrs.
Goodyear must have sparkled in this dress,
which she wore to the 1919-season debutante parties. The garment is silk net embellished overall with thousands of silver
sequins, each sewn on individually by hand.

Clara Becht first appeared in the city
directory in 1903, but she was listed most
consistently from 1914 through 1919. Her
salon was located in the Perin Building, as
was that of Estelle Hart, and later at 413
Race Street, where she operated out of the
Elinor Mae Shop. Becht remained active
until her marriage, in 1920, to Stanley Newton, a grocer, whose market was located

in the Glendale village square. They made their home on Woodbine Avenue in Glendale.

Clara Becht represents not only the long-established apprentice method of entering an artisanal trade but also a dressmaker's success in making the transition from custom to ready-made clothing. Locating herself in a women's dress shop, which surely sold ready-made garments, she probably operated as the custom dressmaker. Many upper-class women still wished to have custom garments made, particularly for special occasions. The Elinor Mae Shop and Clara Becht served the changing needs of twentieth-century women, offering both custom and ready-made garments under one roof. Although Becht served Cincinnati's most elite women as a custom dressmaker, she also represents the end of this occupation's golden age.

Cincinnati's dressmakers were as varied a group as dressmakers in every city and town of nineteenth-century America. Their stories are as individual as the women themselves. As a respectable occupation for women, making custom garments enabled them to maneuver successfully in the business world, to be independent for as long as they

needed or wished. Spinster Minnie Kaufman, who seemed to have enjoyed coming home to a family—her brother's— thrived on her independence for an astounding sixty-two years as a dressmaker. The Kavaneys, whose work spanned forty-eight years, found comfort and success working in a family group. Widows, such as Anna Dunlevy and Martha Wischmeier, found dressmaking a viable means of supporting their families. Dressmakers such as Selina Cadwallader probably did not need to work at dressmaking at all. Some, including Clara Becht and Cordelia Wischmeier, chose to abandon their careers when marriage offered them a "proper" alternative.

Yet all of these women displayed courage and stamina; they represent women's ability to defy society's prescribed boundaries. Dressmakers in the late nineteenth and early twentieth centuries stepped beyond the limitations of their sphere in many ways. They entered man's sphere, a realm that many believed would ruin their health and compromise their morality. In most cases, they entered a sphere far beyond their social standing, yet most were successful beyond their richest dreams, and beyond the boundaries of Cincinnati itself.

The H. & S. Pogue
Company (founded
1863); *Afternoon Dress*,
1899–1900; silk, cotton,
beads, metallic braid;
Label: THE H. & S.
POGUE CO. COS-
TUMES. CINCIN-
NATI, O.; Gift of the
family of Sophia Helen
Fisk Laird, Isabelle
Eastman Fisk, and
Margaret Pogue Fisk,
1996.386a,b.

Ready-Made Garments and the Rise of the Department Store

THE COMPLEX FASHIONS of the nineteenth century had long been the dressmaker's ally but the looser, simpler styles of the 1910s and 1920s signified a grim future for independent dressmakers. The progress of the ready-made garment industry for women's wear accelerated in the twentieth century with the continued simplification of dress construction. As the one-piece, less fitted dress became fashionable, less and less individuation was required. In 1897, only 10 percent of the clothing produced in the United States was ready-made.[1] By 1910, virtually every article of women's dress could be purchased as a ready-to-wear item. Soon, women of every social class were regularly buying clothing off the rack.[2] One dressmaker employed in a Fifth Avenue shop summed up the obvious fate of her occupation: "Our trade is breaking down slowly. Customers who used to order twelve dresses at an order now only take six at a time. Those who ordered only one or two, do not order now at all."[3] At the turn of the century, American women had embraced the convenience and economical advantage of ready-made garments, without considering the effect of their choice on the custom dressmaker.

Even though the growth in production of ready-made garments for women was not dependent on the rise of the department store, the stores provided an outlet for the variety of factory-produced articles that proliferated at the end of the nineteenth century. Ready-made garments provided all Americans with equal access to fashionable attire, whether they lived in the city or on the frontier. The democratization of clothing was complete by the 1920s, when the mass manufacture of women's garments reached maturity. In fact, one midwestern businessman remarked, "I used to be able to tell something about the background of a girl applying for a job . . . by her clothes, but today I often have to wait till she speaks . . . or otherwise gives me a second clew" [sic].[4]

Early ready-made garments, even those for men, did not produce this leveling effect. Often easily recognizable from a distance, they were ill-fitting and constructed of cheap fabrics. Ready-made garments, like women's wear made at home in the mid- to late nineteenth century, were despised as

Advertisements for corsets and bustles were common in women's periodicals. Underwear was one of the few ready-made articles of clothing available for women in the nineteenth century. These items could be purchased in local dry goods stores and by mail order. *Harper's Bazar* (May 1877). *Public Library of Cincinnati and Hamilton County.*

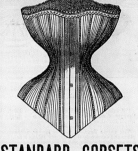

ABOVE RIGHT: *Ladies home Journal* described tailored suits much like the one purchased from the J. M. Gidding Company by Janet March Drewery as part of her trousseau in 1910. *Ladies' Home Journal* (October 1909). *Public Library of Cincinnati and Hamilton County* (see page 161).

disreputable, reflecting on an individual's taste and indicating his or her poverty. High-quality ready-made clothing arose from two main sources: the aspirations of rising lower and middle-class Americans who desired better clothing without the cost of custom-made work, and the custom tailor's response to this need. The result was respectable clothing that could be purchased off the shelf at affordable prices. This process was aided by both progress in industrialization and advances in textile technology in the nineteenth century.[5]

Throughout the 1860s, ready-made women's wear consisted almost exclusively of underwear, cloaks, and wraps. In the next two decades, however, the situation began to change. Independent-minded women sought careers, held jobs, attended institutions of higher learning, played sports, engaged in civic activities, and used modern modes of transportation. These busier, "modern" women viewed ready-made clothing as a convenience: no trips to the dry goods store to buy fabric, buttons, and threads; no frequent and endless visits to the dressmaker for consultations and fittings. A wide selection of household wrappers and a limited number of dresses, suits, and walking costumes were offered through mail-order catalogs and in the burgeoning department stores found in larger cities.[6]

The adoption of the suit as a required element in the female wardrobe spurred the mass production of the "waist." The complete outfit consisted of a jacket, a skirt, and a separate blouse called a shirtwaist or waist. A boon to the working woman, this style was made even more popular by the illustrations of Charles Dana Gibson and his "Gibson Girl." The first shirtwaist manufacturer opened for business in 1891, and in

1892, Lord & Taylor included ready-made ladies' "blouse waists" in their summer catalog, selling for prices ranging from 50 cents to $7. The finer hand-made examples offered at I. Magnin could cost as much as $150. The shirtwaist industry became so prolific and so profitable that in the 1900 census, it was listed as a separate industry. In that year, it was reported that the per capita spending on ready-made clothing had increased to $4 per woman, as compared with 46 cents per capita in 1860.[7]

Those who wished to purchase ready-made items could choose from two convenient sources: the mail-order catalog and the department store. For the customer beyond the reach of a major metropolitan area, the mail-order catalog provided access to commodities, including clothing, that otherwise would have been out of reach. This market was tapped first by Aaron Montgomery

Although ready-made dresses did not have the professional fit of custom-made gowns, they were available in Cincinnati at the Albert I. Straus Company at 411–413 Race Street, around 1900. *Public Library of Cincinnati and Hamilton County.*

140

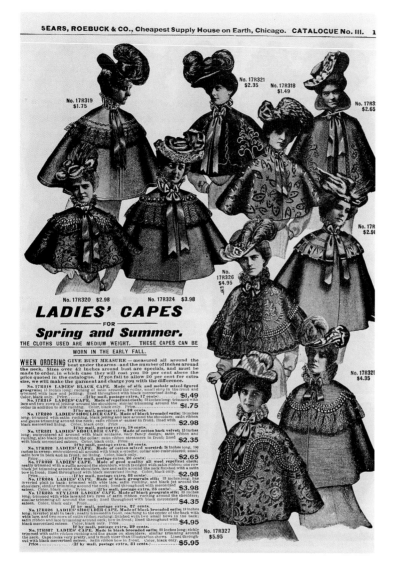

SEARS, ROEBUCK & CO., Cheapest Supply House on Earth, Chicago. CATALOGUE No. III.

No. 17R319 $1.75

No. 17R321 $2.35   No. 17R318 $1.49

No. 17R3 $2.65

No. 17R $2.9

No. 17R326 $4.95

No. 17R320 $2.98   No. 17R324 $3.98

No. 17R321 $4.35

LADIES' CAPES
FOR
Spring and Summer.
THE CLOTHS USED ARE MEDIUM WEIGHT. THESE CAPES CAN BE WORN IN THE EARLY FALL.

No. 17R327 $5.95

Sears, Roebuck & Company offered ready-made coats, capes, jackets, street skirts, underskirts, waists, and wrappers in its 1902 catalog at economical prices.

Ward, in 1872, whose first catalog included everything from plain jet bracelets to grain bags. It seems, however, that the selection of items favored the needs and wants of women rather than men. The majority of the garments and clothing accessories, as well as the household goods, were sure to appeal to the woman of the house, whose progressively public persona increasingly made her the shopper in the late nineteenth century. In three short years, Ward's catalog had expanded from a single sheet advertise-

ment to a seventy-two-page volume. Soon other retailers joined Ward. The Jordan Marsh & Company mail-order catalog was thriving by 1883, and Sears and Roebuck, who printed their first catalog in 1886, were producing it regularly by 1893. In 1897, Sears sent out 318,000 catalogs in the Midwest alone, featuring over 10,000 different items—everything from clothing to pianos.

It was the department store, however, that so profoundly affected the custom dressmaker's fate. In 1829, Frances Trollope built her Bazaar, a forerunner of the modern department store, in Cincinnati. Designed in a mixture of styles, the Bazaar was a product of Trollope's imagination. Egyptian columns graced the side facing south; the Third Street side was formed of three arabesque windows supported by Moorish stone pilasters topped with capitals. Other parts of the building were decorated with stone ornaments, Gothic battlements, and a castellated roofline. The Bazaar was described as "a rich and tasty compound of ancient and modern architecture" and "a good deal of sheer personal whimsy . . . frozen into brick and stone." The second floor of the emporium was organized in separate booths and dedicated exclusively to the sale of fancy goods that Mrs. Trollope had imported from France. It was built as an arcade, with rows of Doric columns supported by connecting arches. The interior was equally impressive, featuring a twenty-four-foot-high rotunda, a curvilinear roof, circular staircases, and paintings and mosaics by noted Cincinnati artist Auguste Hervieu. The Bazaar, lit with gas lamps, was the first public building in Cincinnati to use this means of illumination. Although many came to view both the

The extensive selection and beautiful displays in the millinery, waist, and lingerie department at the John Shillito Company were two of the many ways department stores enticed customers to patronize them (ca. 1916). *Public Library of Cincinnati and Hamilton County.*

goods and the "grotesque" building, Trollope's establishment met with little success and closed in 1831.[8]

Alexander Turney Stewart of New York City, who opened his store in 1846, is generally recognized as the first successful entrepreneur in the field. Previously, retail stores were small and specialized, often beyond reason. One retailer in New York, for example, sold nothing but combs. A woman in search of various articles often had to patronize many shops, no doubt a thoroughly frustrating and time-consuming process. Stewart catered to women and offered a wide variety of items under one roof.[9] This was the single most attractive advantage of department stores.

Many firms were outgrowths of dry goods stores, including both the H. & S. Pogue Company and the John Shillito

Company of Cincinnati. At the outset, department stores offered a limited range of goods, but by the 1870s, their inventory had expanded to include almost everything imaginable. Frequently, these stores were palatial in both size and décor, and their founders pioneered the use of inventive architecture and modern conveniences, much like Trollope's foresighted Bazaar.[10]

A. T. Stewart's establishment, for example, came to be known as the Marble Palace. Dazzling in architecture, size, furnishings, and displays, it was the first building in New York to have a marble exterior and plate-glass display windows: "The interior featured a columned portico leading to a four-storied, domed rotunda. Each floor extended out from the rotunda, which formed a large hollow in the center. There were circular staircases, walls lined

142

The Parisian Corset Store at Race and Opera Place in Cincinnati offered women a wide selection of the newest corset styles. Such stores that specialized in one item were soon obsolete when department stores rose to prominence (ca. 1913). *Public Library of Cincinnati and Hamilton County.*

with mirrors and frescoes, large chandeliers, mahogany showcases and counters, and a special promenade gallery."[11]

Any shopkeeper who specialized in a single line of merchandise had reason to fear the formidable competition posed by the department store, but dressmakers were particularly vulnerable for a number of reasons. Department stores aimed to attract women, the dressmakers' primary customers, with a world of opulence, luxury, and abundance that the typical dressmaker could not provide. Independent dressmakers coexisted for a remarkable length of time alongside the department stores, but by the turn of the century, the balance had shifted in favor of the department stores, and by 1920, they prevailed.

Perhaps the department stores' greatest asset was the fact that they were established

and operated almost entirely by men. Dressmakers lacked the financial power to compete on equal terms with large stores, whose capital and credit ratings far surpassed those of a small, independent salon. Consequently, the department store could keep a large stock of silks, satins, velvets, laces, furs, ribbons, and trimmings of all kinds, as well as coordinating millinery, gloves, stockings, and even jewelry, from which the customer could choose. Only the most successful dressmakers could keep a stock of fabrics and trimmings in their shops at all times. Department stores catered to both the home seamstress and the dressmakers' clients, who purchased fabrics in the stores and took them to the dressmaker to be made up.[12]

Eager to furnish their potential customers with fine fabrics and the most fashionable styles, department store buyers trav-

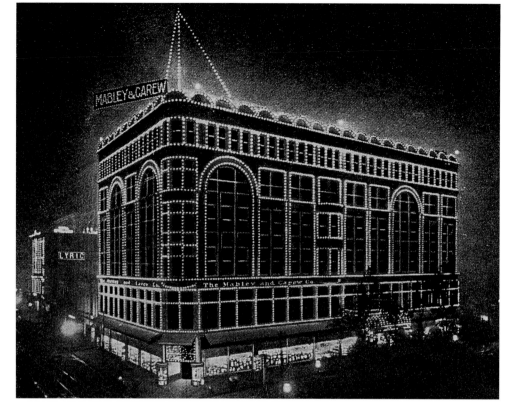

The magnificently illu-
minated Mabley and
Carew store at the
northeast corner of
Fifth and Vine Streets
in Cincinnati, 1920.
*Public Library of Cincin-
nati and Hamilton
County.*

eled to Europe annually to buy model garments from the French couture houses and
the fabrics from which the garments were
made. When the European models arrived,
B. Altman's staged an "opening" for dressmakers—not for retail customers. The
models were not for sale; rather, the intent
was that dressmakers purchase the French
goods from Altman's wholesale fabrics
department. More than a thousand dressmakers from across the country attended
one of these openings.[13]

Advertising was another method used by
department stores to overshadow—and
overwhelm—the custom dressmaker. The
stores were gloriously conspicuous in major
business districts and could hardly go unno-
ticed. Dressmakers' salons were generally
hidden away in homes or commercial buildings. In addition, department stores had

enough capital to spend thousands of dollars
on advertising. They promoted themselves
aggressively in newspapers, recognizing the
need to persuade potential customers that
the ready-made garments they offered were
acceptable and respectable. Some stores even
published their own fashion magazines;
these generally thin catalogs offered fashion
news direct from Paris, with corresponding
illustrations of their offerings. Few individual tradeswomen could afford to compete; their primary mode of advertisement
was word of mouth. Some relied on trade
(business) cards. A few placed occasional ads
or newspaper notices such as that on page
144. But because they were inconspicuous,
new business often was enticed away by
the opulence of the department store windows.

Although department stores had the

144

John Shillito & Co.,

Race, Seventh, and George Streets,

IMPORTERS, JOBBERS, AND DEALERS IN

Staple and Fancy Dry Goods,

CARPETS AND UPHOLSTERY GOODS,

Invite an Examination of their Unusually

Large Stock

OF

CHOICE SPRING FABRICS,

OPEN IN EVERY DEPARTMENT.

They Guarantee the
New Designs, the
Largest Assortments,
And Lowest Prices.

A cordial invitation is extended to all visitors, whether
purchasers or not, to call and see their

MAMMOTH STORE.

THE LARGEST,
BEST LIGHTED, and
BEST ADAPTED

For the Business in this Country, and recognized as one
of the

SIGHTS OF CINCINNATI.

JOHN SHILLITO & CO.

MRS. F. MYRICK,

HAS OPENED HER

Dress - Making - Parlors

AT 18 GARFIELD PLACE.

*Would be glad to see my old patrons
in my new quarters*

Dressmaker Mrs. F. Myrick announces her new quarters at 18 Garfield Place in *Mrs. Devereux's Blue Book* in 1896. Her ad is discreet and unassuming com- pared to the bold advertisements of the department stores. *Public Library of Cincinnati and Hamilton County.*

ABOVE, LEFT: Advertisement for the John Shillito Company, March 19, 1880. *Cincinnati Historical Society Library.*

upper hand, independent dressmakers still offered certain advantages to the discriminating consumer, including privacy, unique design, high quality, and, most important, a relationship that had been built over the years. Those dressmakers who were financially able attempted to compete with the department stores by mimicking them, at least in appearance. They moved to quarters overlooking the street, where they could utilize windows for elaborate signage and eye-catching displays. Salons were furnished and decorated elaborately, often in imitation of luxurious private parlors.[14] Trade journals advised dressmakers to "exploit the fact that you have on exhibition the most complete assortment of everything that is new, popular and fashionable in late designs." They even suggested that the dressmaker employ salespeople whose appearance and personality were pleasing to the customer: "Frumpy saleswomen . . . [are] bad for business."[15] Custom dressmakers now more than ever before needed to entice their customers into their salons. Many who lacked the capital to do so merely relied on their clients' loyalty. The majority of dressmakers found their clientele increasingly limited to the elite, who disdained the ill-mannered masses that thronged to the department stores.[16]

The introduction of the custom dressmaking salon within the department store presented the most significant threat to the independent dressmaker. Department stores, being large concerns, could easily undersell the dressmaker, both for materials and for time and labor. There, under one roof, was everything the customer needed: fabric, notions, trimmings, undergarments, and the dressmaker herself. Conveniently, the customer could shop for other household articles or have an elegant lunch in the store's tearoom, without leaving the premises, perhaps even while she waited for the finishing touches to be completed on her custom-made gown.

Department stores quickly realized that the success of their custom salons depended on providing personal service and high-quality garments that equaled or surpassed the offerings of the individual dressmaker. Although ready-made garments were the bread and butter of store sales, it was the custom salon that eventually lured the wealthier clients away from the independent dressmakers. These salons became elaborate rooms within the confines of the store. They offered "private recesses and French rooms (special showrooms that admitted only the most elite clientele) [that] offered a refuge for wealthy customers."[17] The department stores' appropriation of this last bastion of the custom dressmaker broke down the tradeswomen's last defense by providing a venue in which even the most affluent customers felt at ease.

As a final blow, the department store custom salon was actually a better employer than the independent custom shop. Although wages generally were lower, the work was often steadier and less seasonal. Paychecks were distributed on a predictable, weekly basis, and workrooms usually were brighter and airier than the typical cramped quarters of the custom shop.

At the same time, however, the chances were less certain for the skilled department store seamstress who hoped to rise up the ranks. Few workers achieved the status of the buyer, who, like the independent tradeswoman, enjoyed annual buying trips to Europe and earned some respect in this male-dominated enterprise. In fact, in most cases, the worker's skills often were diluted. The particularly skilled dressmakers employed by the department stores continued to create original designs for fashionable clients; these women differed little from their counterparts in the custom dressmaker's shop and, along with their employers, took great pride in their creative work. Others, however, were relegated to the tasks of trimming or performing alterations on ready-made models, where quantity rather than quality was valued. Alterations became a major service offered by the department store. Only this service made the ready-made garment a viable option for many consumers.[18]

Yet despite such intense competition, the custom dressmaker endured. Women such as Minnie Kaufman and the Tirocchi sisters, who weathered the onslaught of the department store successfully, found ways of adapting to the advent of ready-made garments and their oversized outlets. Clara Becht is a perfect example. Working out of a small shop that offered ready-made garments, she provided the specialized design and care that the most elite women still valued. Other dressmakers coped with the situation through a more specialized division of labor within their own shops. By adding more seamstresses to their staff, they speeded up the process in an effort to mollify consumers who now could be satisfied quickly with an altered, ready-made garment and were impatient with the slow pace of

146

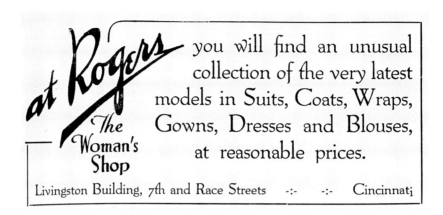

at Rogers you will find an unusual collection of the very latest models in Suits, Coats, Wraps, Gowns, Dresses and Blouses, at reasonable prices.

The Woman's Shop

Livingston Building, 7th and Race Streets   -:-   -:-   Cincinnati

custom work. In a 1908 article in *Ladies' Home Journal* titled "As a Dressmaker Sees Women," a dressmaker related that her staff had grown from just two to an impressive fifty-two girls.[19] Minnie Kaufman may have utilized such a method. Her shop, which lasted until 1944, probably employed a significant workforce, as evidenced by the fact that she hired Katherine Willging as her forelady or overseer of workers.

The transfer of power in dressmaking from women to men is exemplified perfectly in Alfred T. Rogers. From 1919 to 1941, this Irish immigrant was the proprietor of The Women's Shop, located at the corner of Seventh and Race Streets in the Livingston Building in downtown Cincinnati. Rogers advertised women's ready-to-wear garments, millinery, and furs. The Women's Shop resembles the Elinor Mae Shop, where Clara Becht was employed. In a small, select women's dress shop, Rogers probably offered ready-to-wear finished models, garments that could be trimmed to the customer's desires, and possibly custom dressmaking services.

The single surviving piece in the collection that represents Rogers's offerings is the blue chiffon dress, on the opposite page, trimmed with gold metallic lace, a metallic

cummerbund, and hundreds of pink fabric flowers that decorate the bodice and skirt. This is an example of the classically inspired draped design of the early 1920s. Horsehair loops attached between the slip and the chiffon skirt accentuate the hips, exemplifying the *robe de style* that was made popular by French couturiers Paul Poiret and Jeanne Lanvin in that period.

The only element of this dress that needed to fit the body accurately was the wide band of webbing inside the garment at the waist. If this garment was created as a ready-to-wear dress, it would have been easy to take a tuck or two in this inner waistband to fit it to a smaller waistline. Any distortion of the outer construction caused by such an alteration would have been hidden by the wide gathered cummerbund and by the fact that both the bodice and the skirt were gathered at the waist. A far cry from the complex cut and fit of clothing of the second half of the nineteenth century, this dress was worn by Cincinnatian Miss Shirley Kemper, great-great-granddaughter of one of Cincinnati's first settlers, to her cousin's debut party in December 1921. It exemplifies the simplification of garment styles in this period, which allowed dresses to be ready-made.

A. T. Rogers (founded 1919); *Evening Dress,* 1921; silk, cotton, metallic cloth; Label: at Rogers Seventh & Race Sts. CINCINNATI; Gift of Miss Shirley Kemper, 1967.1204.

Miss Shirley Kemper wore this evening dress to her cousin's debutante party in December 1921.

148

John Shillito, founder
of the John Shillito
Company.
*Cincinnati Historical
Society Library.*

As department stores, however, the John
Shillito Company and the H. & S. Pogue
Company figured more prominently than
the smaller shops in this transfer of power
from women to men in Cincinnati. In 1830,
when John Shillito established his dry goods
store, Cincinnati was a growing frontier
town. Shillito offered the (then) 28,000 citizens of the Queen City a variety of goods,
including fabrics, imported from Boston,
New York, London, and Paris.

Born in Greensburg, Pennsylvania, in
1808, John Shillito came to Cincinnati at
age nine and entered the employ of
Blatchley & Simpson as a salesclerk. The
business knowledge he gained during his
thirteen years in their employ certainly contributed to his remarkable success in the
years that followed. In partnership with
William McLaughlin, Shillito opened his
first establishment in a nondescript building
on Main Street between Columbia and
Pearl Streets. Strategically located just a few
blocks away from the bustling public
landing, Shillito had easy access to goods

brought from distant cities on the riverboats.

Shillito's initial concern on Main Street
outgrew both its early partnerships and its
original quarters. In 1833, the business, now
named Shillito, Burnet & Pullen in recognition of Shillito's two new partners, moved to
Fourth Street, between Sycamore and
Main—now employing four clerks. In 1837,
Mr. Shillito purchased his partners' interests
and established the firm of John Shillito &
Company, now in partnership with M. H.
Coates, Isaac Stephens, William Woods, and
Edward Holroyd. By 1857, Shillito had
bought out all of these partners and was
now sole owner. Purchasing a large lot on
Fourth Street between Race and Vine
Streets, Shillito erected a large building,
which housed the store until 1878. Over
time, his sons, Wallace, John, and Gordon,
joined their father as partners.

Again having outgrown the existing
building, Shillito moved his successful business to Race Street, bounded by Seventh
and George Street (now Shillito Place) in an
"uptown" section of Cincinnati devoted to
fine residences and parks. Against the advice
of business consultants but with great foresight and confidence that the city would
continue to prosper and grow, Shillito
erected a magnificent six-story structure
outside the business district.

This new establishment was one of the
"handsomest and best appointed store buildings on the continent."[20] It became known
as one of the "sights" of Cincinnati; travelers
from across the South and the Midwest
came to shop and marvel at the structure.
With a frontage of 176 feet along Race
Street and 270 feet on George Street,
Shillito's new emporium had a floor surface
of seven acres. It boasted an imposing

The John Shillito Company on Race Street, around 1878. *Cincinnati Historical Society Library.*

rotunda and dome sixty feet in diameter and one hundred feet high (see page 150), an architectural achievement for that period and a spectacle few visitors could forget. The store had five elevators, all the latest refinements and conveniences, and a thousand employees. In advertisements, it was described grandly as a "Mammoth Dry Goods House."[21] The new establishment opened in July 1878; on January 1, 1879, John Shillito's youngest son, Stewart, joined the partnership.

John Shillito died on September 10, 1879, at age seventy-one, and the business continued under his sons' direction. In 1882, it was incorporated as the John Shillito Company. In 1928, it was acquired by the F. & R. Lazarus Company of Columbus, Ohio, and in the following year became affiliated with Federated Department Stores. John

Shillito had created a highly successful firm that continued under family ownership for ninety-eight years. It was no less successful after its acquisition by Lazarus and Federated, and remained in business until 1982.

Shillito's success, like that of his peers, was due to many factors. Department stores met the customers' every need in one location. Large stores such as the John Shillito Company offered modern amenities such as elevators, delivery, tearooms, customer credit, knowledgeable and agreeable clerks, lower prices, and special services for those who were willing to pay for them. Department stores enticed consumers by virtue of their sheer size and grandeur alone; small concerns, whatever their offerings, could hardly compete. The custom dressmaking shop within the John Shillito Company created fierce competition for dressmakers such

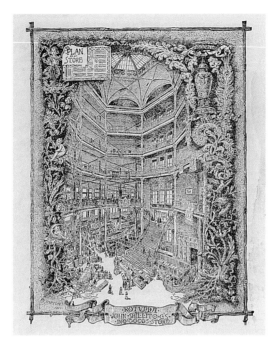

ABOVE LEFT: The impressive rotunda of the John Shillito Company drawn for the *Dramatic Festival Handbook*, 1883. *Cincinnati Historical Society Library.*

as Elizabeth Galvin, Kate Cregmile, and the Kavaney sisters.

Like Selina Cadwallader, Mary Bannon, and Elizabeth Galvin, the John Shillito Company appeared in the Dun and Company credit ledgers. In 1871, it was described as the leading dry goods merchant; there was "none better in this city." Consequently, the store was considered a "very respons[ible] house with unlimited cr[edit]." Even though the credit reporters actually suspected that the store had very large expenses and was not making much of a profit, they still advised creditors to give the establishment unlimited credit.[22] Typical of discriminatory practices against women, Elizabeth Galvin was listed only as a fair credit risk, even though she actually saved money despite her meager earnings.[23]

Despite Shillito's success, only a small number of garments seem to have survived. An afternoon dress (opposite page) created in the Shillito custom salon is indicative of the change in styles in the early 1890s, to a more trim, businesslike look. It is fashioned

in a bold red-and-white-striped fabric with tiny red and white dots reversed out. The vertical stripes accentuate an already slim silhouette; the skirt ruffle, in the same fabric, is made solid red by cleverly concealing the white stripes in the pleating.

Two additional garments, a bridesmaid dress and a wedding gown (also opposite), both bear the Shillito label. Although both date to 1893–1894, they were not worn to the same wedding. The pink bridesmaid dress was worn by Miss Isabel Jelke to her college roommate's wedding. Isabel Jelke, who lived on Clinton Springs Avenue in Avondale, was the daughter of Judge Ferdinand and Louise Faris Jelke. Isabel, who never married, was a member of the Cincinnati Women's Club and treasurer of the first board of the Cincinnati Symphony Orchestra. The provenance of the wedding dress is unknown. Both garments are superb examples of the excessive width of balloon or leg-of-mutton sleeves in the mid-1890s, especially the wedding dress. Its sleeves boast large, tiered puffs framed by strips of fabric

ABOVE: The John Shillito Company (founded 1840); *Afternoon Dress,* ca. 1890; silk; Label: The John Shillito Co. CINCINNATI.; Gift of Mrs. Murat Halstead Davidson, 1969.557a,b.

LEFT: The John Shillito Company (founded 1840); *Bridesmaid Dress,* 1893; silk, linen; Label: The John Shillito Co. CINCINNATI.; Gift of Miss Isabel Jelke, 1935.161, 162.

RIGHT: The John Shillito Company; *Wedding Dress,* 1893–1894; silk; Label: The John Shillito Co. CINCINNATI.; Gift of the Estate of Mrs. Simon Kuhn, 1952.77.

The pink bridesmaid dress was worn by Cincinnati socialite, Miss Isabel Jelke, to her college roommate's wedding. Miss Jelke

never married. The provenance of the wedding dress is unknown.

152

that widen the shoulder line to the extreme. The front of the bodice is designed with wide revers that fold back onto the sleeves, revealing the one soft element—a sheer crepe front inset—in a sea of heavy, off-white satin.

The John Shillito Company was not the only major department store in Cincinnati. One of its leading competitors was the H. & S. Pogue Company. For sixty-three years, from 1849 to 1912, Samuel Pogue and his family—four brothers, two sons, and several nephews—built the family firm into one of the city's largest and most successful department stores.

The Pogue family originated in Cavan County, Ireland. Isabella Crawford, a Scot, married Thomas Pogue, an Irish farmer. By 1840, they had five sons and five daughters. When Thomas Pogue died at age forty-four, their eldest child was only fifteen. The 1848 potato famine forced Mrs. Pogue, a widow in her early forties, to sail with seven of her ten children to America. They came to Cincinnati by steamboat at the invitation of Mrs. Pogue's brothers, John and William Crawford, who operated a dry goods store at 76 West Fifth Street. One of Mrs. Pogue's sons, Samuel, went to work for his uncles in their store.

In 1853, the eldest son, Henry, who had stayed behind in Ireland to complete an apprenticeship with a dry goods merchant, joined Samuel at the Crawford establishment. In 1856, Henry formed a partnership with Edward G. Jones, and the two opened their own staple and fancy dry goods store at 170 West Fifth Street; later, they moved to various other addresses on that same street.

On May 5, 1863, in the middle of the Civil War, Henry, age thirty-four, and

Samuel, thirty-one, purchased their uncles' establishment and changed the name to the H. & S. Pogue Dry Goods Company. In the same year, Henry Pogue bought out Edward Jones's interest in their joint concern, and the Pogue brothers merged the two stores. Soon their brothers, William, Thomas, and Joseph, joined the firm. The business prospered and during the 1860s and 1870s, the Pogue family established itself in the city's business, civic, and social life.

The Pogues' company was definitely a family business in which the brothers took a very personal interest. Not only did they serve as president, secretary, and treasurer of the company, but they also purchased merchandise, knew and waited on customers, and offered custom treatment. Gloves were specially ordered from Paris, shawls from England, and lace from Ireland. Packages were delivered personally, just in time for Christmas. Even their mother, who lived only a few blocks away, was called in to make alterations on the ready-made garments they sold; many of the Pogue women served as seamstresses in the early years.

From 1872 to 1877, the H. & S. Pogue Company was praised in the R. G. Dun and Company credit ledgers as prompt, doing an excellent business with ample means, safe, cautious, and reliable, and accumulating money every year. The brothers Henry and Samuel were described as honorable men who were "good for all they will buy."[24] These adjectives accurately portray two brothers who had survived the potato famine and succeeded, through hard work, in establishing one of the city's most successful ventures—probably, in part, because of their frugality. In fact, Henry and Samuel reportedly took turns acting as night

Henry (left) and
Samuel (right) Pogue,
founders of the H. & S.
Pogue Company.
*Cincinnati Historical
Society Library.*

watchmen to save a salary, and one of the nephews was employed to chase rats from the store each night.

Although the Pogues were frugal with their own time and money, they were known for paying considerably higher wages than most stores in Cincinnati. In most establishments, women clerks were under-paid because, after all, they were in an ideal position to meet wealthy male customers who might become their husbands. The Pogues, however, perhaps because of their strict Presbyterian upbringing, considered this an unhealthy fringe benefit and actually paid their clerks a living wage.

In 1878, the H. & S. Pogue Company moved to a new location at 112-14 West Fourth Street, in the heart of Cincinnati's shopping district. Their new quarters were larger than they needed at the time. When they did not have enough merchandise to fill the shelves, they stocked them with empty boxes to fill the gaps and make the store look full. Business continued to increase, however, and soon the building was too small.

In 1887, the Pogues dropped "Dry Goods" from their name and erected an imposing six-story building at 108 and 110 West Fourth Street. This elegant iron-front structure (see page 154) adjoined their pre-vious buildings on the same block and pro-vided them more than 100,000 square feet of floor room. The store was heralded as "the greatest dry-goods emporium west of New York."[25] It was equipped with modern conveniences, including three large hydraulic elevators and electric lights. At that time, the Pogues employed more than 300 clerks and divided the store into distinct departments. The H. & S. Pogue Company prided itself on serving "the highest class of trade" and providing its customers with the highest quality goods.[26]

The dressmaking and ladies' underwear departments were considered specialties at

The H. & S. Pogue Company, Fourth and Race Streets, around 1900; *Cincinnati Historical Society Library.*

Pogue's. The brothers imported the finest foreign dress goods in large quantities. An advertisement from September 1883 (opposite page) announces their fall importation of elegant novelty and fancy dress fabrics.[27] Not only did Pogue's provide ready-made garments for women but the store also sold fabrics that could be sewn at home or made up in the store's custom salon.

The company continued to prosper and provide superior service to customers despite the deaths of three of the brothers, Thomas, Joseph, and William, in the 1890s. Henry died in 1903 at age seventy-four; Samuel in 1912 at eighty. Robert W. Pogue, Samuel's son, became president of the store. Pogue's, as it was familiarly called by Cincinnatians, remained under the family name until 1984, when it merged with L. S. Ayres of Indianapolis.

The large number of garments that have survived from Pogue's dressmaking salon, eighteen in the museum's collection, are a testament to their popularity, the use of top-quality fabrics, the sturdy construction of the gowns, and the fact that the Pogue women themselves both wore and preserved gowns constructed in the family store. The earliest example dates to the early 1890s. The one-piece gown opposite is constructed of a gold damask fabric in a checkerboard pattern overlaid with an oriental-inspired floral pattern woven so as to catch the light differently across the breadth and the length of the fabric. The neckline, sleeve ends, and lower edge of the bodice are trimmed with a metallic braid, with white, pink, blue, and gold faux pearls, and with thousands of clear and gold-lined seed beads. The pearl fringe hanging from the bodice hem edge is carefully patterned with faux pearls to form diagonal lines of color.

An early 1890s example of exceptional design was donated by the Pogue estate in 1996. The dress on page 156 is constructed of a black, sheer fabric with a woven pattern

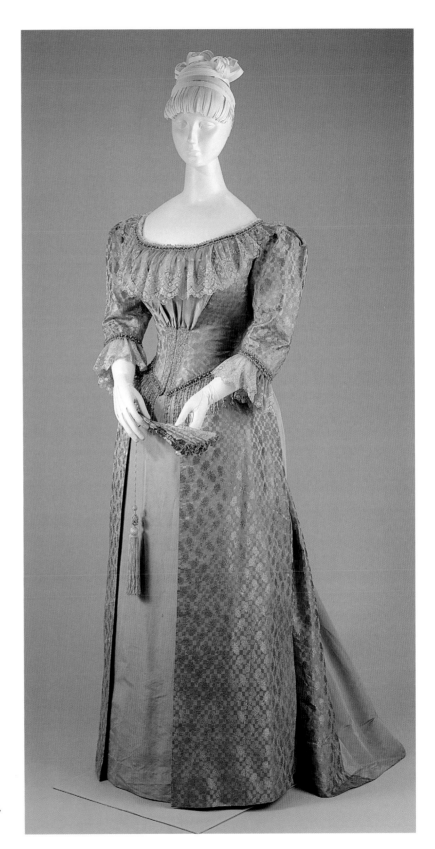

An advertisement for
the H. & S. Pogue
Company, announcing
their newest fabric and
fancy goods imports;
The Week Illustrated
(September 1883).
*Public Library of Cincin-
nati and Hamilton
County.*

The H. & S. Pogue
Company (founded
1863); *Evening Dress*,
1890–1891; silk, beads;
Label: H. & S. Pogue
Co. CINCINNATI;
Gift of Bertrand Kahn,
1962.583.

156

The H. & S. Pogue
Company (founded
1863); *Reception Dress,*
1892–1893; silk, jet
beads; Label: The H. &
S. Pogue Co. Cos-
tumes. CINCINNATI.;
Gift of the family of
Sophia Helen Fisk
Laird, Isabelle Eastman
Fisk, and Margaret
Pogue Fisk,
1996.385a,b.

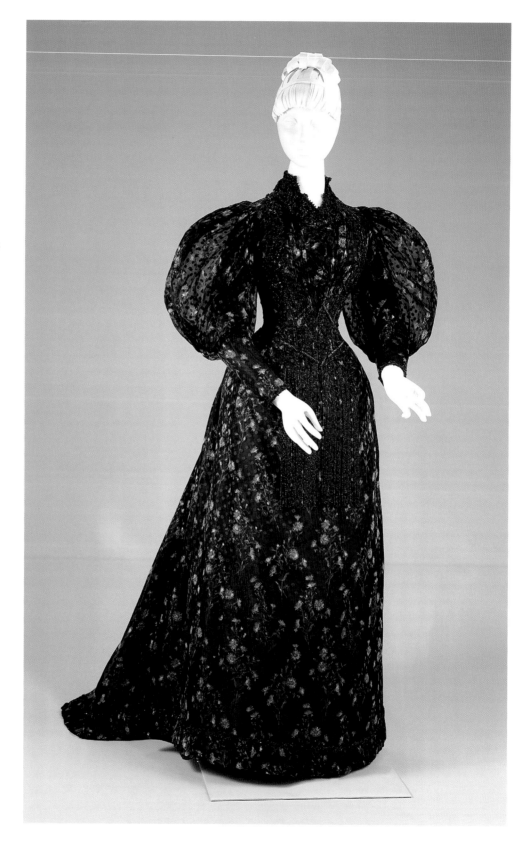

of opaque dots. Overlaid on this structure is a print of daisies in white and green. Under the sheer fabric, a changeable silk of red and black lines the dress, giving it a luminous quality. The balloon sleeves are constructed so as to exploit the sheerness of the fabric, with a tight sleeve underneath. The bodice is richly embellished with jet in a curvilinear pattern. Jet beads hang lavishly in long fringes from the bodice hem edge in both front and back.

Several of the gowns in the collection were worn by members of the Pogue family. Sophia Helen Pogue, sister to Henry and Samuel, wore the Pogue-made dress on page 158 to her daughter Belle's wedding on June 27, 1894. The dress is a beautiful example of a warp print fabric. Set on a beige ground, the yellow, brown, and blue warp print is paired with a woven pattern of dashes that moves diagonally across the fabric. The bodice is trimmed with machine-made lace and pleated pink chiffon. Sophia wore the dress with elbow-length pink gloves.

Many of the city's elite patronized the Pogues' custom salon, including Mrs. Samuel Broadwell (née Lily Lytle). Both the Lytles and the Broadwells were prominent Cincinnati families. Mrs. Broadwell's afternoon dress (on page 159) exemplifies the often harsh color aesthetics of the 1890s. Gold silk faille is paired with a gold-and-brown-patterned fabric for the sleeves and skirt insets. The front of the bodice is overlaid with pleated black chiffon embroidered with gold, pink, and green floss, and gold paillettes. The pink bows at the neck and waistline are an unlikely choice but are true to a period in which such discordant color combinations were not uncommon.

157

DETAIL: H. & S. Pogue *Reception Dress,* 1892–1893; 1996.385a,b.

158

Sophia Helen Pogue in
the gown illustrated at
left. She wore the dress
to her daughter's wed-
ding in 1894.

The H. & S. Pogue
Company (founded
1863); *Evening Dress,*
1894; silk, cotton;
Label: THE H. & S.
POGUE CO. COS-
TUMES. CINCIN-
NATI.; Gift of the
family of Sophia Helen
Fisk Laird, Isabelle
Eastman Fisk, and
Margaret Pogue Fisk,
1996.375a,b.

The H. & S. Pogue
Company (founded
1863); *Afternoon Dress,*
1896–1897; silk,
sequins, metallic
thread; Label: THE
H. & S. POGUE CO.
COSTUMES. CIN-
CINNATI, O.;
Gift of Mrs. Johnson
McGuire & Mrs. Vir-
ginius Hall,
1971.151a,b.

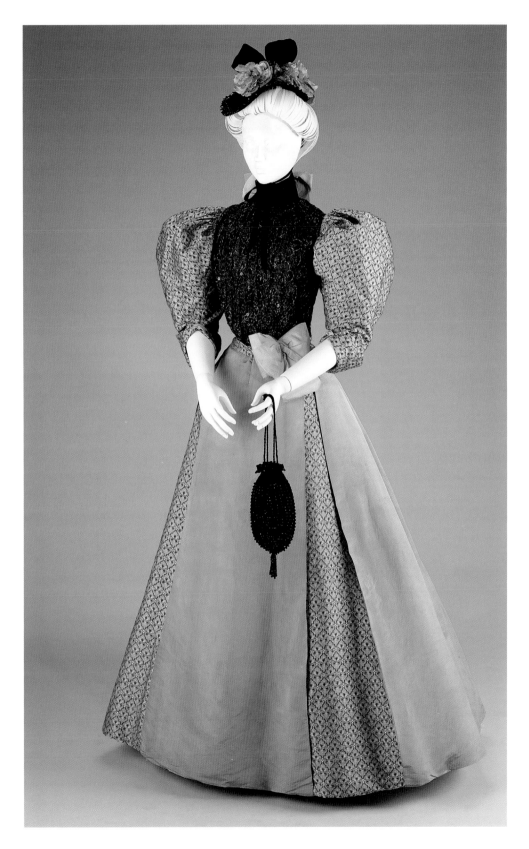

160

10-12 Fourth St., West, CINCINNATI, OHIO   564-68 Fifth Ave., NEW YORK CITY

J. M. Gidding & Co.
IMPORTERS
The "Paris Shop of America"

1510 "H" Street,   1422 Walnut St.,   Superior St. at First Ave.,
WASHINGTON, D. C.   PHILADELPHIA, PA.   DULUTH, MINN.

H

Haas, Mr. and Mrs. Charles,   3570 Washington Avenue,
    Avondale.
Haas, Mr. and Mrs. Marc W. (Weiskopf),   424 Forest
    Avenue, Avondale.
Haas, Mr. and Mrs. Moritz,   610 Forest Avenue,
    Avondale.
Haas, Mr. and Mrs. Sig.,   430 Forest Avenue,
    Avondale.

Although both the John Shillito Company and the H. & S. Pogue Company were examples of the oversized department stores of the second half of the nineteenth century, a smaller-scale retailer, J. M. Gidding & Company, was equally successful. This store was established in Cincinnati in 1907, at 10 West Fourth Street by the Gidding brothers, Jacob M., Benjamin A., Nathaniel, and Joseph, and was advertised as offering "Correct Dress for Women." The façade of the store was decorated by tiles made at the Rookwood Pottery: three-dimensional fruit-and-vegetable cornucopias graced the entrance.

Unlike Shillito's and Pogue's, Gidding's sold only ready-made women's clothing and accessories. The store did not have a custom salon, although it was renowned for superior customer service and surely performed whatever alterations or retrimmings were required to satisfy the clientele. Gidding's catered to the wealthiest members of Cincinnati society and also sold to many fashionable women of the American stage. It was considered a high-fashion store; designers often sold their work there on consignment.

The Gidding brothers came to Cincinnati after operating a retail store in Duluth. They were determined to make the Cincinnati store one of the nation's finest, and they succeeded. By 1914, they had shops in New York at 564-568 Fifth Avenue, in Paris at 34 Rue de Hauteville, in Washington, D.C. at 1510 H Street North, and in Duluth at Superior and First Avenue. The store remained an important part of Cincinnati's retail scene. In 1961, it was purchased by Genesco, Inc. and in 1963 merged with Jenny & Company to form Gidding-Jenny.

The few garments that have survived

J. M. Gidding & Company (founded 1907); *Suit: Coat and Skirt,* 1910; wool, silk; Label: Gidding & Co. DULUTH CINCINNATI NEW YORK PARIS; Gift of Mrs. Richard H. Keys, 1964.243, 244.

Janet March Drewery purchased this suit at J. M. Gidding & Company in 1910 for her trousseau.

162

DETAIL: J. M. Gidding
Evening Dress, 1916–
1918; 1964.330.

J. M. Gidding & Com-
pany (founded 1907);
Evening Dress, 1916–
1918; silk, linen,
metallic cloth, beads,
rhinestones; Label: J.
M. Gidding & Co.
CINCINNATI NEW
YORK PARIS WASH-
INGTON DULUTH;
Gift of family of Mrs.
Charles A. Pauly,
1964.330.

from Gidding's bespeak elegance and quality. Although they are examples of early ready-to-wear clothing, they are made of the finest fabrics and exemplify the highest level of design. A Gidding suit (see page 161) constructed of creamy yellow melton wool is fashionable and elegant in its simplicity. It is trimmed with soft, peach-colored satin on the lapels and buttons. The suit comes from the trousseau of Janet March Drewery, who married James Sutten on October 19, 1910.

Opposite, a sumptuous evening gown from Gidding's is a remarkable example of the elaborate beading popular in the period, combined with the finest fabrics. Both the center front and the back are graced with a complex beaded butterfly motif. Sheer silk brocaded in gold metallic threads is overlaid with green velvet and black net edged with faceted jet beads. Trained, the dress exemplifies the elegance and decorative quality of fashion in that period.

Mrs. Thomas J. Emery (née Mary Muhlenberg Hopkins) wore a plush black coat trimmed with white rabbit fur that bears a Gidding label (at left). Mary Emery was a driving force in Cincinnati society, particularly after her husband's death. With her inheritance, she became an impassioned art collector and philanthropist for many organizations, including the Cincinnati Art Museum. She was a generous supporter of the Episcopal Church, medical programs for children, educational activities, and many local and national charitable agencies. Mrs. Emery's greatest achievement was the establishment of Mariemont, a planned community just to the east of Cincinnati. Mariemont was envisioned as a neighborhood that would offer high-quality rental apartments

J. M. Gidding & Company (founded 1907); *Coat,* 1920; silk, rabbit fur; Label: Gidding CINCINNATI; Gift of Mrs. Virginius Hall, 1971.149.

This coat was worn by Mrs. Thomas J. Emery, philanthropist and founder of Mariemont.

164

The Mabley and Carew store at the northeast corner of Fifth and Vine Streets, around 1920. *Public Library of Cincinnati and Hamilton County.*

to wage earners in an effort to relieve the congested housing conditions in the city. It proved to be a model for later planned communities.

Although only these three retail operations are discussed at length, other Cincinnati retailers were equally successful. Joseph Thomas Carew, born in Peterborough, Ontario, in 1848, first worked for a retail operation in his hometown. In 1869, he secured a position in a large clothing house in Detroit operated by C. R. Mabley. Before long, he was appointed manager of a branch establishment in that city. The business was so successful that Mabley offered Carew the opportunity to become his partner, if he could find an appropriate city for a branch store.

Carew, looking through *Johnson's Cyclopedia*, was excited by the descriptions of

Cincinnati. All he needed was a glance at Fountain Square to be convinced that this was the right location. In 1877, he and Mabley opened their new store on the southwest corner of Fifth and Vine Streets. Their trade continued to prosper, and in 1884, the two men opened yet another branch in Baltimore. Mabley died a year later, but the Mabley and Carew store remained a Cincinnati shopping tradition until 1978, when it was purchased by the Elder-Beerman chain of Dayton, Ohio.

As in every American city, many retailers operated successful businesses in Cincinnati; most of these, however, no longer exist. The George W. McAlpin Company, for example, operated from 1852 to 1996. Many smaller stores catered to Cincinnati women, offering ready-to-wear apparel, including Kline's, Lawton & Company, Irwin's, and La Mode.

Much as the Gilded Age was the golden age for custom dressmakers, the period from 1890 to 1940 might be called the golden age of the American department store. By the turn of the century, most of the major firms had begun to assume their familiar shapes: Marshall Field in 1902, and Carson Pirie Scott in 1903, both in Chicago; Macy's in 1902, in Manhattan; Filene's in 1912, in Boston; and Famous-Barr in St. Louis, in 1913. In that era, large urban stores played a key role in first creating and then satisfying millions of Americans' desires for consumer goods. With the department store acting as an efficient outlet for ready-made garments, merchandise was offered to customers from all walks and levels of life; consumerism was democratized.

This social, cultural, and technological change altered the method by which women had obtained fashionable clothing for a century or more. Consumers were pressed "to buy, dispose of and buy again."[28] The opportunity to create couture garments was severely diminished; the buyer had been lured away by the convenience and lower cost of the ready-made garment. Thousands of women who had once created unique clothing for upper- and middle-class women were no longer needed.

In the dressmaker's place stood a sales clerk who made none of the wares she sold. She had no personal investment in her stock and was trained to avoid a personal relationship with her customers. The gap between maker and consumer widened increasingly, and women became the trimmers, the finishers, the salesclerks, and the consumers in a world that was controlled largely by men.[29]

Anna Dunlevy (active
1889–1913); *Afternoon
Dress,* 1907–1908; silk,
linen; Label: Dunlevy
CINCINNATI,
OHIO.; Gift of Miss
Emily H. Chase,
1941.162, 163.

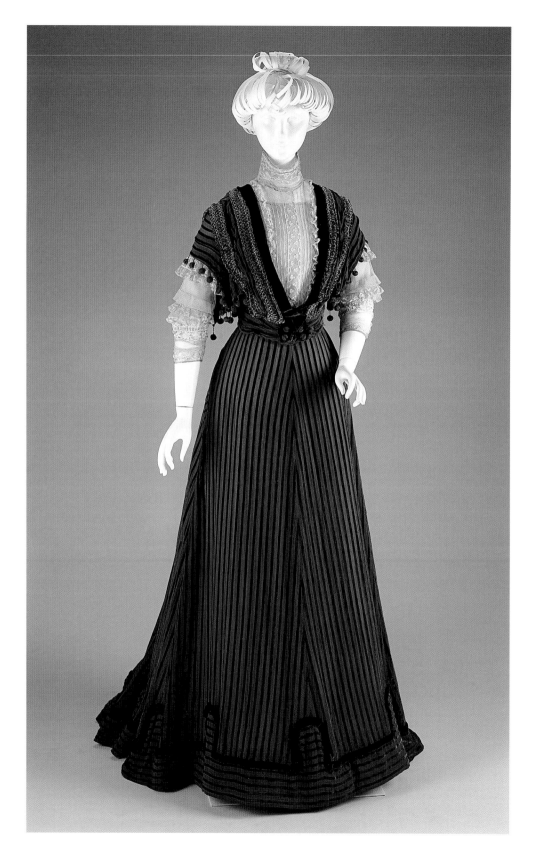

Conclusion

THE RISE OF ready-made clothing and its convenient availability through department stores marked the end of a golden era for the independent custom dressmaker. Once an important figure in a fashionable woman's circle of service providers, she was forced to close her doors. Her creative skills were no longer necessary to endow her clients with the moral superiority and proof of good character that fashionable dress formerly had afforded women. Woman's entry into the "ruthless world" of employment, careers, and higher education integrated men and women in a manner that the Western world had not deemed proper since the late eighteenth century. Segregated from each other's spheres, men and women had lived separate lives; these lives, in the early twentieth century, were becoming intermingled in arenas that previously had accommodated only one sex.

The progress made by women's rights advocates in the early twentieth century provided women with new avenues to success that had been denied them, both legally and culturally, in the past. At the same time, these new freedoms ironically thrust them once again into a male-dominated world. Dressmaking is only one of the entrepreneurial endeavors that offered women great freedom and independence. Perhaps unknowingly, they had created for themselves a separatist strategy that protected a territory in which they moved with, for, and among only women. Within that context, they could operate successfully. With the integration of the male and the female spheres, however, the struggle began again. Men were the supervisors, women the hirelings. Unlike dressmakers, who had operated under their own direction, female clerks, factory workers, and teachers were subject to male authority.[1] Dressmakers, like other independent businesswomen of their time, had offered young women a model, but this model was vanishing.

Women of the nineteenth century faced what must have seemed an impossible obstacle: the concept of the separate sphere, which bound them physically and psychologically to the home. Yet they were able to find means to operate freely, both through confrontation, in the form of the woman's rights movement, and more subtly, in the creative use of their sphere. Cincinnati's dressmakers and their counterparts across the nation are only one example of nineteenth-century women who demonstrated an "Amazonian Spirit"[2] that empowered them to move beyond their prescribed bounds. Historians' relatively recent interest in common people and, specifically, costume historians' interest in milliners and dressmakers, has rendered these women visible.[3] Today, once again, they are important models of ingenuity, perseverance, and tenacity for women young and old.

The 1870s Transformation of the Robe de Chambre

THE SECOND HALF of the nineteenth century was a time of
increased urbanization and changing
socialization. Codes of behavior and dress
were being transformed to establish order
and distinctiveness in a rapidly expanding
bourgeois culture. The study of the *robe de
chambre* and its metamorphosis into the tea
gown in the 1870s is an interesting chapter
in the world of fashion and semiotics.

The dress code of this period was mainly
subdivided in the categories of "undress,"
"half dress," and "full dress." Although the
nomenclature suggests a crescendo from
least to most formal, elevated levels of formality existed within each faction. One's
position in society was conveyed through
the skillful discernment of what was appropriate wear for different times, places, and
company. Because women's social life was
conducted in the home well into the nineteenth century,[1] a wide array of interior
gowns, an important group within the category of undress, was available for events
ranging from the least to the most formal.
All interior gowns were not created for the
same purpose, and one gown could rarely be

appropriate for all occasions. In an era in
which sociability was frequently conducted
in private residences, home was also a public
stage insofar as it was visited by a wide array
of people from a chosen community or
class. The category of undress could thus
have public applications. For instance,
morning garments with a less highly defined
fit or silhouette were not meant to be worn
outside one's bedroom or boudoir. Beyond
this realm, a greater selection of interior
gowns with defined silhouettes could be
worn for more public appearances. As a rule,
fit increased with the degree of formality
and exposure to others.

The *robe de chambre* was an informal
interior gown that had been in use as a form
of undress for both men and women for
many centuries.[2] In the 1870s, it was transformed into a sophisticated garment that
could be worn by hostesses receiving guests
in their homes. During this time, the *robe de
chambre* promoted a new system of sociability, disseminated mostly through the
increase in the production of etiquette manuals and ladies' periodicals.[3] For a price,
these highly popular manuals offered an

170

antidote to the anxieties of the rising middle classes striving to climb the social ladder. Periodicals featured fashion plates, which became an important mode of communication that helped codify existing rules and develop new regulations of dress.

The new system of sociability included the progressive refinement of interior spaces and table etiquette among the middle classes. The semiotics of everyday life are apparent in the study of the house, its contents, and the activities performed there. The specialization of space and the increased refinement in manners gave rise to the adoption of the dining room and parlor.[4] The costs of hosting elaborate dinners and soirées to repay social obligations and entertain friends soon became prohibitive. Equally important was the limited number of guests that could be accommodated. Among the middle classes, anxieties about hosting were so strong that alternative means of refined entertaining were suggested: "An afternoon tea is so cheap that anybody can afford to give one, and involves so little trouble and formality that even the most timid or most lazy hostess need not shrink before the very diminutive lions it brings into her path."[5] Afternoon visits lasted from fifteen minutes to half an hour, a period "sufficient to meet the requirements of politeness"[6]; thus, tea was much more accommodating than other functions.

The development of the parlor or drawing room established in the household a versatile stage for public display. The parlor aimed to give visitors an "artful declaration of its owners' sensibility."[7] For teatime, it was transformed and furnished with a special table that was low enough to enable the hostess to pour tea for her guests while

seated. It is no wonder that the "theatrical" parlor fostered the development of a specialized and whimsical garment that often blended with its setting. In an era keenly aware of the subtle language of clothes and their meaning in society, nothing could be more fitting than the transformation of the *robe de chambre* into the tea gown, a garment worn specifically for a popular, genteel afternoon repast.

The revival of teatime and the development of tea gowns are thus linked to the rise in table etiquette, the growing refinement of dinner as a social event, and the specialization of interior spaces. The modest expense and the lesser formality (by Victorian standards) of teatime appealed to a wider array of middle-class individuals eager to attain social respectability at a lower cost. These factors contributed to the growing popularity of teatime and help explain the relatively large number of elaborate *robes de chambre* and tea gowns found in museum collections, and their differences in styles of execution, ranging from garments "made by loving hands at home" to those executed by Parisian couturiers. Food and dress had long been markers of rank; thus, it is not surprising that the forerunner of the tea gown, the *robe de chambre*, became an ideal indicator of social standing in this artificially constructed system.

By the 1870s, when tea gowns were introduced, tea was no longer an elitist beverage. Teatime, however, remained class conscious, because it entailed a network of reciprocity in which selected individuals achieved group membership.[8] This afternoon repast retained an aura of gentility, because teatime was linked repeatedly to eighteenth-century salons, an association

Selina Cadwallader
(active 1870–1886); *Tea
Gown*, 1877–1878; silk;
Label: S. Cadwallader.
CINCINNATI,
OHIO.; Bequest of
Katherine V. Gano
Estate, 1945.53.

that helped to intellectualize and elevate its
status.[9]

In tracing the origin of the *robe de
chambre* from a modest garment to a gown
of great splendor, one must look to the
revival of teatime in the 1860s and examine
interior gowns from that period.[10] Over-
whelming evidence shows that the tea gown
evolved from what was often labeled in both
English and French as a *robe de chambre*, the
French term for the "interior gown."
Fashion-plate descriptions in periodicals
often used the words *robe* and *toilette* inter-
changeably, as well as substituting *chambre* for
intérieur. The term *house dress* also was used
to describe this type of garment. Just as the
French-speaking world used the English
term *tea gown*, the English-speaking world
used the French terms to describe these
interior gowns.

Many of the elaborate *robes de chambre*
from the early 1870s have all the elements
required for wear at home for 5 o'clock tea
and were thus fit to be labeled as *tea gowns*,
but few were described as such at this point.
As interior gowns, they are often referred to
as possessing "all-in-one constructions,"
because the bodices and the skirts are not
separate. They have the long sleeves and
higher necklines of daytime wear, as well as
a train, and use high-fashion textiles and
trims. Such highly fashionable *robes de
chambre* were cut to fit the figure, and follow
the bustled styles worn by women in the
period.

The tea gown at left from the Cincinnati
Art Museum has all these elements and con-
veys the formal nature of some of the interior gowns from the 1870s. Made in Cincinnati by Selina Cadwallader (d. 1886;
active 1870-1886), it follows the most up-to-

172

Louis XV tea gown, *The Queen* (April 27, 1878).

date European and American trends, and echoes the widespread dissemination of this new style of elaborate interior gown. The sophisticated fabric is inspired by eighteenth-century aesthetics, as are the Watteau back pleats. Named after the French painter Antoine Watteau (1684–1721), who depicted in great numbers the loose gown popular in the early eighteenth century, these pleats became one of the historically inspired elements associated most closely with fanciful tea gown styles. Unlike the wide, floating pleats of the eighteenth-century loose gown, Mrs. Cadwallader's pleats are couched down to define the silhouette more closely.

In the aesthetics of Victorian society, fit was a "product of the highest civilization."[11]

As with many other late nineteenth- and early twentieth-century interior gowns that featured loose-fitting elements such as pleated or draped back and front panels, the *suggestion* of looseness was sufficient to imply informality or an artistic disposition. To ensure respectability and appropriateness in semiprivate and public settings, garments still needed appropriate silhouette definition and corsetry. Like many elaborate 1870s *robes de chambre*, the Cadwallader gown is worn over voluminous underpinnings; the construction of the lower portion follows the typical late-1870s silhouette, which accommodated the fashionable bustle. Because a crinoline or bustle was not worn without corsetry in Victorian times, the contrived silhouette depicted here suggests that a corset was worn. The blue insert at the neck suggests the deeper neckline of a reception gown, while maintaining the decorum of more typical high-necked, long-sleeved interior gowns.

The Cadwallader gown can be described as both a *robe de chambre* and a tea gown. The first *robes de chambre* discovered to date that are specifically labeled as tea gowns appeared on facing pages in the 1878 British periodical *The Queen*.[12] The first, an "afternoon tea gown," retains the patch pocket of the earlier *robe de chambre* but lacks the couched-down Watteau back pleats of its sister, "the Louis XV tea gown" illustrated opposite in two views. Both illustrations show front and back views of the garment. Each garment has a long train and gives the impression of a closely fitted "open robe" and underdress. The Louis XV tea gown is of great interest, because it names its source of inspiration and reinforces the salon connection. These tea gowns coexist with numerous other elaborate gowns of the same type; until the

turn of the century, such garments were as likely to be called by the new term *tea gown* as to be labeled by the variant term *robe de chambre*. Nomenclature is thus a source of confusion, because all tea gowns were interior gowns, but not all interior gowns were appropriate for wear in mixed company at 5 o'clock tea.[13]

As teatime grew in popularity and sophistication, the *robe de chambre* became highly specialized. By the 1890s, it crossed over to the realm of day and evening wear. A product of its time, the elaborate *robe de chambre* emerged in an era marked by historicism, eclecticism, and exoticism, which help define its aesthetics and construction. The elaborate *robe de chambre* of the 1870s and its offshoot, the tea gown, helped to foster major stylistic changes that launched twentieth-century dress. An appropriate venue for fantasy and innovation, they provided respectable women with a place to experiment within the system of nineteenth-century dress and behavioral codes.

174

Josephine M. Kass-
selman (active
1913–1933) *Wedding
Dress,* 1917; silk, linen,
beads, metallic thread;
Label: Josephine 911
NEAVE BLDG.
CINCINNATI: Gift of
Mr. William Schreiber,
1967.1172 (see page
126, left).

Shirley Teresa Wajda

"A Kind of Missionary Work": The Labor and Legacy of Cincinnati's Society Women, 1877–1922

OCTOBER 9, 1880, was Museum Day in Cincinnati. Mayor Charles Jacob had proclaimed it a civic holiday, requesting that all public offices be closed and that all public and private buildings be decorated with flags. The occasion for this celebration was the successful completion of a building fund drive to establish what would become the Cincinnati Art Museum.

Soon thereafter, the Cincinnati Museum Association was organized to oversee the construction and operation of the museum, which was to be located in the city's beautiful aerie, Eden Park. The Association's members included socially prominent men, such as Joseph Longworth, who was its first president, and Alfred Traber Goshorn, who began in 1882 to serve as the Museum's first director.[1]

Although Museum Day crowned one of the Queen City's many efforts to establish public institutions of cultural importance to all its citizens, it also represented the restrictions on American women's civic power. Society women had long been involved in encouraging the arts in Cincinnati and in

working toward the creation of a museum. The Women's Centennial Executive Committee, led ably by Mrs. Elizabeth Williams Perry, had earned national acclaim through the success of the Cincinnati Room at Philadelphia's Centennial Exhibition in 1876. Inspired by this achievement, Mrs. Perry and her colleagues established the Woman's Art Museum Association in April 1877. This group was dedicated to bridging the artificial gulf between the social classes and educating the public in taste through the application of art to industry; it offered lecture series, exhibitions, and art classes to spread its message. In 1878, Mrs. Perry wrote, "I believe there is a brilliant future for the United States in the as yet untrodden field of art applied to industry—and perhaps in none of our cities are the signs of interest more encouraging than here."[2]

By that fateful October day, however, the Woman's Art Museum Association's purpose and power had been eclipsed by Charles West's donation of $150,000 for the museum. (Matching public subscriptions and a subsequent additional donation by West ensured the museum's establishment.)

The Association's successful campaign apparently caused its failure. The women's message promoting public education and the uplift of taste was heeded by the city's civic leaders and became the Museum's central mission—but through the male-only Cincinnati Museum Association. When Mrs. Perry wrote to Charles West in 1880, she chose to frame the experience in a positive light, although her choice of words surely hints at the limits confining her and her colleagues: "The efforts of the Women's Art Museum Association have been limited to a kind of missionary work: if they have performed some service in preparing the way for the Art Museum, they will feel that their labor has not been in vain."[3]

Before it disbanded at the Museum's opening in 1886, the Woman's Art Museum Association used its resources to purchase collections of applied arts, particularly pottery. One of its major purchases, however, from London's South Kensington Museum (now the Victoria and Albert Museum), was a collection of sixteenth- and seventeenth-century European laces and textiles. Women's philanthropic work in the late nineteenth century had ensured the preservation of fashionable handiwork from previous centuries. Both forms of work—the original creation and the subsequent preservation—were symbolized in these laces and textiles. And both were women's work.[4]

This act also symbolized the belief held by many active society women in Cincinnati. Influenced by the Aesthetic Reform movement in Europe and the United States, these women used art to refine daily life through attention to the decorative arts, interior design, and dress. Furthermore, many of these women believed that art edu-

cation could abolish the evils of industrialization and urbanization by reemphasizing workmanship and taste. In this way, the increasing divide between classes—a divide thought to be created by industrialization—could be bridged. As Cincinnatian George Ward Nichols wrote for a national audience, art education meant "artistic and scientific instruction applied to common trades and occupations, as well as to the fine arts. It means that the educated sense of the beautiful is not the especial property of one class, but that it may be possessed and enjoyed by all."[5]

In a very personal way, Cincinnati society women and their dressmakers had already been enacting the artistic life as defined by Ward. Artistic patrons made dressmakers fashionable, and artistic dressmakers made fashionable patrons. A label in a garment was an artist's signature, and the careful crafting of attire, often with exquisitely painstaking detail, certainly was an application of art to industry. Both patron and dressmaker attended to the latest information about aesthetic and fashion trends in Europe and on the East Coast. The relationship between patron and dressmaker was symbiotic, and the history of women in Cincinnati cannot be told without discussing the commercial, social, and philanthropic networks created by the women themselves. United by gender ideology, society women and their dressmakers expressed their social and political gains in the fashionable attire they created together.[6]

Many histories of Cincinnati have been written—many, indeed, were composed in the waning years of the nineteenth century and the first years of the twentieth, just as women were entering more fully into the city's public life. Nevertheless, a reading of these boosterish accounts would support the claim that women (and many other groups) did not participate in the Queen City's civic, economic, or social life. Elite women, as wives, mothers, and daughters, make only brief, rare "guest appearances" in these histories.[7] In matters compatible with traditionally feminine concerns, such as creating and preserving decorative arts and fashion, women could make great gains, but those hard-earned gains could be lost quickly. As revealed by the story of the Woman's Art Museum Association, women's entrance into the public sphere was not easy.

This is not surprising in view of the traditional emphasis on great men and their deeds, and especially on their written accounts. The ideology of separate spheres had long rendered women invisible in the public record: they were legally and socially protected or represented by fathers or husbands. The historian's task is made even more difficult by this cultural tendency to shield women's lives from public view. After all, even while the chroniclers of Cincinnati's Golden Age were proclaiming the city's merits, Cincinnati women were attending college, obtaining legal rights, establishing associations, operating businesses—in short, doing what men did. Also, by the end of the nineteenth century, Cincinnati women were appearing in the society or women's pages of the city's newspapers and in social registers. These successful and Progressive "New Women" were present and active; yet they were overlooked by contemporary historians.[8]

The women were "looked over" and misunderstood by contemporary critics as well. In the years after the Civil War, and increasingly so after the 1899 publication of *The Theory of the Leisure Class*, Thorstein Veblen's caustic study of the wealthy in the United States, Americans often regarded Society as a class of individuals marked by idleness, conspicuous consumption, and fashionable dress. One wonders whether Veblen ever read the society pages of American newspapers. Introduced during Veblen's lifetime (along with an avalanche of etiquette guides), the society page signified not snobbery, but women's increasing political and economic power in American public life. Women rarely were mentioned in newspapers before the Civil War; postbellum society pages in city newspapers appealed directly to women's issues, both within and beyond the home. Spurred also by the home economics movement instituted in high schools and on college campuses across the United States, writers for society or women's pages explained innovations in time-saving home management, from consumer education to updated recipes based on the latest technology. Activities of women's organizations, from early garden and literary clubs to the League of Women Voters, represented a Progressive spirit of public reform that mirrored and influenced the climate in the halls of city, state, and national government—men's traditional sphere of activity. Furthermore, the women's pages displayed the activities of a society reproducing itself, through the publication of wedding, anniversary, and birth announcements; parties; travel itineraries; and the introduction of visitors to the public—all elements of women's traditional sphere. Photographic images in the society section of the daily and Sunday newspapers featured fashionably dressed women (and men) hosting or attending charity balls, participating in public functions such as groundbreaking ceremonies or exhibit openings, and contributing overall to the community's social and cultural welfare.[9]

The cultural shift away from Victorian codes of feminine behavior, which fostered women's privacy, toward the Modern value of publicity, as women gained economic, legal, and civil rights by the 1920s, can be seen in the preference for being known by one's own name rather than that of one's husband. This shift is evident in the pages of Cincinnati's newspapers and in the creation of the society page. Indeed, women became society reporters and editors in this period, thus acquiring much power. Marion Devereux, for example, dominated Cincinnati's social scene from 1910 to 1939, having inherited the job from her mother, Clara. (The Devereux family belonged to Society of Descendants of Colonial Governors, the National Society of Colonial Dames in America, and the Mayflower Society, each a source of social status in its own right.)

Women became even more visible through the publication of social registers, beginning in the 1870s. Peter G. Thomson published the *Cincinnati Society Blue Book and Family Directory* in 1879, eight years before the New York Social Register Association began publishing its more famous directories. The *Graphic Blue Book and Family Directory of Cincinnati,* published in 1887 by the Graphic Press, included illustrations of society members' homes, as well as the "Rules of Cincinnati Society." Mrs. Devereux's *Blue Book of Cincinnati Society*, started in 1894 by Clara and continued by Marion at Clara's death in 1910, was updated every two years until 1929.[10]

If Veblen did condescend to look at the society page, he certainly would have noticed the written descriptions and photographic images of women in fashionable attire, and probably would have disdained what he saw. In fact, a chapter of *Theory of the Leisure Class* was titled "Dress as an Expression of the Pecuniary Culture." Relegating women to mannequins upon which husbands and father displayed their wealth through clothing (in that woman's role was "to consume vicariously for the head of the household"), Veblen overlooked elite and middle-class women's social agency. He decried women's bonnets, the "French heel" of women's shoes, the skirt and its drapery, and the corset as "contrivances" that rendered women "permanently and obviously unfit for work." The demand for novelty in the fashion system fostered Veblen's critique. Veblen saw in the costume of the leisured woman no signs of "productive labor": in Veblen's view, the precise cut of clothing, the lack of wear and tear in a garment, and the large and ever-changing wardrobe demanded by the codes of fashion etiquette revealed its wearer as a "nonproductive" member of society. He criticized American culture for excluding women from "earning a livelihood by useful work" and for mandating that she "beautify" her sphere "within the household."[11]

Yet was Veblen himself not blinded by his theory of fashionable dress? He ignored the varieties of dress worn by women for various aspects of their daily lives, including garments designed for housework. More important, he ignored the dressmakers, whose "productive labor" had created these fashionable costumes. Veblen could not read the society page—nor understand society itself—for what it actually revealed: the changing realities of American women's roles, including the women who wore—and the women who created—fashionable dress. He declared: "Elegant dress serves its purpose of elegance not only in that it is expensive, but also because it is the insignia of leisure."[12] Yet for members of Cincinnati society, leisure could be, and for many women was, the realm of work.

Cincinnati's society women were both fashionable *and* hardworking in ways that escaped Veblen's observation. They maintained family traditions of civic and cultural citizenship. As daughters of city founders, industrialists, merchants, and businessmen, and as wives of leading members of the city's public life, many Cincinnati women learned the lessons of *noblesse oblige* early in their lives. At her death in 1927, Mrs. Mary Muhlenberg Emery (born in 1844) was remembered as "Cincinnati's most beloved and revered philanthropist." Her life in Cincinnati society began after her marriage to Thomas J. Emery in 1866, and continued through their membership in Christ Church on East Fourth Street. There, Mrs. Emery was able to make contacts with many of the city's social leaders. The original Thomas Emery had arrived in Cincinnati in 1832; his sons, Thomas and John, took over their father's prosperous (if malodorous) lard oil business. Thomas Emery's Sons, Incorporated soon was constructing buildings throughout the city, including the Hotel Emery and a large number of apartment houses. The Emerys built Children's Hospital in Mount Auburn, the Colored Orphan Asylum in Walnut Hills, and the Fresh Air Farm in Terrace Park, all to benefit "the people." The distribution of pure milk

to the city's poor, supported by Mrs. Emery, eventually became the Babies' Milk Clinic.

The Emery name has been associated with many buildings and spaces throughout the city. Mrs. Emery's energy and donations ensured the success of the Cincinnati Zoo, the Arboretum in Westwood, and the Bird Reserve in Clifton. In 1911, the Ohio Mechanics' Institute was given a new home, with a gift of $500,000; the Emery Auditorium is located within its walls. In 1925, Mrs. Emery promised that the Edgecliff collection of paintings and a building in which to display them would be given to the Cincinnati Art Museum.

After her husband died in 1906, Mrs. Emery continued her good works. Indeed, Thomas J. Emery had stipulated in his will that his wife was to give away "their fortune where it would do the greatest good." Thus, she devoted the rest of her life to philanthropy and social betterment. She founded the Council of Social Agencies, which later became the Community Chest. The Thomas J. Emery Memorial was established with funds provided by his widow. At her death, the Memorial was in the process of establishing a new garden suburb called Mariemont, named in honor of Mrs. Emery's residence in Newport, Rhode Island. "Mariemont was to have nothing of a charitable or philanthropic motive attached to it," noted *The Cincinnati Enquirer*. "Its sponsor dreamed only of a community with a heart, an ideal place for human beings and their friends," according to Mrs. Emery's personal representative, the aptly named Charles L. Livingood. The severe economic and social dislocations caused by the Great Depression certainly supplied the impetus for such a grand scheme.[13]

Yet the Memorial was created to do more. "As set forth in the articles of incorporation the purpose of the organization is 'to bring about the social, physical, civic, and educational betterment on humanitarian lines of residents of the United States, but preferably of those of the State of Ohio, to produce a more sane citizenry by providing more satisfactory living conditions, and to aid financially such educational institutions used for charitable purposes.'" For her good works, Mrs. Emery was honored many times; in 1920, the University of Cincinnati, a beneficiary of her largesse, awarded its first degree to a woman by bestowing upon her an honorary doctor of laws degree. How fitting that she was the first woman to be awarded a degree *and* the right to vote in the same year (see page 163).[14]

Cincinnati society had its convivial aspects, requiring appropriate dress and manners, and these social rituals strengthened the bonds within and between families. Critics may have condemned these events as showy displays of wealth, but they brought women together in socially approved ways. What did women discuss in their reception rooms? At the supper table? At the edge of the dance floor? By their actions, we know they discussed more than fashionable dress.

"Reception days" were included for many years in *Mrs. Devereux's Blue Book*. Before the reign of Clara and Marion Devereux, the local newspapers listed the receptions days on which society women were "at home" to accept callers. "Calling" was a complicated system of proposing and cementing social ties; it required careful attention to the visitors' street costumes and to the reception gowns of those "at home"

to greet them.[15] Nannie Robinson Maeder's brown silk velvet and satin gown, created in the early 1890s, represents the formality of the ritual. An earlier version of the reception dress (1877–1878) was worn by Mary Swift (Mrs. Joseph C.) Thoms (see pages 86 and 111).[16]

Debutante parties or balls were seasonal events requiring the latest fashions. Etiquette advisors in the late nineteenth century were precise in their specifications for acceptable attire, the order of persons in a reception line, the design of invitations, and types of debut parties. After the turn of the century, and increasingly after World War I, young women chose not to debut, to marry later or not at all, and to take up careers. Perhaps their mothers' increased public activity and club membership offered lessons in individual autonomy to these young women, who, in turn, pushed harder against the limits of the feminine sphere.

This shift is evident in Emily Post's *Blue Book of Social Usage*, first published in July 1922. Mrs. Post offered many more options to young women than did similar advice writers of their mothers' and grandmothers' generations. This book went through seventeen printings between its initial appearance and March 1927, surely a sign of its usefulness and its correct reading of the public mind.[17]

Mrs. Henry Goodyear (born Hannah Taylor Shipley), who graduated from Smith College in 1921, did not debut. Just prior to her marriage, in 1922, to Henry Goodyear, however, she appeared at debutante parties and other social occasions in Cincinnati and elsewhere in an evening dress of white tulle and silver sequins, still participating in a ritual that both expanded and secured the boundaries of Cincinnati's social elites (see page 134).

Miss Shirley Kemper, great-great-granddaughter of the Reverend James S. Kemper (Cincinnati's first pastor and one of its first settlers) wore a blue chiffon evening dress at her cousin's debut in December 1921 (see page 147). That these women preserved these dresses associated with social debuts indicates the importance of such rites of passage in the lives of Cincinnati's young women. Miss Kemper saved her dress very much as her family saved its original home, a log cabin built in 1804, which was moved from Walnut Hills to the Cincinnati Zoo in 1913. Yet these dresses also chronicle their wearers' social service. Miss Kemper belonged to the College Club and the Cincinnati Historical Society, but she spent much of her life teaching third grade at Miss Doherty's School for Girls (which later became the College Preparatory School, and then part of the Seven Hills Schools).[18]

Weddings became public events in the years after the Civil War. They were held increasingly in venues other than private homes, were announced in newspapers, and included more associated rituals, including gift showers and receptions. Specialized clothing for the bride and the guests were also required. Jean Morton Abbott Strader (1883-1959) married Whiteman E. Smith in 1900. Smith, the grandson of the editor of the *Commercial Gazette* and president of the Smith-Gardner Coal Company, died at age thirty-nine in 1919. His cousins included Benjamin W. Strader, Marshall Strader, Clara Whiteman Strader, and John J. Strader, whom Jean Abbott Smith later married in 1920 (see page 112). The Straders and Whitemans were several of Cincinnati's oldest

families. For close to two centuries, the families owned and occupied land along Clifton Avenue. (The house at 3650 Clifton Avenue is still occupied by Mrs. John J. Strader IV.) Strader's Wharf later became the Cincinnati Public Landing, and the family itself was involved in many aspects of Cincinnati's transportation network. Jacob Strader became treasurer, in 1840, and eventually president of the Little Miami Railroad Company and had served as president of the Cincinnati-Louisville Packet Company, which operated river steamers. John J. Strader later served as secretary-treasurer of the Cincinnati Street Railway Omnibus Company, which facilitated suburban development.[19]

The importance of marriage is recognized in the careful preservation of Jean Abbott Strader's wedding dress. This dress, taken together with the wedding dresses of Ruth Grossman (who married Joseph Schild in 1908), Bessie Louise Bradley (who married Monte Jay Goble Sr. in 1909), and Marjory Langdon (who married Clifford R. Wright in 1921), charts not only genealogies of individual families but also a larger social history of shared residence and activities (see pages 103, 105, and 182).[20]

Women within families often united to pursue their interests and to undertake benevolent causes for the city. Yet they also reached out to one another to form women-only associations. Numerous clubs satisfied a variety of interests for Cincinnati women: not only the Ladies' Musical Club and the Cincinnati Woman's Club but also the Ladies' Junior Musical Club, the College Club, the Riding Club, the Woman's Art Club, and the Monday Musical Club. All were (and some remain) in the tradition of

Josephine M. Kas-
selman (active 1913–
1933); *Wedding Dress
and Train,* 1921; silk,
linen, beads; Label:
Josephine 411 RACE
ST. CINCINNATI;
Gift of Mrs. Clifford
R. Wright,
1966.1313a,b.

association that Alexis de Tocqueville had observed as a purely American phenom-enon.[21] Historian Karen J. Blair observes that the early women's club movement helped women develop a sense of civic duty, as well as providing the means to learn skills necessary for public life. Within the meet-ings, women found their common cause and stretched the traditional boundaries of the private sphere.[22]

Clubs also reoriented an increasingly mobile and suburban population. As Cincin-nati matured as a city, its elites and middle

classes established and moved to suburbs such as Clifton, Mount Auburn, and Walnut Hills, located in the hills surrounding the "Basin." The Riding Club, founded in 1902, was located in Mount Auburn, one of Cincinnati's first suburbs. Horse-drawn and (later) electric streetcar lines, inclines, and automobiles facilitated easy transportation to and from club meetings, which often were held in downtown meeting rooms, hotels, and libraries.[23] Day dresses, such as that shown opposite, worn by Mrs. Mary Isabella Crawford Pogue (who died in 1934), would

The H. & S. Pogue
Company (founded
1863); *Afternoon Dress,*
1901–1902; silk, cotton;
Label: Pogue CINCIN-
NATI.; Gift of Mrs.
Herbert Hollomon,
1966.1243a,b.

have been acceptable attire for club meet-
ings and related work. The wife of Henry
Pogue, one of the founders of the H. & S.
Pogue Company, maintained memberships
in the Colonial Dames, the Cincinnati
Woman's Club, the Cincinnati Country
Club, and the Daughters of the American
Revolution.[24]

Mrs. Christian R. Holmes, one of the
wealthiest women in the United States at
her death in 1941, had been born Bettie J.
Fleischmann in Cincinnati. Her father,
Charles Fleischmann, was the founder of the

Fleischmann Company; her brother Julius
served twice as mayor of the Queen City.
Her Danish-born husband (whom she married in 1892) was one of the city's leading
physicians in the first decades of the twentieth century. Dr. Holmes was tireless in his
dedication to Cincinnati and to the construction of the Cincinnati General Hospital. In fact, when the *Cincinnati Enquirer*
reported on Dr. Holmes's death in 1920, his
passing was attributed to overwork. Mrs.
Holmes memorialized her husband and his
devotion to the public by endowing the

deanship of the Medical School of the University of Cincinnati and establishing the Christian R. Holmes Hospital.[25]

Mrs. Holmes was a civic leader in her own right, aiding in the establishment of the Cincinnati Symphony Orchestra in the last decade of the nineteenth century. Five earlier efforts to establish a symphony orchestra had failed, largely because of infighting among (male) benefactors, patrons, and musical directors. In 1891, however, the formation of the twenty-five-member Ladies' Musical Club reinvigorated the movement. The Club soon expanded its active membership to fifty persons, and benefited by the additional support of some 300 associate members, including Mrs. Holmes. In 1894, the Ladies' Musical Club took up the challenge of establishing a permanent orchestra for the city. As historian Robert C. Vitz observed, the Club "provided a new network of relationships that in larger part bypassed the male-dominated connections which had entangled previous efforts." Also crucial to the Orchestra's early success was Cincinnati's Woman's Club, established in 1894 as "an organized center of thought and action among women for the promotion of social, educational, literary, and artistic growth."[26]

Both clubs included as members women crucial to the orchestra's success. Mrs. William Howard Taft, Miss Helen Sparrman, and Miss Emma Roedter ensured this success in 1895, when they pooled $15,000 to underwrite the endeavor. A subsequent Committee of Fifteen Women oversaw the orchestra's business. Mrs. Holmes succeeded Mrs. Taft as president of the Cincinnati Symphony Orchestra in 1900; in her thirteen years of service, she helped to establish

a home for the orchestra and introduced conductor Leopold Stokowski to American audiences. Soon after her husband's death in 1920, Mrs. Holmes moved to Long Island and became a leader in New York philanthropic circles. She memorialized her public service to Cincinnati with her donation to the Art Museum's costume collection in 1920 (see pages 49 amd 113).[27]

Many society women were members of the Cincinnati Garden Club. Helen Rentschler Waldon (who died in 1967) was an "ardent booster" of the garden clubs in Hamilton and Cincinnati, and of the Garden Club of America. A native of Hamilton, Ohio, Mrs. Waldon returned to her hometown in 1941, after a period in Detroit. Her husband, Col. Sidney Dunn Waldon, was vice president and general manager of the Packard Motor Car Company. As a reflection of her various domiciles, Mrs. Waldon was also a member of the Colony Club of New York, the Hamilton City Club, and the Bloomfield Hills Country Club in Detroit. She supported the symphony orchestras of Cincinnati, Detroit, Boston, and New York, was a donor and supporter of the Cincinnati Institute of Fine Arts and the Cincinnati Children's Hospital, and helped to facilitate the merger of the Cincinnati Conservatory of Music with the University of Cincinnati (see page 128).[28]

The women's club movement at the turn of the twentieth century strengthened women's influence on each other and made them more aware of their role in preserving the past. Another member of the Garden Club was Elizabeth Wolcott Henry Chatfield, who in 1919 settled in the Queen City with her husband, William Hayden Chatfield. Mrs. Chatfield's experience in the

DETAIL: Dunlevy *Evening Dress*, 1902–1903; 1993.104a,b.

This evening dress, ornamented with sequins and elaborately draped sleeves, was worn by Elizabeth Wright Blake.

Anna Dunlevy (active 1889–1913); *Evening Dress*, 1902–1903; silk, sequins; Label: Dunlevy CINCINNATI, OHIO.; Gift in memory of Elizabeth Blake Shaffer, 1993.104a,b.

Garden Club surely aided her as a founding member of the Cincinnati Nature Center. She also served as a lady manager of the Children's Convalescent Hospital. Through her estate, the Cincinnati Art Museum possesses the dress worn by Mrs. Chatfield's mother-in-law, Mrs. Albert Hayden Chatfield, also an active clubwoman (see page 115, right).[29] Elizabeth Blake Shaffer, another Garden Club member, was also a Progressive clubwoman: a director of the Garden Club of America, president of the Cincinnati Garden Club, and a member of the Cincinnati Art Museum. Miss Shaffer also was a cofounder of the Junior League of Cincinnati. The Junior League was one of the most successful movements arising from women's participation in public life; it developed trained volunteers in response to community needs. One may not think that a community need is met by the donation of historic and artistic artifacts to the city's museums. Yet Miss Shaffer filled such a need when she presented the gown shown on page 185, worn by her great-grandmother, Elizabeth Wright Blake, as a gift to the Cincinnati Art Museum.[30]

The legacy of Cincinnati's women as Progressive "municipal housekeepers," as volunteers, as philanthropists, and as civic and social leaders has yet to be fully chronicled and assessed. Surely, we have learned that a more inclusive history requires consideration of not only elite women but also all women. Society women depended on others so that they could accomplish the work of civic and cultural good. The history of Cincinnati's society women encompasses the history of the dressmakers, as well as women of other professions and trades.

Women themselves have secured this history through their care in preserving their own or their ancestors' clothing. In the absence of the documents and photographs that more often record men's deeds, these gowns chronicle women's work, both philanthropic and productive. In 1986, Mrs. Murat Halstead Davidson, the former Isabella L. Resor, donated some pieces of clothing, including the reception dress opposite, to the Cincinnati Art Museum. Those items had come down to her from her mother, Mrs. Robert L. (Eunice S. Thoms) Resor (1871–1960), and her grandmother, Mrs. Joseph Clark Thoms (1847–1926).

Mrs. Joseph Clark Thoms was born Mary Swift; her father was Briggs Swift, one of the first settlers in Cincinnati. Her husband was a prominent attorney. Mrs. Thoms had owned property in downtown Cincinnati and had aided her husband in managing a large agricultural initiative called Hueston Farm. She also served her community in her own right as a member of the Woman's Club and as one of the directors overseeing relief efforts during the devastating flood of 1913. Her daughter, Mrs. Robert L. Resor, also pursued an active club life as a member of the Cincinnati Country Club and the Queen City Club.[31]

With her simple act of donation, Mrs. Davidson became a historian; the stuff of women's history was preserved. Through the Cincinnati Art Museum's preservation and exhibition of Mrs. Davidson's gift and those of many other donors, the separate sphere of women in Cincinnati's Golden Age—fashionable ladies, clubwomen, and dressmakers alike—may be revealed. The legacy of the arts as applied to industry, a goal central to the members of the Women's Art Museum Association, has come full circle.

Yet the legacy of Cincinnati society

Selina Cadwallader (active 1870–1886); *Evening Bodice,* 1877–1878; silk; Label: S. Cadwallader CINCINNATI OHIO; Gift of Mrs. Murat Halstead Davidson, 1986.1200b,c. (Skirt by Charles Frederick Worth, 1986.1200c.)

women's activities is much greater than the cultural institutions they helped to establish and that its citizens continue to enjoy today. Cincinnati's society women and the clubs they created and joined at the end of the nineteenth century became the crucibles of larger reforms for women and society across the nation in the twentieth century. In creating supportive environments in which women could establish networks, the club movement offered a potent means of reform. Taking more active roles as citizens, indeed, changing the very definition of the word *citizen* by winning the right to vote, American clubwomen helped to recast women's relationships to their homes, cities, states, and the nation. In so doing, they changed the nation's politics by defining as social problems what was once considered "women's work," particularly issues of inequalities in health, education, housing, and the workplace. Cincinnati society women's work represents an important chapter in a larger history of American women and the politics of the nation.

Appendix

DRESSMAKERS' LABELS

BECAUSE MOST ELITE WOMEN patronized more than one dressmaker, labels served as both a form of advertisement and a signature. Those whose businesses lasted more than a few years often revised the design and color scheme of their labels over time. In some cases, a change of address precipitated a new version. In this collection, labels created in the nineteenth century were generally printed directly onto lengths of ribbon that later were sewn into the waist of the bodice and formed the petersham—a 1- to 1¼-inch-wide band serving as an inner belt that hooked at the center front. By the turn of the century, however, dressmakers had begun to utilize woven labels, which were woven directly into the petersham, or as individual labels on continuous lengths of ribbon that were cut apart and sewn to the petersham after the garment was completed. Most labels simply related the dressmaker's last name and the city and state in which she worked, but some included dressmakers' full names and addresses, the names of commercial buildings in which their salons were located, and an indication of the types of garments they designed. Department stores and specialty shops used labels in the same way. Each dressmaker's style and personal flair is evident in the choice of color and design.

1. *Evening Bodice* on pages 87, 187 [1986.1200b]

2. *Evening Dress* on page 94 [1966.1311a,b]

3. *Afternoon Dress* on pages 98, 99 [2000.78a,b]

7. *Evening Dress* on pages 44 right, 113 [1920.123, 124]

4. *Evening Dress* on pages 49 left, 185 [1993.104a,b]

8. *Evening Dress* on page 115 left [1958.51]

5. *Afternoon Dress* on page 103 right [1971.93a,b]

9. *Wedding Dress* on pages 116, 117 [1977.176]

6. *Evening Dress* on pages 108, 109 [1973.587a,b]

10. *Afternoon Dress* on pages 11, 119 [1975.52a,b]

11. *Evening Dress* on page 121 left [1967.113a,b]

15. *Dress* on page 125 [1948.59]

12. *Wedding Dress* on page 121 right [1986.800a,b]

16. *Wedding Dress* on page 126 left [1967.1172]

13. *Evening Dress* on page 122 left [1973.376a,b]

17. *Wedding Dress* on page 126 center [1966.1313a,b]

14. *Evening Dress* on page 124 [1958.45]

18. *Evening Dress* on page 129 [1986.1156]

19. *Evening Coat* on page 132 [2002.25]

22. *Afternoon Dress* on page 151 far left [1969.557a,b]

20. *Evening Dress* on page 133 [1991.123]

23. *Bridesmaid Dress* on page 151 left [1935.161, 162]

21. *Evening Dress* on page 147 [1967.1204]

24. *Evening Dress* on page 155 [1962.583]

25. *Reception Dress* on pages 156, 157 [1996.385a,b]

28. *Suit: Coat and Skirt* on page 161 [1964.243, 244]

26. *Afternoon Dress* on page 159 [1971.151a,b]

29. *Evening Dress* on page 162 [1964.330]

27. *Afternoon Dress* on page 45 [1963.15a,b]

30. *Coat* on page 163 [1971.149]

Notes

DRESSMAKING AS A TRADE
FOR WOMEN

This essay grew out of a conference session held
at the 2001 annual meeting of the Costume
Society of America (CSA), organized by Christina Bates, Ontario Historian at the Canadian
Museum of Civilization. The session was
intended to explore new directions in research
on women in the dressmaking trades. I am
grateful to Christina for involving me in this
exciting discussion, and to copanelists Pamela
Parmal, Glendyne Wergland, and Jan Loverin, as
well as the audience members, for providing a
stimulating discussion. Finally, I thank Cynthia
Amnéus for attending that CSA session and
inviting me to participate in this project.

1   Robert Blair St. George, *The Wrought
    Covenant: Source Material for the Study of
    Craftsmen and Community in Southeastern New
    England, 1620–1700* (Brockton, Mass.:
    Brockton Art Center, 1979), 16.
2   *Book of Trades: or, Library of the Useful Arts*
    (London: Tabart and Co., 1806–1807).
3   Edith Abbot, *Women in Industry: A Study in
    American Economic History* (New York and
    London: D. Appleton and Company, 1915),
    215.
4   See Wendy Gamber, *The Female Economy: The
    Millinery and Dressmaking Trades, 1860–1930*
    (Urbana and Chicago: University of Illinois
    Press, 1997). The museum community has
    been much quicker to recognize this issue
    and address it in interpretive settings. In 1993,
    for example, Historic Northampton (Massa-
    chusetts) mounted *To Sew a Fine Seam:
    Northampton's Dressmakers, 1880–1905,* curated
    by Lynne Z. Bassett. Most recently, the
    Rhode Island School of Design museum
    produced *From Paris to Providence: Fashion, Art
    and the Tirocchi Dressmakers Shop, 1915–1947.*
    Although the exhibit itself has closed, the A.
    & L. Tirocchi Dressmakers Project
    (http://tirocchi.stg.brown.edu/) is still an
    invaluable online resource. In addition, a
    handful of museum sites address women's
    work in the dressmaking trades in their
    ongoing interpretation. The mantua-making
    and millinery shop at Colonial Williamsburg
    remains among the best-researched examples,
    interpreting women's daily artisanal life. In
    regard to the twentieth century, the Lower
    East Side Tenement Museum in Manhattan
    interprets the experience of Nathalie
    Gumpertz, a German Jewish dressmaker of
    the late nineteenth century; see (http://
    www.tenement.org/vt_gumpertz.html).
5   My own study of women's work in the
    clothing trades in rural New England before
    industrialization is tentatively titled "The
    Needle's Eye: Women and Work in the Age of
    Revolution," and is forthcoming from the
    University of Massachusetts Press.
6   Exceptions include the H. F. duPont Win-
    terthur Museum and Colonial Williamsburg.
    On museum collections as sources for
    women's history, see Helen Knibb, "Present

NOTES

But Not Visible: Searching for Women's History in Museum Collections," *Gender and History* 6 (1994): 352–369.

7 Mary C. Beaudry, "Needlewomen of the Spencer-Pierce-Little Farm: An Archaeological Study of the Material Culture of Sewing and Needlework," *Delaware Seminar in American Art, History, and Material Culture* 8 (December 1994), 8, 11.

8 Lynn Y. Weiner, "Women and Work," in *Reclaiming the Past: Landmarks of Women's History* (Bloomington: Indiana University Press, 1992), 199–223, 201.

9 For one discussion of early American houses as work sites, see Marla R. Miller, "Liberty of the House: Work, Space and Gentility in Rural New England" (paper presented at Vernacular Architecture Forum, Duluth, Minnesota, June 2000).

10 Thomas Dublin, *Transforming Women's Work: New England Lives in the Industrial Revolution* (Ithaca: Cornell University Press, 1994).

11 Gloria Main, "Gender, Work and Wages in Colonial New England," *William and Mary Quarterly* 51 (1994): 39–66, esp. 46.

12 U.S. Bureau of the Census, 1900, 1910.

13 L. H. Guernsey diary, Old Sturbridge Village, 1834–1845.

14 Nathaniel Phelps account book, 1730–1747, Pocumtuck Valley Memorial Association.

15 Sylvester Judd, "Northampton." MSS Vol. 1, 244. Forbes Library, Northampton, Mass.

16. Cooke observes this spectrum among woodworkers in Edward Strong Cooke Jr., *Making Furniture in Preindustrial America: The Social Economy of Newtown and Woodbury, Connecticut* (Baltimore: Johns Hopkins University Press), 1996.

INTRODUCTION

1 Gardiner Spring, *The Excellence and Influence of the Female Character: A Sermon* (New York: F. & R. Lockwood, 1825), 4; *Godey's Lady's Book* (March 1854), 273.

2 Barbara J. Berg, *The Remembered Gate: Origins of American Feminism, The Woman & The City 1800–1860* (New York: Oxford University Press, 1978), ch. 5.

3 Thomas Wentworth Higginson, *Women and the Alphabet: A Series of Essays* (Boston and New York: Houghton Mifflin, 1900).

4 *Ladies' Home Journal* (March 1891), 4.

5 Otto Charles Thieme, *With Grace and Favour: Victorian & Edwardian Fashion in America* (Cincinnati: Cincinnati Art Museum, 1993), 27.

6 Lois W. Banner, *American Beauty* (New York: Alfred A. Knopf, 1983), 19.

1 THE IDEOLOGY OF THE SEPARATE SPHERE

1 Nancy E. Owen, *Rookwood and the Industry of Art: Women, Culture, and Commerce, 1880–1913* (Athens: Ohio University Press, 2001), 16.

2 Barbara J. Harris, *Beyond Her Sphere: Women and the Professions in American History* (Westport, Conn. and London: Greenwood Press, 1942), 3.

3 Berg, 23.

4 Nancy F. Cott, *The Bonds of Womanhood: "Women's Sphere" in New England, 1780–1835* (New Haven, Conn. and London: Yale University Press, 1977), 22.

5 Berg, 24.

6 Cott, 41-42.

7 Ibid.

8 Berg, 28.

9 Cott, 24-25, 35.

10 Ibid., 43.

11 Ibid., 59.

12 Ibid., 61-62.

13 Harris, 33, 56.

14 Jane Swisshelm, *Letters to Country Girls* (New York: J. C. Riker, 1853), 9.

15 Harris, 33.

16 Cott, 65-68. Find original in *Godey's Lady's Book.*

17 Berg, 67-69.

18 Barbara Welter, "The Cult of True Womanhood: 1820–1860." *American Quarterly* 18 (1966): 159.

19 Harris, 48.

20 Mrs. A. J. Graves, *Woman in America: Being an Examination into the Moral and Intellectual Condition of American Female Society* (New York: Harper and Brothers, 1855), 155–156.

21 Harris, 51–54.

22 Berg, 78.

23 Graves, 156.

24 Harris, 51.

25 Welter, 163.

26 Berg, 68-69.

27 Ibid., 79.

28 Cott, 71.

29 Berg, 85.

30 Welter, 160–164.

31 *Godey's Lady's Book* (August 1846), 86.

32 T. S. Arthur, "Bear and Forbear," in *The American Keepsake for 1851* (New York: Cornish, Lamport and Company, 1851), 263–264.

33 Berg, 86.

34 Arthur W. Calhoun, *A Social History of the American Family from Colonial Times to the Present*, vol. II (Ohio: Arthur H. Clark Company, 1918), 84.

35 Alexis De Tocqueville. *Democracy in America*, vol. II (Boston: John Allyn, Late Sever, Francis, & Company, 1882), 245–246.

36 Cott, *Root of Bitterness: Documents of the Social History of American Women* (Boston: Northeastern University Press, 1986), 113.

37 Ibid., 78.

38 Berg, 89–92.

39 Cott, *The Bonds of Womanhood*, 82.

40 William Thomas Venner, *Queen City Lady: The 1861 Journal of Amanda Wilson* (Cincinnati, Ohio: Larrea Books, 1996), 26.

41 Cott, *The Bonds of Womanhood,* 82.

42 Berg, 40.

43 Cott, *The Bonds of Womanhood*, 168.

44 Linda K. Kerber, "Separate Spheres, Female Worlds, Woman's Place: The Rhetoric of Women's History," *Journal of American History* 75 (1988): 23.

45 Cott, *The Bonds of Womanhood;* see chapter 5 for a complete discussion of this phenomenon.

46 Harris, 73–74.

47 Ellen Carol Dubois, "Women's Rights Before the Civil War," in *Our American Sisters: Women in American Life and Thought* (Lexington, Mass. and Toronto: D. C. Heath and Company, 1987), 230–231.

48 Eleanor Flexner, *Century of Struggle: The Woman's Rights Movement in the United States* (Cambridge, Mass.: Belknap Press of Harvard University Press, 1975), 88.

49 Estelle Freedman, "Separatism as Strategy: Female Institution Building and American Feminism, 1870–1930," *Feminist Studies* 5 (1979): 516.

50 Charles Darwin, *The Origin of Species by Means of Natural Selection or The Preservation of Favored Races in the Struggle for Life and the Descent of Man and Selection in Relation to Sex* (New York: Modern Library, 1936), 578–585.

51 Rosalind Rosenberg, *Beyond Separate Spheres* (New Haven, Conn. and London: Yale University Press, 1982), xv, 6.

52 Charles E. Rosenberg, *No Other Gods: On Science and American Social Thought* (Baltimore, Md. and London: Johns Hopkins University Press, 1916), 56.

53 Berg, 114.

54 Rosenberg, *Beyond Separate Spheres,* 7–10.

55 Ibid.

56 Sheila M. Rothman, *Woman's Proper Place: A History of Changing Ideals and Practices, 1870 to the Present* (New York: Basic Books, 1978), 98–99.

57 Gerda Lerner, *The Female Experience: An American Documentary* (Indianapolis, Ind.: Bobbs-Merrill Educational Publishing, 1977), 203–204.

58 Rothman, 56.

59 Ibid., 29.

60 Rosenberg, 12.

61 Ibid.

62 Ibid., 13.

63 Ibid., 17.

64 Swisshelm, 78.

65 Rothman, 42–43.

66 Ibid., 64.

67 Rothman, 65; Kerber, 32.

68 Freedman, 517.

2 WOMEN IN THE WORKPLACE

1 Sharlene Hesse-Biber and Gregg Lee Carter, *Working Women in America: Split Dreams* (New York and Oxford: Oxford University Press, 2000), 26–27.

2 Nancy F. Cott, *No Small Courage: A History of Women in the United States* (Oxford and New York: Oxford University Press, 2000), 270.

3 Ibid.

4 Barbara Mayer Wertheimer, *We Were There: The Story of Working Women in America* (New York: Pantheon Books, 1977), 60.

5 Ibid., 91.

6 Cott, *No Small Courage,* 317.

7 Wertheimer, 102–103; Cott, *No Small Courage,* 277.

8 Lyle Koehler, "Women's Rights, Society, and the Schools: Feminist Activities in Cincinnati,

Ohio, 1864–1880," in *Women in Cincinnati: Century of Achievement 1870–1970,* vol. II, (Cincinnati, Oh.: Cincinnati Historical Society, 1984), 4.

9 Cott, *No Small Courage,* 317.

10 Barbara R. Bergmann, *The Economic Emergence of Women* (New York: Basic Books, 1986), 22.

11 Cott, *No Small Courage,* 11.

12 Angel Kwolek-Folland, *Incorporating Women: A History of Women and Business in the United States* (New York: Twayne Publishers, 1998), 93–94.

13 Rothman, 42.

14. Ibid., 42.

15 Alice Kessler-Harris, "Independence and Virtue in the Lives of Wage-Earning Women: The United States, 1870–1930," in *Women in Culture and Politics* (Bloomington: Indiana University Press, 1986), 5–6.

16 Ibid., 9.

17 Ibid., 10.

18 Irene E. Hartt, *How to Make Money Although a Woman* (New York: J. S. Ogilvie Publishing Company, 1895), 104.

19 Ibid., 11.

20 *Ladies' Home Journal* (September 1899), 26; (December 1897), 28; (January 1891), 4.

21 *Harper's Bazar* (October 1890), 804.

22 *Ladies' Home Journal* (December 1897), 28.

23 Ibid. (April 1893), 18.

24 Ibid.

25 Ibid. (September 1897), 14.

26 Ibid.

27 Ibid. (February 1895), 15.

28 Ibid. (April 1895), 15; (May 1895), 15; (June 1895), 15; (July 1895), 15.

29 Ibid. (March 1900), 16.

30 Berg, 98.

31 Mary Kavanaugh Oldham Eagle, *Congress of Women Held in the Women's Building, World's Columbian Exposition, Chicago, U.S.A., 1893* (Chicago: Wabash Publishing House, 1895), 60.

32 Ibid., 61.

33 *Ladies' Home Journal* (July 1892), 6.

34 Ibid.

35 Jeanne Madeline Weimann, *The Fair Women* (Chicago: Academy Chicago, 1981), 277.

36 Marian Shaw, *World's Fair Notes, A Woman Journalist Views Chicago 1893 Columbian Expo-

sition* (Chicago: Pogo Press, 1992), 61.

37 Weimann, 231.

38 Reid Badger, *The Great American Fair, The World's Columbian Exposition & American Culture* (Chicago: Nelson Hall, 1979), 121–122.

39 C. E. Cabot, "The Carters in Early Ohio," *The New England Magazine* 20 (1899): 347–348.

40 Nancy Elizabeth Bertaux, *Women's Work, Men's Work: Occupational Segregation by Sex in Nineteenth Century Cincinnati, Ohio* (Ann Arbor: University of Michigan, 1987), 31–33.

41 Ibid., 33–34.

42 Nancy Elizabeth Bertaux, "'Women's Work' vs. 'Men's Work'" in Nineteenth Century Cincinnati," *Queen City Heritage* 47 (Winter 1989): 18.

43 Ibid., 19.

3 DRESSMAKING AS A TRADE

1 Gamber, 12.

2 Amy Simon, "She Is So Neat and Fits So Well: Garment Construction and the Millinery Business of Eliza Oliver Dodds, 1831–1833" (Ph.D. diss., University of Delaware, 1993), 101.

3 William D. Howells, *Habits of Good Society: A Handbook* (New York: Carleton Publishers, 1865), 195.

4 Roy Devereux, *The Ascent of Woman* (Boston: Roberts Brothers, 1896), 123.

5 Simon, 94.

6 Claudia B. Kidwell and Margaret C. Christman, *Suiting Everyone: The Democratization of Clothing in America* (Washington, D.C.: Smithsonian Institution Press, 1974), 53.

7 *Cincinnati City Directory,* 1825, 82.

8 Kidwell and Christman, *Suiting Everyone,* 137.

9 Claudia B. Kidwell, *Cutting a Fashionable Fit* (Washington, D.C.: Smithsonian Institution Press, 1979), 1.

10 Joan M. Jensen and Sue Davidson, eds., *A Needle, A Bobbin, A Strike: Women Needleworkers in America* (Philadelphia: Temple University Press, 1984), 12.

11 Kidwell and Christman, *Suiting Everyone,* 15.

12 *Ladies' Home Journal* (April 1906), 20.

13 Otto Charles Thieme, *With Grace and Favour: Victorian & Edwardian Fashion in America* (Cincinnati: Cincinnati Art Museum, 1993), 27.

14 *The Ladies Hand-Book of Millinery and Dress-making, with Plain Instructions for Making the Most Useful Articles of Dress and Attire* (New York: J. S. Redfield, Clinton Hall, 1843), 32.

15 Howells, 176–177.

16 *Ladies' Home Journal* (April 1906), 20.

17 S. A. Frost, *Art of Dressing Well: A Complete Guide* (New York: Dick & Fiztgerald, 1870).

18 Kidwell, *Cutting a Fashionable Fit*, 20.

19 Simon, 50–54.

20 A Lady, *The Workwoman's Guide* (London: Sipkin, Marshall, and Company, 1838), 107.

21 Kidwell, *Cutting a Fashionable Fit*, 13.

22 *Godey's Lady's Book* (July 1855), 65.

23 Kidwell, *Cutting a Fashionable Fit*, 16–18.

24 Gamber, 12.

25 Simon, 55–56.

26 Venner.

27 Michelle Oberly, "The Fabric Scrapbooks of Hannah Ditzler Alspaugh," in *With Grace & Favour: Victorian & Edwardian Fashion in America* (Cincinnati: Cincinnati Art Museum, 1993), 4–13.

28 Gamber, 12–13.

29 *Ladies' Home Journal* (March 1891), 4.

30 Helen L. Sumner, *The History of Women in Industry in the United States* (Washington, D.C.: U.S. Government Printing Office, 1910), 117.

31 *Harpers Bazar* (February 15, 1890), 124–125.

32 *Ladies' Home Journal* (March 1891), 4.

33 Gamber, 10.

34 Diana de Marly, *Worth: Father of Haute Couture*, 2d ed. (New York and London: Holmes and Meier, 1990), 41–42.

35 Caroline H. Dall, *"Woman's Right to Labor"; or, Low Wages and Hard Work* (Boston: Walker, Wise, and Company, 1860), 104.

36 Gamber, 18–19.

37 Ibid., 15–17.

38 Ibid., 15.

39 Ibid., 18.

40 Lucy Eldersveld Murphy, "Business Ladies: Midwestern Women and Enterprise, 1850–1880," *Journal of Women's History* 3 (1991): 65.

41 Gamber, 61.

42 Ibid., 39.

43 Ibid., 53.

44 *Demorest's Monthly Magazine* (January 1870), 24.

45 Caroline H. Woods [Belle Otis], *The Diary of a Milliner* (New York: Hurd and Houghton, 1867), 1, 3, 5.

46 Gamber, 46–52.

47 Murphy, 75.

48 *Ladies' Home Journal* (June 1887), 2.

49 Gamber, 46.

50 Susan Hay, "A. & L. Tirocchi: A Time Capsule Discovered," in *From Paris to Providence: Fashion, Art, and the Tirocchi Dressmakers' Shop, 1915–1947* (Providence: Rhode Island School of Design, 2000), 15.

51 Gamber, 80.

52 *Demorest's Monthly Magazine* (January 1870), 24.

53 *Ladies' Home Journal* (March 1891), 4.

54 Gamber, 74.

55 Amelia Des Moulins, "The Dressmaker's Life Story," *Independent* 56 (1904): 944.

56 Pamela A. Parmal, "Line, Color, Detail, Distinction, Individuality: A. L. Tirocchi, Providence Dressmakers," in *From Paris to Providence: Fashion, Art, and the Tirocchi Dressmakers' Shop, 1915–1947* (Providence: Rhode Island School of Design, 2000), 29–30.

57 Gamber, 100.

58 Ibid., 57.

59 Ibid., 59.

60 Ibid., 84–85.

61 Ibid., 81.

62 Christie Daily, "A Woman's Concern: Millinery in Central Iowa, 1870–1880," *Journal of the West* 21 (1982): 31.

63 Sallye Clark, "Carrie Taylor: Kentucky Dressmaker," *DRESS: The Journal of the Costume Society of America* 5 (1980): 15.

64 Gamber, 102–103.

65 Ibid., 105; Hay, 13.

66 Gamber, 106–107.

67 Susan Porter Benson, "Clients and Craftswomen: The Pursuit of Elegance," in *From Paris to Providence: Fashion, Art, and the Tirocchi Dressmakers' Shop, 1915–1947* (Providence: Rhode Island School of Design, 2000), 63–64.

68 Clark, 19.

69 Parmal, 29.

70 Benson, 61–63.

71 Des Moulins, 945.

72 *Ladies' Home Journal* (December 1887), 3; (April 1887), 16; (February 1898), 22.

73 Ibid. (February 1898), 22.

74 Ibid. (October 1907), 38.

75 Howells, 180–181.

76 Benson, 64.

77 Clark, 21.

78 *Ladies' Home Journal* (March 1891), 4.

79 Justin G. Turner and Linda Levitt Turner, *Mary Todd Lincoln: Her Life and Letters* (New York: Alfred A. Knopf, 1972), 115.

80 Murphy, 164.

81 *Ladies' Home Journal* (June 1901), 14.

82 Benson, 65.

83 *Ladies' Home Journal* (June 1901), 14.

84 Gamber, 119–120.

4 CINCINNATI: A HISTORICAL PERSPECTIVE

1 Clara Longworth De Chambrun, *Cincinnati: Story of The Queen City* (New York and London: Charles Scribner's Sons, 1967), 42.

2 *Cincinnati: 200 Years in Photos and Words,* (Cincinnati, Ohio: *Cincinnati Magazine,* 1988), 201; Daniel Hurley, *Cincinnati: The Queen City* (Cincinnati: Cincinnati Historical Society, 1982), 209.

3 Hurley, 33.

4 Charles Cist, *Sketches and Statistics of Cincinnati in 1859* (Cincinnati: n.p., 1859), 341; Bertaux, 13.

5 Charles Cist, *Cincinnati in 1851* (Cincinnati: William H. Moore and Company, 1851), 257.

6 Hurley, 56–57.

7 Sidney D. Maxwell, *Suburbs of Cincinnati* (New York: Arno Press, 1974), 2.

8 Ibid., 9–10.

9 "Cincinnati: 200 Years in Photos and Words," *Cincinnati Magazine* (1988), 94.

10 Hurley, 86.

11 A. O. Kraemer, *Kraemer's Picturesque Cincinnati* (Cincinnati: A. O. & G. A. Kraemer, 1898), 9.

12 Owen, 2.

13 Ibid., 1.

5 CINCINNATI'S DRESSMAKERS

1 De Chambrun, 134.

2 Ibid., 135–136.

3 Alvin F. Harlow, *The Serene Cincinnatians* (New York: E. P. Dutton & Company, 1950), 160.

4 Timothy Flint, ed., *Travellers in America* (New York: The Knickerbocker 2, 1833), 289–291.

5 Lois W. Banner, *American Beauty* (New York: Alfred A. Knopf, 1983), 18; John Robert

Godley, *Letters from America* (London: John Murray, 1844), 44.

6 Banner, 19–22.

7 Ibid.

8 *Ladies' Home Journal* (June 1901), 15.

9 Eliza Potter, *A Hairdresser's Experience in High Life* (New York and Oxford: Oxford University Press, 1991), 62.

10 Ibid., 276–277.

11 Ibid., 61–62.

12 *Vogue* (October 15, 1917), 35–36.

13 Graydon DeCamp, *The Grand Old Lady of Vine Street* (Cincinnati: The Merten Company, 1991), 83–86.

14 Gamber, 98.

15 *Ohio,* vol. 83, R. G. Dun & Company Collection, Baker Library, Harvard Business School.

16 *Ohio,* vol. 86, R. G. Dun & Company Collection, Baker Library, Harvard Business School; John J. McCusker, *How Much Is That in Real Money?: An Historical Commodity Price Index for Use as a Deflator of Money Values in the Economy of the United States* (Worcester, Mass.: American Antiquarian Society, 2001), 31, 56, 59.

17 *Ohio,* vol. 86, R. G. Dun & Company Collection, Baker Library, Harvard Business School.

18 Patricia Cunningham, "Healthful, Artistic, and Correct Dress," in *With Grace & Favour: Victorian & Edwardian Fashion in America* (Cincinnati: Cincinnati Art Museum, 1993), 25.

19 *Ohio,* vol. 89, R. G. Dun & Company Collection, Baker Library, Harvard Business School.

20 Ibid.

21 Ibid.

22 Interview with Mamie McFaddin Ward by June Smith for the *Beaumont Enterprise and Journal,* August 2, 1974.

23 Thieme, 79.

24 *Ohio,* vol. 89, R. G. Dun & Company Collection, Baker Library, Harvard Business School.

25 Ibid.

26 Ibid.

27 Jacqueline Field, "Dyes and Supplies: The Influence of World War I on Silk Fabrics and Fashions," *Dress* 28 (2001): 77–91.

28 Interview with Bettie McKeon by Otto Charles Thieme, August 19, 1991.

6 READY-MADE GARMENTS AND THE RISE OF THE DEPARTMENT STORE

1 Gamber, 227.

2 Kidwell and Christman, 137.

3 Gamber, 227.

4 Kidwell and Christman, 165–167.

5 Ibid., 15.

6 Ibid., 137.

7 Jessica Daves, *Ready-Made Miracle: The American Story of Fashion for the Millions* (New York: G. P. Putnam's Sons, 1967), 29–31.

8 Frances Trollope, *Domestic Manners of the Americans* (New York: Vintage Books, a Division of Random House, 1949), xl–xlv.

9 Banner, 32–33.

10 Kidwell and Christman, 157.

11 Banner, 34.

12 Gamber, 193–195.

13 Daves, 31, 34.

14 Gamber, 201–203.

15 Ibid., 201, 203.

16 Ibid., 201.

17 Ibid., 195.

18 Ibid., 196–197.

19 *Ladies' Home Journal* (August 1908), 8, 38.

20 Rev. Charles Frederic Goss, *Cincinnati: The Queen City, 1788–1912* (Chicago and Cincinnati: S. J. Clarke Publishing Company, 1912), 608.

21 *Cincinnati Enquirer* (February 13, 1950), 4.

22 *Ohio,* vol. 79, R. G. Dun & Company Collection, Baker Library, Harvard Business School.

23 Ibid., vol. 89.

24 Ibid., vol. 80.

25 Goss, 44.

26 John William Leonard, *The Centennial Review of Cincinnati: One Hundred Years of Progress in Commerce, Manufactures, the Professions, and in Social and Municipal Life* (Cincinnati: J. M. Elstner, 1888), 111.

27 *The Week* (September 1, 1883), 16.

28 William Leach, *Land of Desire: Merchants, Power, and the Rise of a New American Culture* (New York: Pantheon Books, 1993), 92.

29 Gamber, 227–228.

CONCLUSION

1 Gamber, 230.

2 Claudia L. Bushman, *A Good Poor Man's Wife: Being a Chronicle of Harriet Hanson Robinson and Her Family in Nineteenth-Century New England* (Hanover: New Hampshire and London: University Press of New England, 1981), 21.

3 Gamber, 232.

THE 1870S TRANSFORMATION OF THE *Robe de Chambre*

1 Maureen E. Montgomery, *Displaying Women: Spectacles of Leisure in Edith Wharton's New York* (New York: Routledge, 1998), 43.

2 In addition to their prolonged use in the West, *robes de chambre* have been linked periodically since the seventeenth century to Japanese kimonos and their Indian imitations marketed by the Dutch. Aesthetically transformed by Indian interpretation and techniques, these garments were called *banyans* in Great Britain and *indiennes* in France. See Akiko Fukai, "Le japonisme dans la mode," in *Japonisme & mode* (Paris: Musée de la mode et du costume, 1996), 22; François Boucher, *Histoire du costume en Occident de l'antiquité à nos jours* (Paris: Flammarion, 1965; reprint 1983), 282; La Hougue de Bruignac, "Les indiennes: origine et diffusion," in *Touches d'exotisme; XIVe–XXe siècle* (Paris: Union centrale des arts décoratifs, Musée de la mode et du textile, 1977), 4; Edward F. Maeder, "A Man's Banyan: High Fashion in Rural Massachusetts," *Historic Deerfield Magazine* (winter 2001): 1.

3 The last three decades of the nineteenth century witnessed the propagation of etiquette books aimed at a wide variety of individuals and social classes. See John F. Kasson, *Rudeness and Civility: Manners in Nineteenth-Century America* (New York: Hill and Wang, 1990), 5.

4 Ibid., 176, 196.

5 Florence Howe Hall, *Social Customs* (Boston: Estes and Lauriat, 1887), 121.

6 Ibid., 120.

7 Kasson, 176.

8 Rodris Roth, "Tea-Drinking in Eighteenth-Century America: Its Etiquette and Equipage," in Robert Blair St. George, ed., *Material Life in America, 1600–1860* (Boston: Northeastern University Press, 1988), 439.

9 Fanny Douglas, *The Gentlewoman's Book of Dress* n.p., 51; Mrs. Burton Kingsland, "A Talk about Teas," *Ladies Home Journal* (October

1892), 4; Sybil deLancey, "La Mode et les Modes," *Les Modes* 2 (février 1901): 10; see Hall, 124.

10 Florence Howe Hall (p. 121) stated that afternoon teas were revived in England about twenty years before the publication of her etiquette manual, dated 1887.

11 "The real truth of the matter is, that our ancestresses wore these shapeless and senseless garments because *they knew no better* [author's emphasis]. They did not know how to cut out a jacket then; it is the product of the highest civilization, and we should be thankful for it" (Douglas, 8–9).

12 "Dress and Fashion: Description of Illustrations," *The Queen, The Ladies' Newspaper.* Vol. 63, no. 1653 (April 27, 1878), 308-309.

13 Although attendance by gender changed significantly in the nineteenth century, teatime still could be a mixed-gender event. See the 1888 descriptions of debutantes' teas in Montgomery, 49; Hall, 126; Kingsland, 4; "Un Five O'clock Chez Madame ch. de Lassence," in Henry Spont, "Sports d'hiver: la saison à Pau," *Les Modes* 15 (mars 1902):7.

"A KIND OF MISSIONARY WORK": THE LABOR AND LEGACY OF CINCINNATI'S SOCIETY WOMEN, 1877-1922

I thank Cynthia Amnéus for this opportunity to explore the history of the women who helped create Cincinnati, and Marjorie Clayman for her able assistance in researching this essay.

1 Robert C. Vitz, *The Queen & the Arts: Cultural Life in Nineteenth-Century Cincinnati* (Kent, Ohio and London: Kent State University Press, 1855), chap. 9, esp. 218, 221.

2 *The Ladies, God Bless 'Em: The Women's Art Movement in Cincinnati in the Nineteenth Century* (Cincinnati: Cincinnati Art Museum, 1976), 7–9; letter, E. W. Perry to John Bennett, October 11, 1878, quoted in *The Ladies, God Bless 'Em,* 65.

3 As quoted in *Art Palace of the West: A Centennial Tribute, 1881–1981* (Cincinnati: Cincinnati Art Museum, 1981), 26–27.

4 *The Ladies, God Bless 'Em,* 9; *Art Palace of the West,* 31.

5 As quoted in *Art Palace of the West,* 19. From George Ward Nichols, *Art Education Applied to Industry* (New York: Funk and Wagnalls, 1922). On the Aesthetic Reform movement in the United States, see *The Ladies, God Bless 'Em;* Wendy Kaplan, *"The Art That Is Life:" The Arts & Crafts Movement in America, 1875–1920* (Boston: Bullfinch Press, 1987); T. J. Jackson Lears, *No Place of Grace: Antimodernism and the Transformation of American Culture, 1880–1920* (New York: Pantheon, 1981); Mary Warner Blanchard, *Oscar Wilde's America: Counterculture in the Gilded Age* (New Haven, Conn.: Yale University Press, 1988)

6 See, for example, Charles Theodore Greve, *Centennial History of Cincinnati and Representative Citizens* (Chicago: Biographical Publishing Company, 1904); *History of Cincinnati and Hamilton County, Ohio: Their Past and Present, Including . . . Biographies and Portraits of Pioneers and Representative Citizens, Etc.* (Cincinnati: S. B. Nelson and Company, 1894); and Benjamin LaBree, ed., *Notable Men of Cincinnati at the Beginning of the 20th Century* (Louisville, Ky.: George G. Fetter Co., 1904). In *Cincinnati, The Queen City,* the Rev. Charles Frederic Goss dedicated a substantial portion of a chapter titled "Potpourri" (vol. I, 359–86) to women's activities. Even so, the lack of integration of women's lives and work into the city's history is telling.

7 Cincinnati women had successfully organized and executed the Great Western Fair (1863–1864) as part of the United States Sanitary Commission's efforts to fund sorely needed supplies and supervision for army camps, military hospitals, and prisons. This appearance of women in the municipal, state, and national arenas is mentioned in passing in Louis Leonard Tucker, *Cincinnati During the Civil War* (Columbus: Ohio State University Press for the Ohio Historical Society, 1962), 24–26; and in Harlow, 236.

8 Since the 1970s and 1980s, historians (primarily women) have restored Cincinnati women's history: see, for example, Carol Jean Blum, "Women's Culture and Urban Culture: Cincinnati's Benevolent Women's Activities and the Invention of the 'New Woman,' 1815–1895," (Ph.D. diss., University of Cincinnati, 1987) and Dottie Lewis, ed., *Women in Cincinnati: Century of Achievement, 1870–1970* (Cincinnati: Center for Women's

Studies, University of Cincinnati, 1984–1985). For an overview of the difficulties of creating American women's history, see Kerber, 3–39.

9 Thorstein Veblen, *The Theory of the Leisure Class: An Economic Study of Institutions* (New York: Macmillan, 1899); Mary P. Ryan, "Gender and Public Access: Women's Politics in Nineteenth-Century America," in *Habermas and the Public Sphere* (New York: New Viewpoints, 1975); Ryan, *Womanhood in America from Colonial Times to the Present* (New York: New Viewpoints, 1975), 193–248; Montgomery, 143 and chap. 6.

10 Montgomery, chap. 6; *Mrs. Devereux's Blue Book of Cincinnati Society . . . for the Years 1906–7* (Cincinnati: Robert Clarke Company and Author, 1906), 213 and various years; *Social Register,* Cincinnati & Dayton, various years; DeCamp, 87; Harlow, chap. 21.

11 Veblen, chap. 7, 179, 171, 172, 179, 180.

12 Ibid., 171.

13 "Mrs. Mary Emery Passes Away Peacefully; Cincinnati's Most Revered Philanthropist; Built Mariemont, 'City of Contentment,'" *Cincinnati Enquirer* (October 12, 1927), 1, 3; Harlow, 397–399; "Mrs. Emery Gives $300,000 to House Museum Collection, Club Members Learn on Trip," *Cincinnati Enquirer* (May 30, 1925), 10; "Better Citizenry Is Object of Memorial Trusteeship Formed by Mrs. Mary Emery," *Cincinnati Enquirer* (April 27, 1925), 1, 5.

14 "Better Citizenry Is Object of Memorial Trusteeship," 1; "Mrs. Mary Emery Passes Away Peacefully," 3.

15 On calling, see Kenneth L. Ames, *Death in the Dining Room and Other Tales of Victorian Culture* (Philadelphia: Temple University Press, 1992), chap. 1.

16 Accession files 1963.542 (Nannie R. Maeder); 1986.1200 (Mary S. Thoms), Cincinnati Art Museum.

17 Emily Post, *Etiquette: The Blue Book of Social Usage* (New York: Funk and Wagnalls, 1922). For a history of etiquette books consult Arthur M. Schlesinger, *Learning How to Behave: A Historical Study of American Etiquette Books* (New York: Macmillan Company, 1946).

18 *Alumni Biographical Register, 1871–1935* (Northampton, Mass.: Smith College, 1936);

accession file 1991.123 (Hannah Taylor Shipley Goodyear), Cincinnati Art Museum; "Shirley Kemper, of Settler's Family," *Cincinnati Enquirer* (March 24, 1978), D-12; accession file 1967.1204 (Shirley Kemper), Cincinnati Art Museum.

19 Accession file 1967.440, Cincinnati Art Museum; "Mrs. Jean Strader, of Pioneer Family," *Cincinnati Enquirer* (October 14, 1959), 2C; "Whiteman E. Smith Dies," *Cincinnati Enquirer* (March 25, 1919), 7.

20 Accession files 1969.533 (Ruth Grossman Schild); 1986.116 (Bessie Louise Bradley Goble Sr.); 1966.1313 (Marjory Langdon Wright), Cincinnati Art Museum.

21 Alexis de Tocqueville, *Democracy in America,* trans. Henry Reeve (Boston: John Allyn, 1862), vol. 2, sec. 2, chap. 5.

22 Karen J. Blair, *The Clubwoman as Feminist: True Womanhood Redefined, 1868–1914* (New York: Holmes and Meier Publishers, 1980), 117–19.

23 Luke Feck, "Yesterday's Cincinnati," in Writer's Digest Books, (Cincinnati: F&W Publications, 1975), 70; Zane L. Miller, *Visions of Place: The City, Neighborhoods, Suburbs, and Cincinnati's Clifton, 1850–2000* (Columbus: Ohio State University Press, 2001), chap. 1.

24 "Mrs. Henry Pogue Expires; Widow of Noted Merchant," *Cincinnati Enquirer* (December 31, 1934), 1; accession file 1966.1243, Cincinnati Art Museum.

25 "Patron of Music Dies at 70," *Cincinnati Enquirer* (September 30, 1941), 15; "To Bury Mrs. C. R. Holmes in Spring Grove Today," *Cincinnati Enquirer* (October 2, 1941), 10; "Active Life of Physician Ends: Major C. R. Holmes Dies After Long Illness," *Cincinnati Enquirer* (January 10, 1920), 16.

26 Mrs. Holmes is listed as an associate member in the Ladies' Musical Club annual programs (Season 1895–96, Season 1896–97, and Season 1897–98); Vitz, 126; Goss, vol. I, 372, 374–375; Goss, vol. II, chap. 21, enumerates the various clubs and societies.

27 Vitz, 125–130; Harlow, 347–349; accession file 1920.123, 124, Cincinnati Art Museum.

28 "Helen Rentschler Waldon Dies; Widely-Known Hamilton Native," *Cincinnati Enquirer* (September 12, 1967), 18; "Col. Sidney D. Waldon Dies; Developer of Liberty Motor,"

Cincinnati Enquirer (January 21, 1945), 1.

29 "Elizabeth Chatfield, Charity, Civic Leader," *Cincinnati Enquirer* (July 18, 1973), 11.

30 Accession file 1993.104, Cincinnati Art Museum; Sharon Morgan, "Elizabeth Shaffer: She Helped Found Junior League," *Cincinnati Enquirer* (March 7, 1993), B7.

31 Accession files 1986.1200, 1986.1156, Cincinnati Art Museum; "Editor's Grandson, Murat H. Davidson," *Cincinnati Enquirer* (March 13, 1965), 8; "Mrs. Mary Swift Thoms," *Cincinnati Enquirer* (October 23, 1936), 7; *Mrs. Devereux's Blue Book, 1906–7,* 229; "Mrs. R. L. Resor," *Cincinnati Enquirer* (September 2, 1960), 11.

Bibliography

A Lady. *The Workwoman's Guide*. London: Sipkin, Marshall and Company, 1838.

Abbot, Edith. *Women in Industry: A Study in American Economic History*. New York and London: D. Appleton and Company, 1910, 1918.

Allinson, May. *Dressmaking as a Trade for Women in Massachusetts*. Washington, D.C.: U.S. Bureau of Labor Statistics, 1916.

Alumni Biographical Register, 1871–1935. Northampton, Mass.: Smith College, 1936.

Ames, Kenneth L. *Death in the Dining Room and Other Tales of Victorian Culture*. Philadelphia: Temple University Press, 1992.

Art Palace of the West: A Centennial Tribute, 1881–1981. Cincinnati: Cincinnati Art Museum, 1981.

Arthur, T. S. "Bear and Forbear." In *The American Keepsake for 1851*. New York: Cornish, Lamport and Company, 1851.

Austerlitz, E. H. *Cincinnati from 1800 to 1875 with Exposition Guide for 1875*. Cincinnati: Bloch and Company, 1875.

Badger, Reid. *The Great American Fair, The World's Columbian Exposition and American Culture*. Chicago: Nelson Hall, 1979.

Banner, Lois W. *American Beauty*. New York: Alfred A. Knopf, 1983.

Beaudry, Mary C. "Needlewomen of the Spencer-Pierce-Little Farm: An Archaeological Study of the Material Culture of Sewing and Needlework." Paper presented at the Delaware Seminar in American Art, History, and Material Culture, n.p., 8 December 1994.

Benson, Susan Porter. "The Customers Ain't God: The Work Culture of Department-Store Saleswomen, 1890–1940." *Working-Class America: Essays on Labor, Community, and American Society*. Urbana, Chicago, and London: University of Illinois Press, 1983.

———. "Clients and Craftswomen: The Pursuit of Elegance." In *From Paris to Providence: Fashion, Art, and the Tirocchi Dressmakers' Shop, 1915–1947*. Providence: Rhode Island School of Design, 2000.

Berg, Barbara J. *The Remembered Gate: Origins of American Feminism, the Woman and the City 1800–1860*. New York: Oxford University Press, 1978.

Bergmann, Barbara R. *The Economic Emergence of Women*. New York: Basic Books, 1986.

Bertaux, Nancy Elizabeth. *Women's Work, Men's Work: Occupational Segregation by Sex in Nineteenth Century Cincinnati, Ohio*. Ann Arbor: University of Michigan Press, 1987.

———. "'Women's Work' vs. 'Men's Work' in Nineteenth Century Cincinnati." *Queen City Heritage* 47, no. 4 (1989): 17–31.

Blair, Karen J. *The Clubwoman as Feminist: True Womanhood Redefined, 1868–1914*. New York: Holmes and Meier Publishers, 1980.

Blanchard, Mary Warner. *Oscar Wilde's America: Counterculture in the Gilded Age*. New Haven, Conn.: Yale University Press, 1998.

Blewett, Mary H. *We Will Rise in Our Might: Working Women's Voices from Nineteenth-Century New England*. Ithaca, N.Y. and London: Cornell University Press, 1991.

Blum, Carol Jean. "Women's Culture and Urban

Culture: Cincinnati's Benevolent Women's Activities and the Invention of the 'New Woman,' 1815–1895." Ph.D. dissertation, University of Cincinnati, 1987.

Book of Trades: Or, Library of the Useful Arts. London: Tabart and Company, 1806–1807.

Boucher, François. *Histoire du Costume en Occident de l'Antiquité à nos Jours.* Paris: Flammarion, 1965; reprint 1983.

Brew, Margaret Louise. *American Clothing Consumption, 1879–1909.* Chicago: University of Chicago Press, 1945.

Broughton, Catherine. *Suggestions for Dressmakers.* N.p., 1896.

Brown, F. W. *Cincinnati and Vicinity with Map and Illustrations.* Cincinnati: C. J. Krehbiel and Company, 1898.

Bryner, Edna. *Dressmaking and Millinery.* Cleveland: Survey Committee of the Cleveland Foundation, 1916.

Bushman, Claudia L. *A Good Poor Man's Wife: Being a Chronicle of Harriet Hanson Robinson and Her Family in Nineteenth-Century New England.* Hanover, New Hampshire and London: University Press of New England, 1981.

Cabot, C. E. "The Carters in Early Ohio." *The New England Magazine* 20, no. 3 (May 1899) 344–351.

Calhoun, Arthur W. *A Social History of the American Family from Colonial Times to the Present,* vol. II. Cleveland, Ohio: Arthur H. Clark Company, 1917–1919.

"The Changing Face of Fountain Square." *Cincinnati Historical Society Bulletin* 27, no. 8 (fall 1969): 239–241.

Cincinnati: 200 Years in Photos and Words. Cincinnati: *Cincinnati Magazine,* 1988.

Cincinnati Society Address Book. Cincinnati and Buffalo: Dau Publishing Company, 1898.

Cincinnati, the Queen City. Cincinnati: The Cuvier Press Club, 1914.

Cist, Charles. *Cincinnati in 1851.* Cincinnati: William H. Moore and Company, 1851.

———. *Sketches and Statistics of Cincinnati in 1859.* Cincinnati: n.p., 1859.

———. *Cincinnati Miscellany, Antiquities of the West.* Cincinnati: Caleb Clark, 1845.

Clark, Sallye. "Carrie Taylor: Kentucky Dressmaker." *DRESS: The Journal of the Costume Society of America* 5 (1980): 13–23.

Cogan, Frances B. *All-American Girl: The Ideal of Real Womanhood in Mid-Nineteenth-Century America.* Athens: University of Georgia Press, 1989.

Cooke, Edward Strong Jr. *Making Furniture in Preindustrial America: The Social Economy of Newtown and Woodbury, Connecticut.* Baltimore: Johns Hopkins University Press, 1996.

Cott, Nancy F., ed. *The Bonds of Womanhood: "Women's Sphere" in New England, 1780–1835.* New Haven, Conn. and London: Yale University Press, 1977.

———. *No Small Courage: A History of Women in the United States.* Oxford and New York: Oxford University Press, 2000.

———. *Root of Bitterness: Documents of the Social History of American Women.* Boston: Northeastern University Press, 1986.

Cott, Nancy F., and Elizabeth H. Pleck, eds. *A Heritage of Her Own: Toward a New Social History of American Women.* New York: Simon and Schuster, 1979.

Cummins, Virginia. *Hamilton County Ohio: Court and Other Records,* vol. III. Cincinnati: General Printing Company, 1966–1969.

Cunningham, Patricia. "Healthful, Artistic, and Correct Dress." In *With Grace & Favour: Victorian & Edwardian Fashion in America.* Cincinnati: Cincinnati Art Museum, 1993.

Daily, Christie. "A Woman's Concern: Millinery in Central Iowa, 1870–1880." *Journal of the West* 21 (1982): 26–32.

Dall, Caroline H. "'Woman's Right to Labor'; or, Low Wages And Hard Work: In Three Lectures." Delivered in Boston, November, 1859.

Darwin, Charles. *The Origin of Species by Means of Natural Selection or the Preservation of Favored Races in the Struggle for Lie* and *The Descent of Man and Selection in Relation to Sex.* New York: Modern Library, 1936.

Dau's Blue Book of Selected Names of Cincinnati And Suburban Towns. New York: Dau Publishing Company, 1904.

Daves, Jessica. *Ready-Made Miracle: The American Story of Fashion for the Millions.* New York: G. P. Putnam's Sons, 1967.

de Aguirre, Gertrude G. *Women in the Business World.* Boston: Arena Publishing Company, 1894.

de Bruignac, La Hougue, "Les Indiennes: Origine et Diffusion." *Touches d'Exotisme; XIVe–XXe Siècle.* Paris: Union Centrale des Arts Décoratifs, Musée de la Mode et du Textile, 1977.

DeCamp, Graydon. *The Grand Old Lady of Vine Street*. Cincinnati: Merten Company, 1991.

De Chambrun, Clara Longworth. *Cincinnati: Story of the Queen City*. New York, London: Charles Scribner's Sons, 1939.

de Lancey, Sybil. "La Mode et les Modes," *Les Modes* 2 (février 10, 1901): 10–19.

de Marly, Diana. *Worth: Father of Haute Couture*, 2d ed. New York and London: Holmes and Meier, 1990.

Des Moulins, Amelia. "The Dressmaker's Life Story." *Independent* 56 (April 28, 1904): 936–939.

De Tocqueville, Alexis. *Democracy In America*. Boston: John Allyn, 1862.

Devereux, Clara Anna Rich. *Mrs. Devereux's Blue Book of Cincinnati: A Society Register and Convenient Reference Book*. Cincinnati: Author, 1896.

———. *Mrs. Devereux's Blue Book of Cincinnati Society . . . for the Years 1906–07*. Cincinnati: Robert Clarke Company and Author, 1906.

———. *Mrs. Devereux's Blue Book of Cincinnati Society . . . for the Years 1912–13*. Cincinnati: Author, 1914.

———. *Mrs. Devereux's Blue Book of Cincinnati Society . . . for the Years 1919–20*. Cincinnati: Author, 1919–1920.

———. *Mrs. Devereux's Blue Book of Cincinnati Society . . . for the Years 1921–22*. Cincinnati: Author, 1921–1922.

Devereux, Roy. *The Ascent of Woman*. Boston: Roberts Brothers, 1896.

Douglas, Fanny. *The Gentlewoman's Book of Dress*. N.p., n.d.

Dublin, Thomas. *Transforming Women's Work: New England Lives in the Industrial Revolution* (Ithaca: Cornell University Press, 1994).

Dubois, Ellen Carol. "Women's Rights Before the Civil War." In *Our American Sisters: Women in American Life and Thought*. Lexington, Mass. and Toronto: D.C. Heath and Company, 1987.

Eagle, Mary Kavanaugh Oldham. *Congress of Women Held in the Women's Building, World's Columbian Expostion, Chicago, U.S.A., 1893*. Chicago: Wabash Publishing House, 1895.

Ellis, Anita. *Rookwood Pottery: The Glorious Gamble*. New York: Rizzoli, 1992.

Feck, Luke. "Yesterday's Cincinnati." In *Writer's Digest Books*. Cincinnati: F&W Publications, 1975.

———. *Yesterday's Cincinnati*. Miami: E. A. Seeman, Publisher, 1975.

Field, Jacqueline. "Dyes and Supplies: The Influence of World War I on Silk Fabrics and Fashions." *Dress* 28 (2001): 77–91.

Flexner, Eleanor. *Century of Struggle: The Woman's Rights Movement in the United States*. Rev. ed. Cambridge, Mass.: Belknap Press of Harvard University Press, 1975.

Flint, Timothy, ed. "Travellers in America." *The Knickerbocker* 2, no. 4 (October 1833): 283–301.

Frank, Leonie C. *Musical Life in Early Cincinnati and the Origin of the May Festival*. Cincinnati, Ohio: Ruter Press, 1932.

Freedman, Estelle. "Separatism as Strategy: Female Institution Building and American Feminism, 1870–1930." *Feminist Studies* 5, no. 1 (1979): 512–529.

Frost, S. A. *Art of Dressing Well: A Complete Guide*. New York: Dick and Fitzgerald, 1870.

Fukai, Akiko. "Le Japonisme dans la Mode." In *Japonisme & Mode*. Paris: Musée de la Mode et du Costume, 1996.

Gamber, Wendy. *The Female Economy: The Millinery and Dressmaking Trades 1860–1930*. Urbana and Chicago: University of Illinois Press, 1997.

Gilman, Amy. "Cogs to the Wheels: The Ideology of Women's Work in Mid-Nineteenth-Century Fiction." *Science and Society* 47 (1983–84): 178–204.

Godley, John Robert. *Letters from America,* vol. 1. London: John Murray, Albemarle Street, 1844.

Goshkin, Ira and Wertheimer, Ellen. *We Were There: The Story of Working Women in America*. New York: Pantheon Books, 1977.

Goss, Rev. Charles Frederic. *Cincinnati: The Queen City, 1788–1912*. Chicago and Cincinnati: S. J. Clarke Publishing Company, 1912.

Graves, Mrs. A. J. *Woman in America: Being an Examination into the Moral and Intellectual Condition of American Female Society*. New York: Harper and Brothers, 1855.

Greve, Charles Theodore. *Centennial History of Cincinnati and Representative Citizens*. Chicago: Biographical Publishing Company, 1904.

Guernsey, L. H. Diary, Old Sturbridge Village, 1834–1845.

Hall, Florence Howe. *Social Customs*. Boston: Estes and Lauriat, 1887.

Harlow, Alvin F. *The Serene Cincinnatians*. New York: E. P. Dutton and Company, 1950.

Harris, Barbara J. *Beyond Her Sphere: Women and the Professions in American History*. Westport, Conn. and London: Greenwood Press, 1942.

Hartt, Irene E. *How to Make Money Although a Woman*. New York: J. S. Ogilvie Publishing Company, 1895.

Hay, Susan. "A. & L. Tirocchi: A Time Capsule Discovered." In *From Paris to Providence: Fashion, Art, and the Tirocchi Dressmakers' Shop, 1915–1947*, Providence: Rhode Island School of Design, 2000.

Hays, Elinor Rice. *Morning Star: A Biography of Lucy Stone 1818–1893*. New York: Octagon Books, 1978.

Herbert, Jeffrey G. *Restored Hamilton County Ohio Marriages 1860–1869*. Bowie, Md.: Heritage Books, 1996.

Hesse-Biber, Sharlene, and Gregg Lee Carter. *Working Women in America: Split Dreams*. New York and Oxford: Oxford University Press, 2000.

Hicks, Mrs. Rebecca. *The Milliner and the Millionaire*. Pennsylvania: Lippincott, Grambo and Company, 1852.

Higginson, Thomas Wentworth. *Women and the Alphabet: A Series of Essays*. Boston and New York: Houghton Mifflin, 1900.

Hill, Joseph A. *Women in Gainful Occupations*. Washington, D.C.: U.S. Government Printing Office, 1929.

History of Cincinnati and Hamilton County, Ohio; Their Past and Present, Including . . . Biographies and Portraits of Pioneers and Representative Citizens, Etc. Cincinnati: S. B. Nelson and Company, 1894.

Howells, William Dean. *Habits of Good Society: A Handbook*. New York: Carleton Publishers, 1865.

———. *A Woman's Reason*. Boston: James R. Osgood and Company, 1882.

Huenefeld, Catherine, ed. *A Centennial Review: The First Hundred Years of the Cincinnati Woman's Club, 1894–1994*. Cincinnati: Cincinnati Woman's Club, 1994.

Hunt, Harriet K. *Glances and Glimpses or Fifty Years Social, Including Twenty Years Professional Life*. Boston: John P. Jewett and Company, 1856.

Hurley, Daniel. *Cincinnati: The Queen City*. Cincinnati: Cincinnati Historical Society, 1982.

Jensen, Joan M. and Davidson, Sue, eds. *A Needle, a Bobbin, a Strike: Women Needleworkers in America*. Philadelphia: Temple University Press, 1984.

Jerde, Judith. "Mary Molloy: St. Paul's Extraordinary Dressmaker." *DRESS: The Journal of the Costume Society of America* 7 (1981): 82–89.

Judd, Sylvester. "Northampton," MSS vol. 1, 244. Forbes Library, Northampton, Mass.

Kaplan, Wendy. *"The Art That Is Life": The Arts & Crafts Movement in America, 1875–1920*. Boston: Bullfinch Press, 1987.

Kasson, John F. *Rudeness and Civility: Manners in Nineteenth-Century America*. New York: Hill and Wang, 1990.

Kenny, D. J. *Illustrated Cincinnati: A Pictorial Hand-Book of the Queen City*. Cincinnati, Ohio: Robert Clarke and Company, 1875.

Kerber, Linda K. "Separate Spheres, Female Worlds, Woman's Place: The Rhetoric of Women's History." *Journal of American History* 75 (1988): 9–39.

Kessler-Harris, Alice. "Independence and Virtue in the Lives of Wage-Earning Women: The United States, 1870–1930." In *Women in Culture and Politics*. Bloomington: Indiana University Press, 1986.

Kidwell, Claudia B. *Cutting a Fashionable Fit*. Washington, D.C.: Smithsonian Institute Press, 1979.

Kidwell, Claudia B., and Margaret C. Christman. *Suiting Everyone: The Democratization of Clothing in America*. Washington, D.C.: Smithsonian Institute Press, 1974.

Kingsland, Mrs. Burton. "A Talk about Teas." *Ladies Home Journal* (October, 1892).

Knibb, Helen. "Present But Not Visible: Searching for Women's History in Museum Collections." *Gender and History* 6 (1994): 352–369.

Koehler, Lyle. "Women's Rights, Society and the Schools; Feminist Activities in Cincinnati, Ohio, 1864–1880." In *Women in Cincinnati: Century of Achievement 1870–1970*, vols. I–III. Cincinnati: Cincinnati Historical Society, 1984.

Kraditor, Aileen S. *Up from the Pedestal: Selected Writings in the History of American Feminism*.

New York: Quadrangle/New York Times Book Company, 1968.

Kraemer, A. O., and G. A. Kraemer. *Kraemer's Picturesque Cincinnati*. Cincinnati: Authors, 1898.

Kwolek-Folland, Angel. *Incorporating Women: A History of Women and Business in the United States*. New York: Twayne Publishers, 1998.

The Ladies, God Bless 'Em: The Women's Art Movement in Cincinnati in the Nineteenth Century. Cincinnati: Cincinnati Art Museum, 1976.

LaBree, Benjamin, ed., *Notable Men of Cincinnati at the Beginning of the 20th Century*, Louisville, Ky.: George G. Fetter Co., 1904.

The Ladies Hand-Book of Millinery and Dressmaking, with Plain Instructions for Making the Most Useful Articles of Dress and Attire. New York: J. S. Redfield, Clinton Hall, 1843.

Leach, William. *Land of Desire: Merchants, Power, and the Rise of a New American Culture*. New York: Pantheon Books, 1993.

Lears, T. J. Jackson. *No Place of Grace: Antimodernism and the Transformation of American Culture, 1880–1920*. New York: Pantheon, 1981.

Leonard, John William. *The Centennial Review of Cincinnati: One Hundred Years of Progress in Commerce, Manufactures, the Professions, and in Social and Municipal Life*. Cincinnati: J. M. Elstner, 1888.

Leonardo, Michaela di. "Women's Work, Work Culture, and Consciousness." *Feminist Studies* 11 (1985): 490–496.

Lerner, Gerda. *The Female Experience: An American Documentary*. Indianapolis: Bobbs-Merrill Educational Publishing, 1977.

———. *The Majority Finds Its Past: Placing Women in History*. New York and Oxford: Oxford University Press, 1979.

Lewis, Dottie L., ed. *Women in Cincinnati: Century of Achievement 1870–1970*. Cincinnati: Center for Women's Studies, University of Cincinnati, 1984–1985.

Maeder, Edward F. "A Man's Banyan: High Fashion in Rural Massachusetts." *Historic Deerfield Magazine* (winter, 2001): 1–6.

Main, Gloria. "Gender, Work and Wages in Colonial New England." *William and Mary Quarterly* 51 (1994): 39–66.

Maxwell, Sidney D. *Suburbs of Cincinnati*. New York: Arno Press, 1974.

McCusker, John J. *How Much Is That in Real Money?: An Historical Commodity Price Index for Use as a Deflator of Money Values in the Economy of the United States*. Worcester, Mass.: American Antiquarian Society, 2001.

Miller, Marla. *The Needle's Eye: Women and Work in the Age of Revolution*. Amherst: University of Massachusetts Press, forthcoming.

Miller, Marla R. "Liberty of the House: Work, Space and Gentility in Rural New England." Paper presented at the Vernacular Architecture Forum, Duluth Minnesota, June 2000.

Miller, Zane L. *Visions of Place: The City, Neighborhoods, Suburbs, and Cincinnati's Clifton, 1850–2000*. Columbus: Ohio State University Press, 2001.

Montgomery, Maureen E. *Displaying Women: Spectacles of Leisure in Edith Wharton's New York*. New York: Routledge, 1998.

Murphy, Lucy Eldersveld. "Business Ladies: Midwestern Women and Enterprise, 1850–1880." *Journal of Women's History* 3, no. 1 (1991): 65–81.

Musselman, Barbara L. "The Shackles of Class and Gender: Cincinnati Working Women, 1890–1920." *Women in Cincinnati: Century of Achievement, 1870–1970*, vol. I. Cincinnati: Cincinnati Historical Society, 1984.

———. "Businesswomen and Separate Spheres in the Midwest, 1850–1880." *Illinois Historical Journal* 80 (1987): 15–176.

Newstedt, J. Roger. *Mrs. Frances Trollope in Cincinnati: The 'Infernal Regions' and the Bizarre Bazaar, 1828–1803. Queen City Heritage* 57, no. 4 (1999): 37–45.

Nichols, George Ward. *Art Education Applied to Industry*. New York: Funk and Wagnalls, 1922.

1902 Edition of the Sears, Roebuck Catalogue. New York: Bounty Books, a division of Crown Publishers, Inc., 1969.

Notable Men of Cincinnati at the Beginning of the 20th Century. Louisville, Ky.: George G. Fetter Company, 1903.

Oberly, Michelle. "The Fabric Scrapbooks of Hannah Ditzler Alspaugh." In *With Grace & Favour: Victorian & Edwardian Fashion in America*. Cincinnati: Cincinnati Art Museum, 1993.

O'Neill, William L. *Feminism in America: A History*. New Brunswick, N.J.: Transaction Publishers, 1989.

Owen, Nancy E. *Rookwood and the Industry of Art:*

Women, Culture, and Commerce, 1880–1913. Athens: Ohio University Press, 2001.

Parmal, Pamela A. "Line, Color, Detail, Distinction, Individuality: A. L. Tirocchi, Providence Dressmakers." In *From Paris to Providence: Fashion, Art, and the Tirocchi Dressmakers' Shop, 1915–1947,* Providence: Rhode Island School of Design, 2000.

Penny, Virginia. *Think and Act: A Series of Articles Pertaining to Men and Women, Work and Wages.* New York: Arno Press and New York Times Book Company, 1971.

———. *Working Women.* Boston: Walker, Wise and Company, 1863.

Phelps, Nathaniel account book, 1730–1747. Pocumtuck Valley Memorial Association.

Porter, Rev. James A. M. *The Operative's Friend, and Defence: Or, Hints to Young Ladies, Who Are Dependent on Their Own Exertions.* Boston: Charles H. Peirce, 1850.

Post, Emily. *Etiquette: The Blue Book of Social Usage.* New York: Funk and Wagnalls, 1922.

Potter, Eliza. *A Hairdresser's Experience in High Life.* New York and Oxford: Oxford University Press, 1991.

Roe, George M., ed. *Cincinnati: The Queen City of the West.* Cincinnati, Ohio: C. J. Krehbiel and Company, 1895.

Rogers, Millard F. Jr. *Rich in Good Works.* Akron, Ohio: University of Akron Press, 2001.

Rogers, Ruby. "Samuel Pogue's Store and Family." *Queen City Heritage* 52, no. 4 (winter 1994): 2–6.

Rosenberg, Charles E. *No Other Gods: On Science and American Social Thought.* Baltimore and London: Johns Hopkins University Press, 1916.

Rosenberg, Rosalind. *Beyond Separate Spheres.* New Haven, Conn. and London: Yale University Press, 1982.

Roth, Rodris. "Tea-Drinking in Eighteenth-Century America: Its Etiquette and Equipage." In Robert Blair St. George, ed., *Material Life in America, 1600–1860.* Boston: Northeastern University Press, 1988.

Rothman, Sheila M. *Woman's Proper Place: A History of Changing Ideals and Practices, 1870 to the Present.* New York: Basic Books, 1978.

Ross, Steven J. *Workers on the Edge.* New York: Columbia University Press, 1985.

Ryan, Mary P. *Cradle of the Middle Class: The Family in Oneida County, New York, 1790–1865.*

Cambridge, London, and New York: Cambridge University Press, 1981.

———. "Gender and Public Access: Women's Politics in Nineteenth-Century America." In *Habermas and the Public Sphere.* New York: New Viewpoints, 1975.

———. *Womanhood in America from Colonial Times to the Present.* New York: New Viewpoints, 1975.

Schlesinger, Arthur M. *Learning How to Behave: A Historical Study of American Etiquette Books.* New York: Macmillan Company, 1946.

Schneider, Dorothy. *Women in the Workplace.* Santa Barbara, Calif.: ABC-CLO, Inc., 1993.

Scott, Anne Firor. *Natural Allies: Women's Associations in American History.* Urbana: University of Illinois Press, 1992.

Severa, Joan L. *Dressed for the Photographer: Ordinary Americans and Fashion 1840–1900.* Kent, Ohio and London: Kent State University Press, 1995.

Shaw, Marian. *World's Fair Notes, A Woman Journalist Views Chicago 1893 Columbian Exposition.* Chicago: Pogo Press, 1992.

Shepherd, Anne B. "Setting the Stage: Cincinnati in 1894." In *A Centennial Review: The First Hundred Years of The Cincinnati Woman's Club, 1894–1994,* Cincinnati: Cincinnati Woman's Club, 1994.

Simon, Amy. *She Is So Neat and Fits So Well: Garment Construction and the Millinery Business of Eliza Oliver Dodds, 1831–1833.* Ph.D. dissertation, University of Delaware, 1993.

Smith-Rosenberg, Carroll. *Disorderly Conduct: Visions of Gender in Victorian America.* New York and Oxford: Oxford University Press, 1985.

Spont, Henry. "Sports d'hiver: la saison à Pau," *Les Modes* 15 (Mars 1902): 4–10.

Spring, Gardiner. *The Excellence and Influence of the Female Character: A Sermon.* Preached in The Presbyterian Church in Murray Street. New York: F. & R. Lockwood, 1825.

St. George, Robert Blair. *The Wrought Covenant: Source Material for the Study of Craftsmen and Community in Southeastern New England, 1620–1700.* Brockton, Mass.: Brockton Art Center, 1979.

Stanton, Elizabeth Cady. *Address to the Legislature of New York.* Albany: Weed, Parsons and Company, 1854.

Storer, Maria Longworth. *History of the Cincinnati Musical Festivals and of the Rookwood Pottery.* Paris: Herbert Clarke, 1919.

Sumner, Helen L. *The History of Women in Industry in the United States.* Washington, D.C.: U.S. Government Printing Office, 1910.

Swisshelm, Jane. *Letters to Country Girls.* New York: J. C. Riker, 1853.

Tate, Skip, and Felix Winternitz. *The Insider's Guide to Cincinnati.* Manteo, N.C.: Falcon Publishing, 1998.

Thieme, Otto Charles. *With Grace and Favour: Victorian & Edwardian Fashion in America.* Cincinnati: Cincinnati Art Museum, 1993.

Trollope, Frances. *Domestic Manners of the Americans.* New York: Vintage Books, a Division of Random House, 1949.

Tucker, Louis Leonard. *Cincinnati During the Civil War.* Columbus: Ohio State University Press for the Ohio Historical Society, 1962.

Turner, Justin G., and Linda Levitt Turner. *Mary Todd Lincoln: Her Life and Letters.* New York: Alfred A. Knopf, 1972.

U.S. Bureau of the Census. *Fourteenth Census of the United States Taken in the Year 1920 Population: Volume IV. Report on Occupations.* Washington, D.C.: U.S. Government Printing Office, 1923.

———. *Historical Statistics of the United States Colonial Times to 1970: Part 1.* Washington, D.C.: U.S. Government Printing Office, 1975.

———. *Index to the Executive Documents of the House of Representatives for the Second Session of the Fiftieth Congress.* Washington, D.C.: U.S. Government Printing Office, 1889.

———. *Ninth Census: Volume 1: The Statistics of the Population of the United States.* Washington, D.C.: U.S. Government Printing Office, 1872.

———. *Report on Manufacturing Industries in The United States at the Eleventh Census: 1890. Part I: Totals for States and Industries.* Washington, D.C.: U.S. Government Printing Office, 1895.

———. *Special Reports, Occupations at the Twelfth Census.* Washington, D.C.: U.S. Government Printing Office, 1904.

———. *Statistics of the Population of the United States at the Tenth Census (June 1, 1880).* Washington, D.C.: U.S. Government Printing Office, 1883.

———. *Statistics of Women at Work.* Washington, D.C.: U.S. Government Printing Office, 1907.

———. *Thirteenth Census of the United States Taken in the Year 1910 Population: Volume IV. Report on Occupation Statistics.* Washington, D.C.: U.S. Government Printing Office, 1914.

Veblen, Thorstein. *The Theory of the Leisure Class: An Economic Study of Institutions.* New York: Macmillan, 1899.

Venable, M. L. *Kraemer's Picturesque Cincinnati.* Cincinnati: A. O. and G. A. Kraemer, 1898.

Venner, William Thomas. *Queen City Lady: The 1861 Journal of Amanda Wilson.* Cincinnati: Larrea Books, 1996.

Vexler, Robert I., comp. and ed. *Cincinnati: A Chronological & Documentary History 1676–1970.* Dobbs Ferry, NY: Oceana Publications, 1975.

Vitz, Robert C. *The Queen & the Arts: Cultural Life in Nineteenth-Century Cincinnati.* Kent, Ohio and London: Kent State University Press, 1989.

Weimann, Jeanne Madeline. *The Fair Women.* Chicago: Academy Chicago, 1981.

Weiner, Lynn Y. "Women and Work." In *Reclaiming the Past: Landmarks of Women's History.* Bloomington: Indiana University Press, 1992.

Welter, Barbara. "The Cult of True Womanhood: 1820–1860." *American Quarterly* 18 (1966): 151–174.

Wertheimer, Barbara Mayer. *We Were There: The Story of Working Women in America.* New York: Pantheon Books, 1977.

Who Was Who in American Art 1564–1975: 400 Years of Artists in America: Vol II. G-O. Madison, Wisc.: Sound View Press, 1999.

Williams' City Directory. Cincinnati: Williams Directory Company, 1850–1945.

Woods, Caroline H. [Belle Otis] *The Diary of a Milliner.* New York: Hurd and Houghton, 1867.

Woodward, Helen. *The Lady Persuaders.* New York: Ivan Obolensky, Inc., 1960.

Index